242 01 /DSL   50

W9-BBP-727

au not in BCL
in BIP
3-30-00

The Abstract Journal,

1790-1920:

Origin, Development and Diffusion

by

BRUCE M. MANZER

The Scarecrow Press, Inc.
Metuchen, N.J. & London
1977

Library of Congress Cataloging in Publication Data

Manzer, Bruce M   1936-
    The abstract journal, 1790-1920.

    Bibliography: p.
    Includes index.
    1.   Abstracts--Periodicals--History.   2.   Abstracting
--History.   I.   Title.
Z695.9.M35   016-05   77-24143
ISBN 0-8108-1047-6

Manufactured in the United States of America

To

My Family

ACKNOWLEDGMENTS

    I wish to express my appreciation to Professor Herman Fussler, Dean Howard Winger, and Professor Don Swanson of the University of Chicago Graduate Library School, whose guidance and encouragement made this study possible. I would like also to acknowledge the teaching of Mr. Robert Wadsworth of the Graduate Library School who instilled in me a keen appreciation for both the theory and practice of enumerative bibliography.

TABLE OF CONTENTS

LIST OF TABLES

LIST OF ILLUSTRATIONS

CHAPTER I

INTRODUCTION

This study is an investigation of the origins and development of the abstract journal in all subject areas, in all
languages, and from all countries, in the period from 1790
through 1920. On the one hand it proposes to examine by
the historical method the origins and development of the abstract journal in the context of the evolution of the bibliographic apparatus for the control of the periodical literature
and, on the other, to examine by quantitative statistical analysis the developmental characteristics of the abstract journal
in this period. The former aspect is treated by examination
of: 1) the literature of the subject, 2) the abstract journals
themselves, and 3) the conditions attending their emergence
and development; grouping and chronicling as much evidence
as possible into meaningful patterns to permit conclusions.
The latter aspect is treated by a quantitative statistical analysis of such characteristics as growth, duration, type of publication, sponsorship, geographic diffusion, language diffusion, subject diffusion, arrangement, frequency, and indexing.
Tabulation, graphing, and analysis of the resulting data are
carried out to supply conclusions about these developmental
characteristics as well as additional and supportive data to
that derived from the historical method described above.

Definitions

The literature is replete with definitions of abstracts
rather than abstract journals. Customarily, these definitions,
as in Webster's,[1] take the form of a synonymy in which
words of similar meaning are discriminated from each other.
The word abstract is thus discriminated from such other
words as: abridgment, digest, epitome, extract, précis,
summary, and synopsis.

The term "abridgment" properly suggests reduction in
compass with retention of relative completeness. In an abridg-

1

ment there may be omission of minor points. A "digest" presents a condensation of information gathered from many sources and is usually methodically arranged for ready reference. "Epitome" suggests the briefest possible treatment of a complex whole that still has independent value, citing the chief points. In the epitome emphasis is placed on extreme accuracy of presentation. The word "extract" implies a selected passage from a larger work, usually in the language of the original. A "précis" is simply a concise statement or re-statement of essential facts, often being a report suggesting the tone of the original. "Summary" is a generic term applying to the entire category of synonyms. The term "synopsis" implies a skeletal presentation, usually in the form of a series of headings or an outline of an argument, or a narrative suitable for rapid examination. In this context the word "abstract" is defined as being a summary of a document, treatise, or proposed treatment, giving the salient points, usually in the order of presentation, with usually no claim to independent utility.

It is obvious that precise definition of the term "abstract" is not easy, very probably because of the highly variable application of abstracting historically to a wide range of activities in bibliography, librarianship, and elsewhere. [2] Categorization of a journal as an abstract journal must depend on a more pragmatic definition of the term "abstract."

As used in this study, in the context of a technique of bibliographic organization, the term "abstract" is probably best defined as it was at the International Conference on Science Abstracting in 1949: "An abstract is a summary of a publication or article accompanied by an adequate bibliographical description to enable the publication or article to be traced."[3]

The literature further categorizes abstracts thus defined as: 1) indicative, written with the intention of enabling the reader to decide whether he should refer to the original publications, 2) informative, presenting all the principal arguments and principal data of the original, or 3) evaluative, commenting on the worth of the original. Since the nature of the abstracts does not affect the definition used here and since in practice the boundaries between these categories tend to blur, these factors do not enter into the definition used in this work.

As to the abstract journal itself, Harrod states:

> Abstracting [is] a form of current bibliography in
> which sometimes books, but mainly periodicals are
> summarized.   They are accompanied by adequate
> bibliographical description to enable the publication
> or article to be traced, and are frequently arranged
> in classified order.   Periodicals which contain ab-
> stracts are known as journals of abstracts or ab-
> stract journals. [4]

An abstract journal, then, as defined in this study is
a form of serial bibliography in which books and related materials, but primarily periodical articles published elsewhere,
are summarized and accompanied by adequate bibliographic
description to enable the original publication to be traced.
It may constitute a cover-to-cover publication, independently
issued, or a section of a primary journal.   Arrangement is
usually, though not necessarily, classified.

By way of context, it should be noted that abstract
journals are only one of the elements of current bibliography
which are generally understood, in the period under review,
to consist, in addition, of the index journal and the review
or collective synthesis (the German Jahresbericht).   The latter type of publication is not to be confused with the review
journal which serves an evaluative purpose and is primarily
concerned with the monographic literature.   All these elements, the abstract, the index, and the review journals,
provide access on a current and retrospective basis to primary journal literature.   The abstract journal is differen-
tiated from the other two forms primarily by its arrangement
(generally being classified) and its inclusion of abstracts of
the cited publications.   It further differs from the review in
its lack of a critical or evaluative nature.

Admittedly the lines between the principal types of
current bibliography are not hard and fast.   The differentiation between serial annotated bibliography and the abstract
journal in the early period when there was considerable overlap of all types of bibliography and when a critical review
style had not yet developed is, similarly, a difficult one.

Delimitation

Early in the study it was realized that, in addition to

the problems due to the blurring of types of bibliography,
there were difficulties caused by several other categories of
bibliographic publication besides the index and review journals which also overlapped with the abstract journal in nature
and function but which did not meet the definition as here set
forth.   Special efforts were made to distinguish these and to
exclude them from the study.   These forms are: 1.   Law
reports and digests; 2.   Patent bulletins; 3.   Journals abstracting only papers presented at professional meetings;
4.   Journals abstracting articles from a single journal;
5.   Statistical abstracts; 6.   Digest journals; 7.   Abstract
journals with a restricted distribution; 8.   Critical review
journals; 9.   Serials containing abstracts of theses; 10.   Serials containing précis; and 11.   Homotopic abstracts.

The reporting and digesting of legal literature as a
form of bibliographic control, abstracting, as it were, stat-
utes and case reports, is considered outside the scope of
this work since it does not deal with the periodical literature, rather representing a separate, yet collateral, line of
bibliographic development. [5]

The abstracting of patents, yet another, collateral,
line of bibliographic development, is also outside the scope
of this work.   Primarily included in this category are the
official patent gazettes.

Journals abstracting only papers presented at professional meetings are few in number, being represented by such
publications as the Geological Society of America's <u>Abstracts
of Proceedings</u> and the Linnean Society of New York's <u>Ab-
stracts</u>.

Journals abstracting articles from a single journal are
outside the definition used in this study.   An important example here is the <u>Philosophical Transactions of the Royal
Society</u>.   Two noteworthy exceptions to this are, however, included since they otherwise fulfill the definition, viz., the
<u>New York Times Index</u> and the <u>Times Index</u>.

Statistical abstracts, while included in some studies of
abstract journals, are clearly a genre apart from that defined here.

Digest journals, such as <u>Science Digest</u>, present
lengthy condensations of journal articles and are, of course,
outside the purview of this study.

Abstract journals with a restricted distribution, usually taking the form of a house organ, have been excluded from the study for obvious reasons of inaccessibility.

Critical review journals are excluded since, as mentioned above, they are evaluative in nature and almost exclusively confined to the monographic literature.

Serials comprised of summaries of theses accepted at institutions of higher learning are sometimes issued independently, at other times such summaries are part of university publications. In any event, because of their scope, they are outside the definition of this study.

Précis writing, a technique almost wholly confined to the summarizing of government administrative reports, and its manifestations are not included, similarly, because of their limited scope.

Homotopic abstracts, i.e., abstracts which accompany the piece which they summarize whether it be a monograph or an article, are a phenomenon apart from, but not unrelated to, abstracting as defined here.

Significance of the Study

Designed primarily as a vehicle to permit the rapid communication of research findings, the learned journal, with its currency, speed of publication, and guaranteed circulation, is the principal source of up-to-date contributions to knowledge. [6] These same features which make the periodical an important source for those seeking information account also for its importance in meeting the scholars' need to establish priority by providing an outlet for the rapid publication of research findings.

A number of secondary, but nonetheless important factors similarly deriving from the nature and format of the learned journal combine to enhance further its significance to the scholar. Principal among these is the inclusion by most periodicals of correspondence columns, permitting an exchange of views; bibliographic notices of varying kinds; news notes; and advertisements. Their inclusion along with original articles enables the journal to fill a unique informational and bibliographical role in the transfer of knowledge. [7]

While it may seem a minor point, it should be mentioned here that there are many topics about which no information in book form has been published. Often the only source of such published information is a journal article.

One further important aspect of the learned journal, and one which is often overlooked, is its role in peer group judgment. Since it is largely on the basis of his published papers that a scholar makes his reputation the peer group judgment exercised by editorial review boards and referees, as well as that by readers afterwards, is an important element in maintaining the discipline of a field.

Because of their importance, then, learned journals have been the object of considerable effort at bibliographic control on a number of levels and by a variety of devices from the earliest times. [8] Here we are particularly interested in the mechanism which has developed for the bibliographic control of their contents.

The first learned journals were characterized by the inclusion of tables of contents and indexes, indexes at first to individual volumes, and later cumulative and, still later, collective indexes to more than one title. From the earliest times bibliographic sections of journals took note of articles published in other journals and, with the growth of the journal literature, the bibliographic apparatus of the day, comprised principally of monographic bibliographies, compendia, encyclopedias, etc., slowly began to take note of the contents of the journal literature. Much later, especially from the mid-nineteenth century onward, libraries too attempted to deal with the problems posed by these publications.

Most of this effort at bibliographic control of the journal literature in the seventeenth and eighteenth centuries proceeded, as indicated above, as a minor aspect of the bibliography of monographs, then characterized by a definite bio-bibliographical slant. This treatment was, however, probably adequate at the time considering the volume of the journal literature and the needs of scholars of the period.

Soon after the beginning of the nineteenth century, however, burgeoning scholarship, particularly in the sciences and technology, resulted in a shift of emphasis in publication from the monograph to the journal as scholars sought both to establish priority and to keep abreast of their fields. The volume of journal publication, which had been relatively

small, now began to increase at a greatly accelerated pace
paralleling that of the growth of scholarship.   With this rapidly growing body of journal publication it soon became difficult for scholars to keep up with developments either on a
current or on a retrospective basis and there accordingly developed a need for a more methodological and systematic apparatus to provide bibliographic control of the journal literature as the traditional monographically-oriented apparatus of
the past proved increasingly inadequate to the task.   In short,
the first decades of the nineteenth century witnessed a tremendous increase in the growth of journal publication and a
concomitant crisis in its bibliographic control.

It is at this point in the first decades of the nineteenth
century that such an apparatus designed to meet this need
emerged, an apparatus consisting ultimately of three elements
(in the period covered by this study): the abstract journal,
the index journal, and the major review journal (or Jahresbericht).

Beyond being the earliest of the three elements to appear, the abstract journal may also be considered, at least
in the time period here under review, the primary element
in that, unlike the index and review journals, it attempted to
respond simultaneously to the fundamental twin bibliographic
problems of current awareness and retrospective coverage.
The former problem it sought to meet by the presentation on
a current basis of systematically arranged summaries of
journal articles designed to provide rapid and accurate an-
nouncement of new research in a manner intended to keep
scholars abreast of developments in their fields; the latter
problem it attempted to meet through cumulation and indexing
of the abstracts, providing an "encyclopedic" repository in
summary form of the published knowledge in a given field. [9]

While it is an element of the guiding hypothesis of
this study that the abstract journal emerged and developed
to meet the problems of current awareness and retrospective
coverage, its current awareness function is today recognized
by some writers as having become one of relatively minor
importance.   Indeed, in the period covered by this study it
can be seen that, as the volume of primary journal literature
increased, accompanied by a corresponding growth in the abstract journal population, further layers of bibliographic control were required resulting in the appearance of the index
journal to provide a more efficiently produced alternative to
the abstract journal and control of the growing body of general

periodical literature; and the appearance still later of the
major review journal to provide the needed synthesis and
evaluation of the burgeoning periodical literature.

Several secondary features of the abstract journal
which contribute to its importance should be mentioned here.

It has been pointed out in the literature[10] that abstracts
can serve as surrogates for original articles, in many cases
precluding the necessity of seeing the original reference.
Further, abstracts provide convenient access to foreign language publications, since most abstract journals are universal in their coverage and provide translated abstracts of foreign language materials.[11]   Given the limited distribution of
some of these primary journals and the language limitations
of many users this is a distinct advantage of the abstract
journal.

The importance of the abstract journal to the scholar,
then, is as one element of a total bibliographic apparatus,
an element designed primarily to serve as a systematic repository of knowledge in a given field.

Secondarily the abstract journal is important as a
device to enable the scholar to learn of new, pertinent published information, though as pointed out above, its importance here is coming increasingly into question.   More
broadly, it has been suggested that, to the extent that the
abstract journal fulfills its current awareness function, it
delineates the frontiers of a field thereby suggesting areas
for further research.[12]

Beyond its importance to scholars in meeting their
informational and bibliographic needs, the abstract journal
is an important tool for librarians, bibliographers, documen-
talists, information scientists, and others concerned with
identifying, locating, and obtaining needed information and
materials.[13]

Mention was made above of the emergence of further
layers of bibliographic control beyond that provided by the
abstract journal.   As the nineteenth century progressed, the
second element of the bibliographic apparatus for the control
of the contents of periodicals, the index journal emerged.
The index journal, developing especially after the middle of
the nineteenth century, seems to have been a response to
the need for a more efficiently produced alternative to the

abstract journal (a capability which was now afforded by technological developments of the period in printing and photography) and for a device for the control of the contents of the
general periodical literature, which had been growing at a
considerable pace. The fact that many journals did not have
indexes and that such indexes as did exist varied widely in
usefulness, were additional factors in the emergence of the
index journal.

The third element of the bibliographic apparatus, the
major review publication, seems to have emerged at the end
of the nineteenth century as stated above in response to the
need for a device to provide evaluation and synthesis of the
ever-growing body of periodical literature.

Given the continuing importance of the journal as a
source of primary information and as a publication outlet and
the need for its bibliographic control the reader might naturally wonder about the nature of the emergence and development of this tripartite bibliographic apparatus which appeared
in the period under study and the forces which shaped it.

It is the purpose of this study to trace the origins,
growth, and diffusion of this system which developed in the
period from 1790 through 1920 for the control of the contents
of the journal literature with special emphasis on the abstract journal. This is done in the context of the historical
development of systematic bibliography and under the guiding
hypothesis that the abstract journal emerged and developed
as an integral element of a larger apparatus comprised also
of the index journal and the review journal. It is further
hypothesized that this system developed in response to the
demand for bibliographic control of the contents of the periodical literature as an organic synthesis and logical extension of the tools used by scholars in the seventeenth and
eighteenth centuries and earlier, altered significantly in
form and role.

More specifically, by the use of historical and statistical methods, this study proposes to examine the emergence
and development of the abstract journal in the period from
1790 through 1920 in an effort: 1) to determine the nature
of the emergence and growth of the abstract journal; 2) to
characterize the abstract journal in the period under study
and to differentiate it from the other two elements of the
bibliographic apparatus for the bibliographic control of the
contents of periodicals, the index journal and the review

journal; 3) to identify, examine, describe, categorize, and analyze as many as possible of those abstract journals published in the period under study; 4) using the data thus collected, to attempt to discover the prevailing factors which shaped the development of the abstract journal.

As is pointed out below in the "Review of Related Literature" [p. 11] this topic is characterized by a dearth of substantive investigation. The literature that does exist is widely scattered among numerous disciplines, and there seems to be some controversy over the exact nature of the origins of the abstract journal. Some writers claim that the first abstract journal was the Journal des sçavans, the first learned journal, since it contained, among other things, summaries of articles published elsewhere; others claim that the abstract journal is the logical extension of the index journal, developed in the nineteenth century by the inclusion of abstracts with the citations; while still others believe that the abstract journal is the nineteenth century "innovation" of the documentalist seeking to meet his bibliographic needs. Kronick and Malclès, among others, see the abstract journal as an organic synthesis and logical extension of the traditional bibliographic apparatus of the seventeenth and eighteenth centuries in a new form and role emerging and developing in response to the need for a systematic device to provide control of the periodical literature.   This controversy is discussed in more detail below. [14]

Because there is little or no substantive information on the emergence and growth of the abstract journal and the factors which shaped its development; and because the literature contains competing and contradictory explanations about this phenomenon, it is felt that this study can make a contribution to its understanding by presenting a substantive investigation of these areas.   Beyond any significance derived from illumination of the origins and development of the abstract journal and resolution of the controversy regarding this emergence, there is added significance in that the study brings together much information previously widely dispersed. Important also is the study's identification, examination, description, categorization, and analysis of some 310 abstract journals published during the period from 1790 through 1920, a group unrestricted in geographic or subject scope.

Further, it is hoped that this study will assist in the identification of the forces which shaped this bibliographic phenomenon, identifying which are constant and which are variable, not only because such an understanding of the past is an appropriate end in itself but because it can be assumed that these same forces still control the development of periodical bibliography (and perhaps even more broadly, systematic bibliography).   Possibly such an understanding will lead to a better knowledge of the future direction and potential of such bibliographic effort.

The period from 1790 through 1920 was chosen because: 1) this period represents that of the emergence and development of the bibliographic apparatus under study; 2) the period preceding this, in which the apparatus existed in a desultory state, has been investigated by Kronick;[15] 3) the interruption of the old bibliographic tradition by the effects of World War I, with its dissipation of German hegemony in the field of bibliography and the rise of a new concept of systematic bibliography, provides a convenient ending point for the study; and 4) the rapid growth in the number of abstract journals following World War I similarly suggests this period as a cutoff point in terms of a manageable number of titles.

As already mentioned this work is primarily concerned with the origins of the abstract journal in the context of the development of a bibliographic apparatus in response to the growth of the periodical literature.   Since it is possible to write about these origins and developments in several contexts we should point out areas which are not the primary concern of this study but which the author recognizes as meriting full, independent investigation in their own right. Such aspects as intellectual and social history, the growth of specific areas of knowledge, particularly the sciences and technology, the contributions of social organizations, printing practice, the book trade, and the development of the postal service and improved methods of distribution, all merit study in an effort to understand their impact and influence on the development of the abstract journal.

Review of Related Literature

Material relating to the origins and development of the abstract journal is not plentiful.   The literature that does exist is diffused throughout several disciplines and is characterized by a singular lack of historical perspective.   Almost nothing of a monographic nature exists.   The reason for this neglect of abstract journals is not clear.   It is possible that, since most abstract journals are in the area of the sciences,

they have suffered from the same neglect that the entire subject of scientific journalism, or all of learned journalism for
that matter, has suffered. It is perhaps also attributable to
the nature and historical role of the abstract journal itself,
being cumulated and superseded by the literature that follows
it.

The literature pertinent to this study may be classified
according to the following scheme.

I.   Bibliographic Organization
      A.   Bibliographic Organization in General
      B.   Bibliographic Control of the Periodical Literature
      C.   The Abstract Journal
II.   Subject Bibliography
      A.   Subject Bibliography in General
      B.   Guides to the Literature of Specific Subject Areas
      C.   Historical Bibliography of Specific Subject Areas
III. Librarianship
      A.   Treatment of Periodicals in Libraries
      B.   Reference Service
IV.   Documentation
      A.   Introductory Works
      B.   Studies, Analyses, and Evaluations
      C.   The Practice of Abstracting
      D.   Problems, Current State, and Future Trends
V.   Communication in Science
VI.   History of Science
VII. Learned Journalism
VIII. Bibliographies of Abstract Journals

Relevant material is found at several levels of the
literature of bibliographic organization. At the general level
some information on the development of the abstract journal
can be gleaned from such classic works as Besterman's The
Beginnings of Systematic Bibliography, Malclès' La Bibliographie and Les Sources du travail bibliographique, Schneider's
Handbuch der Bibliographie, Shera and Egan's Bibliographic
Organization, and Taylor's General-Subject Indexes Since 1548
and A History of Bibliographies of Bibliographies, as well
as in such introductory works as Robinson's Systematic Bibliography and Staveley's Notes on Modern Bibliography.
Works in this category mention the abstract journal in the
broad survey of the historical development of bibliographic
organization, serving to place it in context with the other
tools for the control of the periodical literature. Brief definitions and a few examples characteristically illustrate the

abstract journals in these works.   The principal value of
works in this category is to provide the bibliographical setting in which the abstract journal developed.

On the level of bibliographic control of the periodical
literature there exist a number of articles, one of the more
important ones being Murra's "History of Some Attempts to
Organize Bibliography Internationally," while on the specific
matter of the abstract journal there exists Clapp's "Indexing
and Abstracting; Recent Past and Lines of Future Development," and "Indexing and Abstracting Services for Serial
Literature," and Mayer's "Abstracting and Review Journals."
In addition to these articles, the principal monographs on the
subject are Collison's Abstracts and Abstracting Services,
which devotes a chapter to historical development, and Polzovics' Adatok és felismerések a szakirodalmi dokumentáció
történerének kezdeteihez [A Contribution to the Early History
of Documentation].   In addition to providing identification of
some of the early abstract journals included in this study,
this category of material provided substantive discussion of
the development of bibliographic control of the periodical
literature in general and its control by the abstract journal
in particular, touching upon the role of the abstract journal,
the motivation of sponsors of abstract journals, as well as
characteristics of growth, subject, and geographic diffusion
(Collison's work being particularly helpful in this regard).

The literature of subject bibliography also contains
some material pertinent to this investigation.   At the general
level such works as Staveley's Introduction to Subject Study,
Hale's Subject Bibliography in the Social Sciences and Humanities, and Grogan's Science and Technology; an Introduction to the Literature proved useful as well as the more specific guides to the literature such as Crane and Patterson's
A Guide to the Literature of Chemistry, Littleton's The Literature of Agricultural Economics, Pearl's Guide to Geologic
Literature, Blake's Medical Reference Works, 1679-1966,
and Brodman's Development of Medical Bibliography.   This
category of material was primarily useful for its discussion
of the role of the abstract journal in subject bibliography.
With the exception of Brodman's work, however, there was
little of a historical nature.   Several works in this category,
notably Brodman's and Blake's, were useful in the identification of early abstract journals.

The literature of librarianship contains some material
pertinent to this study in that segment devoted to the treatment

of periodicals in libraries.   Allen's <u>Serial Publications in
Large Libraries</u>, Davinson's <u>The Periodicals Collection</u>,
Grenfell's <u>Periodicals and Serials</u>, and Osborn's <u>Serial Pub-
lications</u> are examples.   In the area of reference service in
libraries Foskett's <u>Information Service in Libraries</u> touches,
similarly, on the topic at hand.   The literature here was
marginally useful to the extent that it defined the abstract
journal and its role in the bibliographic control of the periodical literature, though such treatment was usually brief.

The literature of documentation contains a comparatively small amount of material pertinent to this study.
About this, Ember says: "Many of the available historical
accounts are modestly hidden in prefaces and introductions
to textbooks and treatises, usually with an apologetic reference to the obscurity of the genesis and infancy of documentation."[16] This statement might well be extended to the bulk
of the literature.

In the field of documentation works such as Loosjes'
<u>On Documentation of Scientific Literature</u> and Casey's <u>Punched
Cards</u> are typical of the literature in this area where the
historical development of abstract journals, if discussed at
all, is treated only by way of introduction to the subject as
a whole.   The few serious historical and theoretical works
in this area such as Bradford's <u>Documentation</u>, Otlet's <u>Traité
de documentation</u>, and Shera's <u>Documentation and the Organization of Knowledge</u> were invaluable aids in providing information about the origins of the abstract journal, particularly
the growth of the periodical literature, the emerging needs of
the subject specialists, and the motivation of the early sponsors of abstract journals.   The literature of studies, analysis,
and evaluation (largely comprised of use, overlap, coverage,
and cost studies) contains little germane to this study.   Similarly, the literature of the practice of abstracting (the technique of writing abstracts, standardization of abstracting
practice, the mechanics of editing and publication) contains
little of direct interest.   The literature of problems, current
state, and future trends (dealing primarily with the rationali-
zation of service and the application of machine methods) has,
likewise, little relevance to this study.

Surprisingly, the literature of the history of science
also deals very little with the phenomenon of the abstract
journal.   Price's works, such as his <u>Little Science, Big
Science</u>, are notable exceptions.   Beyond providing identification of several early titles the literature in this category

was primarily useful for the data it yielded on abstract journal growth and opinions expressed as to the reasons for this
growth.

     The literature of communication in the sciences has
occasional references to the development of the abstract journal, primarily in that portion comprised of conference proceedings dealing with the problems of scientific information
handling. Here again, though, it is usually of minor importance and only by way of introduction to discussion of current
problems and, hence, not very useful from the standpoint of
this study. Examples are the proceedings of such meetings
as the International Conference on Scientific Information, held
in 1959, the Symposium on Communication in Science, 1967,
and the Royal Society of London's Scientific Information Conference, 1948. It is, of course, possible to trace back into
the nineteenth century the concern of subject specialists, particularly in the sciences, with bibliographic control of the
periodical literature as expressed at their meetings. Such
references are not uncommon in the proceedings of such
groups as the American Association for the Advancement of
Science, the Smithsonian Institution, the American Chemical
Society, the Royal Society of London, and the British Association for the Advancement of Science. These references,
though, are mainly concerned with the immediate problem at
hand of providing access to their respective literatures.
Their main value is in supplying some insight into the motivation of the sponsors of such bibliographic enterprises, although the bulk of them were confined to indexing services.

     The meager literature of learned journalism, while
containing little directly applicable to the present study, was
invaluable in supplying personal data, bibliographic information and, to a limited extent, data on the characteristics of
early abstract journals. Notable examples here are Kronick's
A History of Scientific and Technical Periodicals: the Origins
and Development of the Scientific and Technological Press,
1665-1790 (particularly helpful for its discussion of the abstract journal in the period covered), Kirchner's Das deutsche
Zeitschriftenwesen, Lehmann's Einführung in die Zeitschriftenkunde, Menz's Die Zeitschrift, Mott's History of American
Magazines, Garrison's Medical and Scientific Periodicals of
the Seventeenth and Eighteenth Centuries, Porter's "The
Scientific Journal--300th Anniversary," McKie's "The Scientific Periodical from 1665-1798," and Barnes' "The Beginnings of Learned Journalism."

Bibliographies of abstract journals, useful for identifying candidate titles, are discussed below in the "Plan of the Study" [p. 20].

Summary of Findings

It is proposed here to summarize the findings or opinions, some of which are general, others of which are conflicting, as found in the literature described above and, further, to identify those which the author proposes to test in this study.

Regarding the practice itself of abstracting there seems to be general agreement in the literature that abstracting has existed in various forms throughout the whole of recorded history:[17] as scholia and marginal glosses in medieval manuscripts; in the form of calendaring; in the form of précis writing; as legal digests and reports; and as bibliographies. An early seventeenth century example of the so-called homotopic abstract is cited by Clarke.[18]

Regarding the origins of the abstract journal there seems to be a difference of opinion. Some writers[19] consider it to be the logical outgrowth of the practice of periodical indexing which is viewed by them as having gone through two principal stages: the retrospective stage of the eighteenth and nineteenth centuries characterized in its beginnings by indexes to individual periodicals, later by cumulative indexes to individual periodicals, and, finally by collective indexes to more than one periodical; and the second stage from the late nineteenth and early twentieth centuries onward: current, ongoing indexes to more than one periodical, as typified by the Wilson and various subject-oriented periodical indexes. The abstract journal in this thesis is usually treated as a consequence of the latter stage of development.

Some other writers[20] see, rather, the development of the abstract journal as one paralleling the development of the indexing journal. These writers see it as an organic synthesis of the following devices, designed to do more effectively the same job that they had been trying to do, viz., to provide a means of disseminating knowledge, and at the same time, providing a means of access to recorded knowledge, especially to the periodical literature, for the community of scholars:

1. The periodically issued handbooks and literature guides

of the seventeenth and eighteenth centuries, which usually included extensive annotations.
2. The review journals of the seventeenth and eighteenth
    centuries primarily concerned with reviewing the con-
    tents of periodicals. (It should be borne in mind that the
    early review journals essentially only summarized the
    contents of other publications, and that a critical re-
    view style as we know it today did not begin to develop
    until the first decades of the nineteenth century.)
3. The monumental monographic subject bibliographies of
    the late eighteenth and early nineteenth centuries, often
    heavily annotated.

These devices were, in turn, seen as successors to
the medieval pandects, encyclopedias, and other compendia
which strove in their own way to provide scholars with access to the literature.

Others[21] see the origins of the abstract journal with
the birth of the first learned journal, the Journal des sçavans,
in 1665 since this publication contained summaries of books
and journal articles. The Journal was widely emulated in
style and content and many of the journals of that time down
to the early nineteenth century similarly contained extracts,
translations, reprints, and abstracts of materials published
elsewhere.

Still others[22] see the abstract journal as an "innovation" of the new art of documentation which developed in
Europe in the first half of the nineteenth century in response
to the subject specialists' need for current information amid
the rising tide of periodical publication, and the inability of
the library as an institution to deal effectively with their information needs. These writers usually cite the Pharmaceutisches Centralblatt, which first appeared in 1830 and which
is the predecessor of Chemisches Zentralblatt, as the earliest
known abstract journal.

Polzovics[23] develops at some length the interesting
theory that the emergence of the abstract journal was a
socio-economic response to the stimulus of mercantilism
which brought a corresponding pressure on science and technology, and not a direct result of the growth of the journal
literature as most other writers suggest.

Loosjes[24] suggests a strong developmental influence
on the part of annotated accession lists and catalogs of early
special libraries.

As to the reasons for the development of the abstract journal, writers generally agree[25] that it arose as a device to provide effective bibliographic control of the fast growing periodical literature with the specific purpose of: providing current awareness of newly published periodical literature; providing the facilities for retrospective bibliographic control of the periodical literature; providing access to foreign language publications as, increasingly, an interest developed to know of foreign experiences; and providing a surrogate for original publication.

The abstract journal was seen, even more fundamentally, as a basic means of achieving an important objective of many disciplines, viz., the improvement of the quality of that discipline by means of rapid and accurate communication of domestic and foreign professional knowledge.[26]

This development is usually viewed in the larger context of the evolution of a whole complex of bibliographic devices consisting, besides the abstract journal, of indexing journals, review journals, and ultimately the newer elements of bibliographic control such as table-of-contents journals, permuted title lists, and citation indexes, all designed to organize and make available the literature of a subject field.

Very little in a substantive way has been written on the developmental characteristics of the abstract journal, such as growth, duration, sponsorship, geographic, subject, and language diffusion. With the exception of Kronick's study, this writer knows of no work which reports on these characteristics of abstract journals based on first hand examination.

Regarding the subject development of the abstract journal, there seems to be general agreement[27] that the development was from the polymathic journals of the late seventeenth and early eighteenth centuries to the appearance of abstract journals in the sciences (chemistry, physics, and mathematics), followed closely by appearance in the field of medicine. There soon followed in the nineteenth century proliferation and increased specialization in the sciences, technology, and medicine. In the latter half of the nineteenth century there were tentative abstract publications in the social sciences, followed in the twentieth century by appearance, even more tentatively, in the humanities. Overall, in terms of numbers, abstract journals predominated in the period under study (and still do) in the sciences and

technology.   Collison[28] attributes this to the competitive nature of these fields and their support by business, government, and industry, as well as to their high degree of organization.   Some writers also attribute this to the fact that the
information of the sciences and technology is more susceptible
to such treatment than the literature of the social sciences
and the humanities. [29]

The author found no substantive studies in the literature pertaining to the growth of abstract journals in the time
period under review.

Sponsorship of abstract journals, as indicated by Collison, [30] follows a pattern of individual initiative by subject
specialists, at first singly or in small groups, for the earliest abstract journals, declining in the nineteenth century to
be replaced by organized efforts in the form of sponsorship
by professional societies and associations, later by government and industrial sponsorship, and, still later, by commercial enterprise.   Only with the twentieth century do we
see the rise of the independent abstracting service and the
first tentative beginnings of international cooperation in abstracting.   Cooperation by this time among professionals
within subject fields, and often within national boundaries,
had long since superseded personal enterprise.

The literature[31] reflects an early and sustained effort
at abstract journal production in Germany, an effort which
resulted in German preeminence in the field until World War
I when, because of the associated economic, social, and political disruption, German efforts were superseded by the
English language abstracting services.

No relevant literature seems to exist pertaining to the
bibliographic characteristics of abstract journals: their format, indexing, arrangement, frequency, etc.

The opinions expressed above can be categorized as
relating to: 1) the development of the practice of abstracting,
2) the origins of the abstract journal, 3) the reasons for the
development of the abstract journal, 4) the developmental
characteristics of the abstract journal, and 5) the factors in-
fluencing the development of the abstract journal.   Since
there seems to be general agreement in the literature about
points 1 and 3, the validity of opinions expressed on points
2 and 4 will be examined.   Further, the study will attempt
to shed some light on the factors which influenced the

development of the abstract journal, a subject not substantively treated in the literature.

Plan of the Study

Concurrent with the literature review phase of the study, the author undertook to develop a list of abstract journals meeting the criteria described above to serve as the basis for the chronological and statistical portions of the study as well as to supply supplemental data, from prefatory and similar matter, for the literature review phase.

Since no comprehensive directory of abstract journals exists, and since the criteria used in this study are not necessarily those used by compilers of bibliographies of abstract journals, it was necessary to collect as many "candidate" titles as possible from secondary sources for examination on an issue-by-issue basis throughout the period covered by the study (since a given "candidate" title could change in character at any time) to insure that they met the criteria of the study, and, if so, for the collection of needed data.

The initial file of "candidate" titles was culled, on the general level, from the several bibliographies of abstract journals which follow: the various guides of the International Federation for Documentation (its Abstracting Services in Science, Technology, Medicine, Agriculture, Social Sciences, Humanities; Abstracting Services: an Index to Material Collected by FID in 1962/1963; and List of Current Specialized Abstracting and Indexing Services); the four editions of FID's Index Bibliographicus; the Science Museum's Bibliography of Current Periodical Abstracts and Indexes Published in the British Commonwealth and Contained in the Science Museum Library; the seventh through the fourteenth editions of Ulrich's International Periodicals Directory; and Collison's The Annals of Abstracting, 1665-1970.

At the general level of science and technology additional titles were obtained from the Library of Congress' Guide to the World's Abstracting and Indexing Services in Science and Technology (two editions); Cobb's Periodical Bibliographies and Abstracts for the Scientific and Technological Journals of the World; Hulme's Class Catalog of Current Serial Digests and Indexes of the Literature of Pure and Applied Science; the World Health Organization's Current Indexing and Abstracting Periodicals in the Medical and

Biological Sciences; Mayer's "Abstracting and Review Journals;" and Blake's Medical Reference Sources, 1679-1966.

Such specialized and selective lists of abstract journals
were consulted as Fleming's "Medical Abstracting Journals
and Services;" Blanchard and Ostvold's Literature of Agricultural Research; Milek's "Abstracting and Indexing Services
in Electronics and Related Electrical Fields;" Lederman's
"Abstracting and Indexing Periodicals of Chemical Interest
Published in the United States;" and Gray's "Abstracting and
Indexing Services of Physics Interest."

A handful of additional candidate titles were gleaned
from Kronick's A History of Scientific and Technical Periodicals; Kirchner's Die Grundlagen des deutschen Zeitschriften-
wesens; Bolton's A Catalogue of Scientific and Technical Periodicals, 1665-1895; and Scudder's Catalogue of Scientific
Serials of All Countries. Several titles were added by being
noted in the introductory matter of already-identified journals
and 'chaining' backward.

The compilation of such a candidate file by this method
was complicated by the fact that most of the above-mentioned
tools included both abstracting and indexing services, and,
further, by the fact that nearly all were restricted to current
services only.

The next step in the study concerned the determination
of the "data elements" needed to produce the required data
for the study. The following were decided upon, codified,
and a work sheet for the collection of data was prepared:

Beginning Decade	Supplement
Ending Decade	Sponsor
Status	Multiple Sponsor
Type	Change of Sponsor
Change of Type	Language
Relationship to Predecessor	Country
Relationship to Successor	Duration
Format	Subject
Arrangement	Editorial Comment
Change of Arrangement	Anomaly
Indexes	Generic
Change of Indexes	Frequency

Nine hundred and twenty-seven "candidate" titles were
thus identified of which eight hundred and sixty-two were

examined in libraries in Chicago, Washington, D.C., New
York City, and Cambridge, Massachusetts. Of the 862 titles
examined, 310 were determined to be abstract journals within
the definitions of this study. Several additional titles, identified by asterisks in the text, are included. These latter
were not examined but were included on the strength of the
evidence of secondary sources.

That a high number of titles was discarded is largely
attributed to the fact that many of the sources from which
the file was compiled did not differentiate between abstract
and index publications. This was especially the case for the
editions of Index Bibliographicus. The following reasons,
then, account for the discarding, upon examination, of "candidate" titles: 1) they were not bona fide abstract journals
within the definitions of this study (i.e., they were some
other form of current serial bibliography); 2) they contained
no abstracts in the time period covered, though they may
have begun to carry abstracts after 1920; 3) they contained
fewer than 100-150 abstracts per year

The results of the examination of the 310 journals
were transferred to punched cards and tabulated for statistical analysis.

It is recognized that the discoveries set forth here
may be limited because of the definitions stated above or because of failure to discover pertinent items, but the study is
based on an effort to identify, examine, and describe the
entire corpus of relevant material.

At this point it might not be inappropriate to state
that the author has long felt a need to present a study of
this kind, bringing together widely scattered information and
supplying data where none existed previously. Accordingly,
the study is cast in the broadest of terms. By electing to
do this, the author realizes that certain sacrifices have to
be made. The personal involvement of responsible individuals, the role of professional and learned societies, the in-
terrelationships of subject and bibliographical development,
the complex sociological implications--all of these facets
must necessarily receive what seems a cursory treatment in
such a study. Still further, the text runs the risk of degen-
erating into a dry narrative and enumeration of titles. Nonetheless, it is hoped that this study fulfills its purpose of
painting the broad lines of the subject. Future scholars,
hopefully, can fill in the details.

Finally, several "housekeeping" points should be made. In identifying titles in the text, the titles as of 1920 (or the latest title if the publication has ceased) are used; the dates are dates of publication, not dates of inclusion of abstracts (if these latter dates are different this fact is indicated in the text). Open dates indicate that the title is still current. Translations are, unless otherwise noted, the author's.

Notes

1. Webster's Third International Dictionary of the English Language, Unabridged, s.v. "Abridgment."
2. This point is developed further below, pp. 52-54.
3. International Conference on Science Abstracting, Paris, 1949, Final Report (Paris: Unesco, 1957), p. 34.
4. Leonard M. Harrod, The Librarians' Glossary, 3d ed. (New York: Seminar Press, 1971), p. 25.
5. For further discussion of this point see below, p. 54.
6. Denis J. Grogan, Science and Technology; an Introduction to the Literature, 2d ed. (London: Clive Bingley, 1973), p. 110.
7. Ibid., p. 111.
8. A more extensive discussion of the historical development of efforts to provide bibliographical control of the contents of journals is presented below, pp. 31-51.
9. Robert L. Collison, Abstracts and Abstracting Services (Santa Barbara, Calif.: ABC-Clio, 1971), p. 1. U.S. Congress, House, Committee on Science and Astronautics, Dissemination of Scientific Information. 86th Cong., 2d sess., 1959, p. 99.
10. See, for example, Sidney Passman, Scientific and Technological Communication (New York: Pergamon Press, 1969), p. 73.
11. Donald E. Davinson, The Periodicals Collection; Its Purpose and Uses in Libraries (London: Deutsch, 1969), p. 64.
12. Collison, p. 1.
13. It is recognized here that, to a certain extent, the value of a specific abstract journal is a function of its comprehensiveness, editorial policy, and standards. On this point see especially Paul Vesenyi, An Introduction to Periodical Bibliography (Ann Arbor: Pierian Press, 1974), pp. 27-28.
14. See pp. 16-18.
15. David A. Kronick, A History of Scientific and Technical Periodicals: the Origins and Development of the

24 The Abstract Journal

Scientific and Technological Press, 1665-1790
(Metuchen, N.J.: Scarecrow Press, 1962 [c1961]).

16. George Ember, Review of Adatok és felismerések a
szakirodalmi dokumentáció történerének kezdeteihez,
by Iván Polzovics, in American Documentation 16
(January 1965): 39.

17. See, for example, George Chandler, Libraries in the
Modern World (New York: Pergamon Press, 1965),
p. 6.

18. Clarke, Archibald, "Abstracts and Extracts in General
Professional Literature," Library Association Record
13 (January 1911): 40.

19. See, for example, Verner Clapp, "Indexing and Abstracting; Recent Past and Lines of Future Development,"
College and Research Libraries 11 (July 1950): 197-
206.

20. See, for example, Kronick, pp. 149-158; Claudius
Mayer, "Abstracting and Review Journals," in
George Sarton, Guide to the History of Science
(Waltham, Mass.: Chronica Botanica, 1952), p.
105; and Robert S. Casey and James W. Perry,
eds., Punched Cards (New York: Reinhold, 1958),
p. 577.

21. Most notably Collison, pp. 59-60.

22. See especially Derek Price, Little Science, Big Science
(New York: Columbia University Press, 1963), p.
96; Samuel C. Bradford, Documentation, with an
Introduction by Jesse H. Shera and Margaret Egan,
2d ed. (London: Lockwood, 1953), p. 27; and
Estelle Brodman, The Development of Medical Bibliography (Washington: Medical Library Association,
1954), p. 27.

23. Iván Polzovics, Adatok és felismerések a szakirodalmi
dokumentáció történerének kezdeteihez (Budapest:
Országos Müszaki Könyvtár és Dokumentációs Köz-
pont, 1964), p. 76.

24. Th. P. Loosjes, On Documentation of Scientific Literature, trans. A. J. Dickson (Hamden, Conn.: Ar-
chon Books, 1967), p. 27.

25. See, for example, Collison, pp. 4-6; Christopher W.
Hanson, Introduction to Science-Information Work
(London: Aslib, 1971), pp. 83-84; and Grogan, p.
185.

26. Abstracts for Social Workers 1 (Spring 1965): [2].

27. See particularly California. University. University
at Los Angeles. School of Library Service, The
Annals of Abstracting, 1665-1970, ed. Robert L.

Collison (Los Angeles: School of Library Service and University Library, University of California, 1971), pp. iii-iv.

28. Collison, Abstracts and Abstracting Services, p. 64.
29. Christopher Ricks, "Learned Journals," Times Literary Supplement, 4 July 1968, p. 709.
30. Collison, Abstracts and Abstracting Services, pp. 60-64.
31. Ibid., pp. 60-61. Brockhaus Enzyklopädie in zwanzig Bänden, 17. Aufl., s.v. "Dokumentation."

CHAPTER II

THE BIBLIOGRAPHIC CONTEXT

In order to understand more completely the origin and growth of the abstract journal as a device for the bibliographic control of the periodical literature it is first important to examine it in the overall context of its development, i.e., as one component of the total bibliographic mechanism that has evolved for the control of published materials, placing special emphasis on the development of control of the periodical literature.

Historical Sketch

It is beyond the scope of this present work to trace in detail the complex historical development of systematic, or enumerative, bibliography. The interested reader is referred to such works as those of Besterman,[1] Schneider,[2] and Malclês.[3] Here we can only outline its salient features.

Systematic bibliography has as its aims the recording, description, identification, location, and accessing of the graphic records of man.[4] As such it is an art that has existed since antiquity as, early on, scholars saw the importance of organizing the literature for use.[5] Typically working independently in his own field, the medieval scholar, ignorant of any scientific nature of his efforts and using his own techniques, produced the bibliographies necessary for his studies (usually as a by-product of his scholarly activities).[6] Admittedly these bibliographies differed in character from modern bibliographies in that they lacked a clearly defined role. That is, they partook equally of a literary, historical, and enumerative nature, approaching bio-bibliographical dictionaries of today. Indeed it has been stated that the primary role of bibliography of this period was to save the texts of the past from oblivion.[7] This lack of a clear role for bibliography persisted well into the eighteenth century and, to a certain extent, into the nineteenth.[8]

The monographic bibliographies thus produced, supplemented by the encyclopedias, pandects, and other compendia of the day (and to a lesser extent by libraries and
their catalogs) sufficed to meet the needs of the early polymaths in an age when men could carry all knowledge in their
heads, relying principally on their own memory and intuition.[9]

Events of the seventeenth and eighteenth century were
to change all this.

The crisis in scholarly communication which had given
rise to the learned journal[10] was superseded by a new crisis
due in large part to the unrelenting growth of periodical publication. No longer could an individual scholar rely on his
own faculties to keep abreast of his field. As learning grew
and proliferated so too did its record, and the less adequate
became the system of retrospective bibliographies and other
devices described above in providing bibliographic control.
A need now arose for a methodological device to provide this
control.[11]

There were, of course, other contributing factors to
this crisis beyond the growth and increasing specialization of
knowledge and its record. Before proceeding it might be
useful here to enumerate several of these. Among the more
important factors creating new demands on the traditional
bibliographic apparatus were: 1) the progress of public education; 2) the creation of major universities and institutes
and the increase in learning and research which they fostered;
3) the establishment of libraries and archives and their concern with organizing the records of mankind; 4) the growth
and stabilization of the book trade; 5) the creation of learned
and professional societies (many of which demonstrated a concern for exercising bibliographic control over their subject
literature); and 6) the development of new technology.[12]

By the early nineteenth century scholars in the sciences had become reliant on the learned journal for the reporting of new knowledge (i. e. , for the establishment of
priority) as well as for obtaining up-to-date, exact information. As the century progressed other sectors of society,
including government and industry, also became reliant on
the journal for such information.[13] A need now existed for
current awareness of advances in learning to support these
activities. Accordingly, the traditional bibliographic apparatus which had served the needs of scholars to this point
underwent a distinct change.

First, a significant change in the role of systematic
bibliography came about as it assumed the functions associated with modern bibliography, viz. , the recording, description, location, and accessing of the records of mankind. [14]

Second, a major change in the kind and form of bibliography took place.   The pressures for dissemination for
current advances in learning led to the rise of current bibliography, superseding the great monographic retrospective
bibliographies of the past.   Further, the increasing proliferation of knowledge fostered a growth in subject bibliography,
largely replacing the universal bibliography which had gone
before.   The emerging current bibliography utilized forms of
systematic bibliography which had existed from the earliest
times: the index, the abstract, and the review. [15] Each of
these types of bibliography now took on new importance as
the instrument of control over the burgeoning literature--the
index journal, the abstract journal, and the review journal.

Finally, it should be noted that, with the value of
systematic bibliography now becoming generally recognized,
the field profited from increasing attention.   Whereas formerly lone scholars or small groups of collaborating scholars
had been responsible for much of the bibliographic enterprise,
throughout the nineteenth century a pattern of sponsorship
succeeded this characterized first by professional and learned
society sponsorship of bibliographic activity followed later in
the century by such enterprise on the part of government,
academic, and research institutions. [16] Library activity in
the bibliographic control of the literature was uneven and intermittent, being primarily concerned with local control through
classification of the book collection. [17] An important development resulting from this increased corporate attention to bibliographic activity was the rise of subject field bibliographic
responsibility and the increasing application of system and
method to a field previously characterized by its diffuse nature and lack of method. [18]

It should be noted that leadership in bibliographic activity came largely from Germany. [19] For the whole of the
nineteenth century down to World War I Germany was in the
forefront of the bibliographic movement, probably due to the
strong scientific tradition of her universities with their emphasis on graduate instruction and research.   Germany's example was soon followed throughout Europe resulting in a
rapid growth of bibliographic activity. [20] Only with the interruption caused by World War I did German bibliographic

efforts cede the field, principally to English-language, and more especially to American, publications. [21]

By the turn of the twentieth century bibliographic activity in general was in a state of ferment and vigorous development. This was a period which witnessed methods and standards brought to cataloging, classification, and other library techniques as a partial consequence of the formation of library associations. [22] This ferment in the library world seems, however, to have been motivated more by the pragmatic need to deal with the vast increase in publication and knowledge than a theoretical belief in the value of bibliographic control. [23] In retrospect the period must be viewed as a relatively dormant one so far as the larger issues of bibliographic organization go. [24]

It was in the world of the subject specialist that significant developments were occurring, the period up to World War I being a crescendo of bibliographic activity.

As early as mid nineteenth century scholars had been making emphatic statements at their national meetings about the need for reliable, comprehensive, current bibliographies, [25] and a number of bibliographic ventures attempting to meet this need dominated the scene before World War I. Here we can only cite such activities as those of La Fontaine and Otlet, the International Institute of Bibliography, the Concilium Bibliographicum, and the International Catalogue of Scientific Literature, enterprises which sought not only to provide comprehensive control of the literature but to develop the techniques necessary for their production. [26]

By the beginning of the twentieth century, bibliography as a profession had, as Malclès states "attained its majority and won its freedom. It has defined its goals, discovered its rules, and forged its methods. There was no one who was not aware of its "functional" definition, and of the possibilities which bibliography now presented."[27]

But the continued needs of science and industry combined with the newly emerging needs of the social sciences and the humanities produced even greater pressures on the bibliographic apparatus as the world entered the period of the World War. [28] Universal bibliography was again the dream of bibliographers until interrupted by the disruptive economic and social effects of the War.

Several trends in the development of bibliography in the period under review become immediately apparent even from so short an historical sketch as this.

First, the tremendous increase in the volume of publication through the eighteenth and nineteenth centuries, along with the growth and proliferation of learning, combined with other social and economic factors to produce heightened pressures on the traditional bibliographic apparatus which had long served the needs of scholars but which could not supply their needs for current bibliographical control.

Second, a new kind and form of bibliography arose to meet this need, current subject bibliography manifested in a range of secondary services, the index journal, the abstract journal, and the review journal, superseding the universal, retrospective, and usually monographic, bibliographies of the past. These devices utilized already existing techniques of bibliography with increasing standardization and method.

Third, the role of systematic bibliography emerged clearly in this era as that generally attributed to modern systematic bibliography.

Fourth, numerous enterprises prefiguring present-day interest in universal bibliography on an international basis arose in the late nineteenth century, usually on the part of subject specialists, though these efforts were unsuccessful in meeting their goals. Countless subject-oriented enterprises on a smaller scale were attempted but their efforts were largely uneven in coverage, intermittent, and uncoordinated. The disruptive effect of World War I dealt a severe blow to much of this enterprise.

Fifth, a genuine social need for bibliographic control of the literature seems to have been recognized increasingly throughout the nineteenth century by widely divergent groups, though each group, generally subject or national or both, seems largely to have worked in isolation and with a disregard for past experiences. [29]

Sixth, leadership in the effort to exert bibliographic control over the growing literature seems to have come from a German model spreading to other countries rapidly. This leadership was dealt a severe blow by the effects of World War I which also seriously interrupted bibliographic development throughout the world.

Seventh, the greatest efforts toward control seem to have been concentrated from the earliest times to the present day in the fields of science and technology, perhaps due to the early maturing and academic acceptance of these fields as well as their high degree of organization, characteristics which did not apply to the social sciences and humanities.

Eighth, the importance of the learned journal and the problems of bibliographic control which it presented must be counted as a major element in the increased pressures for effective bibliographic organization.

We now review some of the high points in the development of bibliographic control of the learned journal.

Bibliographic Control of the Learned Journal

The beginnings of the learned journal are discussed in detail below. [30] Suffice it to say here that the growth of learning and publication in the sixteenth and seventeenth centuries generated a need for a better system of scholarly communication than that afforded by the system of letters and oral presentation at meetings which had characterized scholarship to that point. The learned journal emerged to fill this role in scholarly communication.

The journals which developed, provided from the earliest times problems of bibliographic control, [31] problems of identification, location and content access. It is this latter control that we are concerned primarily with here.

Initially the bibliographic control of the contents of learned journals was provided by two devices and somewhat later by a third.

The first of these devices was the bibliographic sections of learned journals which listed, abstracted, extracted, or reviewed the contents of other journals. [32] Indeed the first learned journal, the Journal des sçavans, devoted a major portion of its contents to this function as did other journals which followed and emulated it. These bibliographic sections, and this bibliographic function of the learned journal, became increasingly important as the volume of publication increased and the ability of scholars to cope with it decreased.

The second device for the content control of the journal literature also began with the first journal, viz., the index. [33] Indexes to individual volumes were published from
the earliest times, followed eventually by cumulated indexes
to individual volumes and ultimately by collective indexes to
more than one periodical. [34]

A third device for the control of the periodical literature which existed in the late seventeenth and eighteenth centuries was the abstract journal. These publications, intermittent in appearance and polymathic in scope, did not survive the demise of the polymathic journals at the end of the
eighteenth century and were more of a bibliographic anomaly
than a direct lineal antecedent of the modern abstract journal. [35]

Mention has already been made of the traditional bibliographic devices, the encyclopedias, pandects, guide-books,
and other compendia which, to a certain extent, provided bibliographic control of the periodical literature. Their efforts
were, however, primarily confined to the monographic literature.

With the tremendous growth in volume of publication
mentioned above, which characterized the seventeenth and
early eighteenth centuries this system of control, comprised
of the three devices just enumerated, proved not to be systematic, timely, or comprehensive enough as it was overwhelmed by the flood of journal publication and the increased
demands on the part of scholars for current information.

The pressures for current bibliography described
above now caused these three devices to be transformed into
new forms as current subject bibliography. Additional pressures came in the early decades of the nineteenth century
from journal editors who, anxious to increase the substantive
content of their publications, sought to pre-empt the ever-
growing space devoted to bibliographical material for original
articles. [36] The total effect was to force two of the devices
for the bibliographic control of the periodical, the bibliographic
section and the index, to assume a new format independent
of primary journal publication, and to cause the abstract
journal to be reconstituted as a form of current subject bibliography. [37] Put another way, the abstract journal, the index journal, and the review journal emerged as the vehicles
of current bibliography as logical extensions of the earlier
devices which had existed for this purpose. This extension

was not a complete one, however, in the sense that the
learned journal still performs an important bibliographic
function.

These modern devices which emerged in the nineteenth
century for the control of periodical contents can be categorized as follows: 1) journal-dependent bibliography, consisting
of sections of primary journals and ranging from minor unannotated notices to extensively annotated and systematically
arranged bibliographies; and 2) independent bibliography, which
may be further subdivided into: a) current forms (the indexing,
abstract, and review journals) and b) monographic bibliography of periodical articles.   Let us briefly examine some
of the principal developments in these categories before we
examine the abstract journal in detail.

Journal-Dependent Bibliography

As mentioned above it was the practice of early journal editors to note the contents of other journals (often re-
printing entire articles or extracts from them).   There soon
developed in most primary journals sections of so-called
"collectanea" consisting of book and journal article notices,
correspondence, news notes, etc.   Sometimes their inclusion
was prompted by competitive considerations but more often
they were probably due to a genuine concern on the part of
the editor to spread knowledge. [38]   Generally those sections
were very informal becoming, with the passage of time, more
comprehensive in their scope and more systematically arranged.   Many of our present day specialized bibliographies
can be traced to these early sections of collectanea.

By the dawn of the nineteenth century these collectanea sections had become standard features of many learned
journals.   Some had even become extensive sections of bibliographical notices.   As many of these journals underwent a
change in sponsorship and nature, those bibliographic sections that remained within the covers of primary journals
thrived, growing in scope and extensiveness and becoming
increasingly systematically arranged.

Before about 1800 these sections, generally called
simply "bibliography" or some equivalent term, usually noted
both books and periodical articles not distinguishing between
the two, though this lack of differentiation diminished as the
periodical came less to be considered a book issued in parts
and more to have a nature of its own.   Up to this point the

periodical had not become significant enough in terms of numbers, nor had the need for current awareness become critical
enough to pose a bibliographic problem, and the coverage of
current periodical literature in this manner was generally
adequate.

With the dawn of the nineteenth century, for the reasons cited above, this form of bibliographic control became
less and less adequate.   Until the alternative of current subject bibliography developed, however, the bibliographic sections of periodicals continued to play a major role in the
control of the periodical literature.

In an effort to meet the bibliographic needs of the
nineteenth century these bibliographic sections underwent significant change.   Among these changes were: 1) an increasing tendency to segregate bibliography from other materials
previously included in "collectanea" sections of journals, particularly the separating out of the bibliography of periodical
articles into sections bearing titles such as "Current Periodical Literature," "Index analytique," or "Zeitschriftenschau";
2) an increasingly systematic arrangement of the contents of
these bibliographic sections, from random to journal title
arrangement to elaborate systems of classification; 3) an increasing use of annotations; 4) an increasing standardization
of entry and citation, author entry and fuller citations becoming the rule, and 5) an increasing occurrence of indexes to
these bibliographic sections, either as part of the journals'
indexes or issued separately.

Still later in the century, particularly after mid century, these trends intensified while several other trends now
became discernible: principally an increasing emphasis on
comprehensiveness and the emergence of a number of these
sections in independent form, generally as annual bibliographies.

By the beginning of the twentieth century almost every
journal of a major subject field had its "Current Periodicals"
or "Zeitschriftenschau" presenting more or less comprehensively and systematically and on a more or less timely basis
annotated or unannotated references to the periodical literature of that field.   While many of them were inconsequential
in terms of their effectiveness in providing adequate control
some others were major bibliographic achievements.   The
"Critical Bibliography of the History and Philosophy of Science and the History of Civilization"; the "Übersicht" of

Just's Botanische Jahrbücher; the "Index to American Botanical Literature"; "Medizinische Bibliographie des in- und ausländischen gesamten Medizin"; and the "Bibliographie géographique internationale," to name but a few, were such major bibliographical efforts.

The beginnings of bibliography of the periodical literature of librarianship hark back to this format, the Bibliographie des Bibliotheks- und Buchwesens, a pioneer work in the field, began as an annual cumulation of the classified bibliography of books and periodical articles published from 1904 in the Zentralblatt für Bibliothekswesen. Also, the predecessor to Library Literature, the "Library Work" section of Library Journal, was itself a continuation of the bibliography section of Library Work, having begun in April 1906.

As the nineteenth century progressed the problem of the subject control of the periodical literature became steadily more critical and alternative formats, chiefly the independent serial subject bibliography superseded the bibliographic sections of journals as the principal device for control, attempting to provide it on a more comprehensive, systematic and timely basis than the sections were then able to do. Appendix V is a selected list of journals which contained important sections of bibliographic notices in the time period under review here.

Independent Bibliography of Periodical Articles

The current independent bibliographies of periodical articles which existed in the period from 1790 through 1920 are: the index journal, the abstract journal, and the review journal.

a. The Index Journal.

The early history of periodical indexes is well documented by Kronick[39] and Malclès.[40] Broadly, the pattern of development is that cited above, viz., the retrospective stage of the seventeenth, eighteenth, and early nineteenth centuries, characterized in its beginnings by individual indexes to individual periodicals, and later by cumulative indexes to individual periodicals, and finally by collective indexes to more than one periodical title; and the second stage from the middle and late nineteenth century onward: current, ongoing indexes to more than one periodical title.

The index, like other bibliographic devices, was already well established in the monographic literature at the
time of the birth of the learned journal in the latter half of
the seventeenth century, its adoption being an extension of its
use in the monograph. The first volumes of the Journal des
sçavans and the Philosophical Transactions, as well as other
journals of the period, were supplied with indexes. By the
end of the eighteenth century the index was a well established
feature of most periodicals.

The next logical extension of the use of the index was
to a series of volumes of one periodical title, i.e., the issuance of a cumulative index. An example of this is Maty's
A General Index to the Philosophical Transactions from the
First to the Seventieth Volume published in London in 1787.
Kronick, Taylor, and Haskell[41] cite many other examples of
this sort of index.

The next logical development in periodical indexing
was the development of collective indexes. It is with this
development that we truly begin to move into the area of
systematic bibliographic control of the periodical literature
by means of indexing publications. Examples of this type of
publication are Philip Gesner's Die Entdeckungen der neuesten
Zeit in der Arzneygelahrtheit (Nördlingen, 1778-88) and Paul
Usteri's Repertorium der medicinischen Literatur (Zurich,
1768-95), both indexes to medical journals.

Kronick[42] gives an account of the collective indexes
to periodicals which have been variously accorded the honor
of being the first true periodical index as we know it today;
Cornelius â Beughem's La France sçavante (Amsterdam,
1683) (being basically a classified index to the Journal des
sçavans for the years 1665 to 1681); Beughem's Apparatus ad
historiam litterariam (Amsterdam, 1689-81) (similar to its
predecessor and covering some nine journals); Beutler's Allgemeines Sachregister über wichtigsten deutschen Zeitschriften
(Leipzig, 1790) (a systematic index to some eight journals);
Ersch's Repertorium über die allgemeinen deutschen Journale
und andere periodischen Sammlungen für Erde beschreiben,
Geschichte und die damit verwante Wissenschaften (Lemgo,
1790-92) (which Lehmann[43] cites as the first systematically
arranged bibliography of the contents of periodicals); Reuss'
Das Gelehrte England, oder Lexikon der jetzt lebenden
Schriftsteller in Grossbritanien, Irland und Nordamerika,
nebst einem Verzeichnis über Schriften vom Jahre 1770 bis
1790 (Berlin, 1791) (which analyzed some twenty periodicals)

and Reuss' Repertorium commentationum a societatibus litter-
aris editarum (Göttingen, 1801-21) (a classified subject index
to the publications of learned societies before 1800). This
work was later taken up by the Royal Society's Catalogue of
Scientific Papers.

This enumeration brings us down to the beginning of
the nineteenth century when periodical bibliography, as described above, was in the throes of a crisis because of the
inability of traditional devices to deal with the growing body
of literature and the increased demands of scholars.

It was in this period that the prototypes of the modern
abstract journal, such as the Retrospect of Philosophical,
Mechanical, Chemical and Agricultural Discoveries and the
Bulletin universel, dating from 1805 and 1823 respectively,
made their appearance. The independently issued current indexing journal was still, however, in its formative stages.

John Edmands (1820-1915), librarian of the Brothers
in Unity, a literary and debating society at Yale University,
prepared in 1847 a pamphlet entitled Subjects for Debate,
with Reference to Authorities. This pamphlet, a selective
subject classified index to the periodicals in the library, met
with such success that in 1848 William Poole (1821-1894),
who had become librarian, proceeded to enlarge upon Ed-
mand's work. Instead of an index to selected references,
Poole analyzed the contents of the Society's periodical hold-
ings which had no indexes of their own. This effort aroused
such interest that Poole took his manuscript to George Put-
nam who proceeded to publish it under the title An Alphabetical Index to Subjects Treated in the Reviews and Other Periodicals, to Which no Indexes have been Published. This
publication indexed the contents of some thirty nine periodicals down to 1848 in addition to some miscellaneous material. Poole immediately began the preparation of another,
expanded edition which appeared in 1853 and which contained
five or six times the material in his original work.[44]

In the meantime the London firm of Sampson Low,
Son and Company published in 1859 the first issue of its
quarterly periodical index entitled Index to Current Literature. This publication, not unpretentiously, subtitled itself
an "author and subject index to every book in the English
language, and to articles in literature, science, and art, in
serial publications" and indexed the contents of some twenty-
six American and British publications.[45] It ceased publication with 1861.

It was about this time also, the 1870's to be more
precise, that the American librarian, now almost forgotten,
William McCrillis Griswold (1853-1899) published at his own
expense a series of indexing publications culminating in his
Monthly Index to Current Periodical Literature, Proceedings
of Learned Societies, and Government Publications (New York,
July 1880-Dec. 1881).   Griswold continued for some time to
publish other periodical indexes under the pen name "Q. P.
Index," but their usefulness seems to have been marred by
Griswold's eccentricities in spelling and alphabetization, according to one biographer, who described him as "having
more of a passion than a gift for indexing."[46]

Librarians as a group had not yet been heard from in
this matter of periodical indexing.   The subject had become
so important as the need for such indexes became increasingly recognized that it was taken up at the first meeting of
the American Library Association in 1876[47] where much interest was expressed in a revival of Poole's Index to Periodical
Literature.   After considerable discussion a plan was developed for the indexing of periodicals on a current basis
through a system of allocation of titles to a group of cooperating libraries with Poole providing the overall editorial control.[48]   Fifty one libraries cooperated voluntarily in this
project and produced in 1882 the Index to Periodical Literature comprising 1442 pages of subject references to the contents of 6,245 volumes of 232 serials covering the years from
1802 through 1881.[49]

After the issuance of this third edition of Poole's
Index in 1882 W. K. Stetson of the Wesleyan University Library proposed a cooperative enterprise to continue the
work.[50]

Under the editorship of William I. Fletcher (1844-1917),
who had been an associate editor of the third edition of
Poole's Index, and with the volunteer cooperation of the staff
of the American Library Association, a monthly Cooperative
Index to Current Numbers of Leading Periodicals was issued
as a supplement to Library Journal from March 1883.   The
Cooperative Index soon ran into problems of failure on the
part of some of the cooperating libraries to carry their share
of the burden, exacerbated by the growing body of literature
to be indexed and economic problems of the enterprise.[51]
The annual issue for 1891 was the last volume in this series
as the Cooperative Index was succeeded by the Annual Literary Index.

The Annual Literary Index, edited by William Fletcher
and Richard Bowker (1848-1933), again with the cooperation
of members of the American Library Association, carried on
the work of the Cooperative Index on an expanded basis, covering a larger list of periodicals, and incorporating as a new
feature the indexing of portions of books and the listing of
significant bibliographies of the year. [52]   The Annual Literary
Index was in turn succeeded by the Annual Library Index
which was succeeded by the American Library Annual in 1911.
The Annual discontinued the indexing of periodical articles as
this function was now taken over by Readers' Guide to Periodical Literature.

Meanwhile, the Germans had begun in 1896 their Bibliographie der deutschen Zeitschriftenliteratur, at first as an
annual, and later as a semi-annual index to German periodical literature with a very comprehensive scope. This was
followed in 1911 by a companion publication covering periodicals in the principal non-German languages, the Bibliographie
der fremdsprachigen Zeitschriftenliteratur. Both of these
publications continue today reconstituted as the Internationale
Bibliographie der Zeitschriftenliteratur.

At the same time the Bibliographie was getting under
way in Germany American librarians were relying on the
Annual Literary Index and Poole's Index for coverage of the
general periodical literature. There was, however, growing
dissatisfaction with their lack of timeliness, [53] resulting in
proposals for yet another index. [54]

The staff of the Cleveland Public Library had been
compiling a card index to the contents of its periodicals, not
unlike a good many other libraries of the period, when in
1895 the librarian, William H. Brett (1846-1918), offered
at the American Library Association meeting to undertake to
publish a monthly catalog from these cards. After surveying
leading libraries as to the titles to be covered, the Library
began to issue in June 1896 the Cumulative Index to a Selected List of Periodicals, a monthly, cumulative index in
dictionary form. The idea behind the enterprise, as stated
in its introduction, was to make available on a timely basis
the contents of the most widely used periodicals in American
public libraries. [55]   The Cumulative Index soon began to run
into problems of production costs and inadequate support before merging in 1903 with Readers' Guide. [56]

At the beginning of the twentieth century, then, there

existed four major periodical indexes: (1) Poole's <u>Index</u>;
(2) the <u>Annual Literary Index</u>; (3) the <u>Bibliographie der</u>
<u>deutschen Zeitschriftenliteratur</u>; and (4) the <u>Cumulative Index</u>
<u>to a Selected List of Periodicals.</u> As mentioned above these
publications were being plagued by problems of costs or lack
of cooperation or lack of timeliness. The English-speaking
world was in the early years of this century effectively without a current index to the general periodical literature. This
was the situation when H. W. Wilson (1868-1954), a Minneapolis bookseller, applied his bibliographical, technological,
and merchandizing genius to the problem.

Wilson had been intrigued for some time by the problems associated with providing an efficient and comprehensive periodical indexing service. [57] He now devised a scheme
which called for a central bibliographical effort to index the
periodicals and to produce the publication; he also developed
the so-called "service basis" concept whereby libraries pay
according to their actual subscription lists. These innovations enabled him to launch successfully in 1901 <u>Readers'</u>
<u>Guide to Periodical Literature</u> followed soon by periodical
indexes in subject fields. [58]

Several English language periodical indexes followed,
such as Faxon's <u>Annual Magazine Subject Index</u> and the British <u>Subject-Index to Periodicals</u> but the Wilson indexes had
paved the way for current indexing publications produced on
a sound basis.

While all this activity was being expended in indexing
the general literature by librarians and bibliographers, a
concomitant demand arose among the subject specialists for
the indexing of their literature, particularly in the sciences
and in technology.

In 1851 Joseph Henry, perhaps influenced as Clapp[59]
suggests by Charles Coffin Jewett, the imaginative librarian
at the Smithsonian Institution, or, as Coulson[60] suggests,
smarting because of the neglect of his scientific contributions
by Europeans, inserted in his report as Secretary of the
Smithsonian a passage calling attention to the need for a better means of disseminating information about scientific research and the need for some kind of index to it:

> It is estimated that about 20,000 volumes, in-
> cluding pamphlets purporting to be additions to the
> sum of human knowledge, are published annually;

and unless this mass be properly arranged, and the means furnished by which its contents may be ascertained, literature and science will be overwhelmed by their own unwieldy bulk. The pile will begin to totter under its own weight, and all the additions we may heap upon it will tend to add to the extension of the base, without increasing the elevation and dignity of the edifice.

One of the most important means of facilitating the use of libraries, particularly with reference to science, is well digested indexes of subjects, not merely referring to volumes or books, but to memoirs, papers, and parts of scientific transactions and systematic works. [61]

As it became apparent that the Smithsonian could not do the job single-handedly, and as money to implement a project of this sort was not forthcoming, Henry conceived a plan for dividing the work. To this end he addressed a letter to the British Association for the Advancement of Science soliciting their cooperation with the Smithsonian Institution; a plan in which he himself would undertake to index the American literature. [62] The Association took up this plan at its Glasgow meeting the following year and a committee, all of whose members belonged to the Royal Society of London, was appointed to study it. [63] Although the cooperation proffered by Henry on the part of the Smithsonian Institution was not forthcoming due to the reasons cited above, the Royal Society decided to undertake the entire project itself, obtaining a subsidy from the British Treasury to publish the work. The result was the Catalogue of Scientific Papers, 1800-1900, the first volume of which appeared in 1867.

The monumental Catalogue, which forms for general purposes the principal index to the scientific literature of the nineteenth century, consists of nineteen volumes of author-title entries arranged alphabetically by author and provides a record of the contents of 1555 periodicals, transactions, reports, etc. Four volumes of a projected seventeen volume subject index were published.

At the beginning of the twentieth century the Royal Society conceived of a plan of so organizing the record of scientific production on an annual basis in a single publication that the need for competing publications would be eliminated. This attempt, the International Catalogue of Scientific Literature, in seventeen subject sub-series, was heroic.

It continued until World War I when, due to a lack of money and international cooperation, it ceased publication. [64]

While the Royal Society was preparing to issue its Catalogue of Scientific Papers one the earliest ongoing subject indexes to periodicals was born--Zoological Record.

Founded in 1864, Zoological Record was the product of a group of zoologists, principally associated with the British Museum and the Zoological Society of London, who wished to provide each year a comprehensive bibliography of zoological literature. The Record was first issued by Van Vorst, a London publisher interested in natural history, but after five volumes, when it had proved to be an unprofitable venture, it was taken over by the Zoological Association and ultimately the Zoological Society of London. Generous grants for its subsidy from the British Association for the Advancement of Science and the Royal Society have enabled it to continue to this day.

In 1876 John Shaw Billings (1838-1913) inaugurated his Index-Catalogue of the Library of the Surgeon-General's Office. This publication was designed to serve both as an index for users of the library and as a bibliography of medical literature.

Since the Index-Catalogue found a wide favorable reception as a bibliographic tool for medical literature, Billings undertook to improve its effectiveness by undertaking to publish monthly editions known as Index Medicus; a Monthly Record of Current Medical Literature, listing books and journal articles in a dictionary catalogue. Index Medicus soon became a major tool of medical bibliography, discontinuing, however, in 1927 when it merged into the American Medical Association's Quarterly Cumulative Index to Current Medical Literature, begun in 1916, to form Quarterly Cumulative Index Medicus.

It was in the area of chemistry where the need for indexes to the periodical literature next became critical.

At the annual meeting of the American Association for the Advancement of Science in 1882 the subject of indexing the chemical literature was discussed and a Committee on Indexing Chemical Literature appointed, chaired by Henry Carrington Bolton[65] (1843-1903). In its first report the next year the Committee recommended, among several alternatives, that a system of journal indexing be adopted which relied on the utilization of volunteer chemists who would index journals available to them for the element of interest to them. [66] This recommendation was adopted by the association and for the next twenty years numerous indexes, or more accurately "one-shot" bibliographies, of this type were produced, though their publication and distribution left much to be desired. Some were published in the <u>Annals of the New York Academy of Sciences</u>, others appeared as <u>Smithsonian Miscellaneous Contributions</u>, while still others were apparently never published. The Smithsonian Institution did, however, circulate a list periodically of these independently prepared subject bibliographies of the chemistry of various elements.

By the 1890's it had become apparent that the system just described was not working and that the situation had grown even more critical when, at the Congress of Chemists held in 1893 in Chicago, Bolton presented another plan for the control of the chemical literature, this one calling for an international index. [67] Bolton's plan called for the chemical society journal of each country to publish an index to the current literature of that country according to a set of internationally agreed upon rules of entry (to be drawn up by an international committee of experts from each society). Bolton expressed the concern that attempts on the part of each nation to provide foreign coverage of the literature were diluting national efforts, and that the way to achieve true international bibliographic control was through 'building blocks' of thorough national control. [68] He further proposed that an international committee on chemical bibliography be established to investigate a scheme, his or any other, for cooperative international indexing. Retrospective coverage would, he felt, be provided by the subject indexes of the Royal Society's <u>Catalogue of Scientific Papers</u>.

A resolution was passed at the Congress to implement Bolton's plan and the next annual report of the Committee on Indexing Chemical Literature expressed a hope that the future International Congress of Applied Chemistry would arrange the publication of an exhaustive index to the chemical literature of the world by means of international cooperation. [69]

The Congress, meeting in Brussels under the aegis of the Belgian Government in 1894, was presented with such a plan by H. Van Laer in the name of the Belgian Chemists Association.

Van Laer proposed that an international bureau be set up which would carry on liaison between chemical societies; provide for the exchange of publications; and prepare an index to the literature of applied chemistry which the Belgian Association would publish as a journal. Material was to be supplied to the central bureau by national committees set up for the purpose. [70]

Nothing further seems to have come of any of these plans.

Meanwhile, Herbert Field, an American zoologist, developed a plan for an international subject index to the zoological literature. This plan called for a central bureau with headquarters in Zurich with various sub-bureaus located in the principal countries of the world. The central bureau would issue a classified bulletin of bibliographic references on cards. With the backing of the canton, the city of Zurich, various professional societies, and probably some of his own money, Field established such a bureau, the Concilium Bibliographicum, in 1896. The Concilium provided a bibliographical service on cards with decimal classification numbers on each and a bibliographic index in journal form, one edition of which was printed on one side of the page only.

It was about this time that the Belgian lawyers Paul Otlet and Henri La Fontaine set up, with the support of the Belgian Government, the International Institute of Bibliography in Brussels (sometimes called the Brussels Institute). Broadly speaking, it was the purpose of the Institute to act as a world bibliographical information center. While the Institute never published its projected Répertoire bibliographique universel, its accomplishments in the field of international bibliography were significant, among them: 1) the publication of a journal which served as a medium for the exchange of information on bibliographic organization; 2) serving as a clearinghouse on bibliographical information; 3) the development and issuance of expanded schedules of the Universal Decimal Classification; and 4) the convening of international meetings on bibliographic organization. The Institute found no easy solutions to the problems of bibliographic control and even came under suspicion from librarians and bibliographers who distrusted its centralization of the bibliographic function and its preoccupation with the Universal Decimal Classification. [71]

Other indexes to subject areas of the sciences followed.

In 1902 the Bibliographie scientifique française began publication on a bimonthly basis under the auspices of the French
National Ministry of Education, attempting to index the literature of the pure sciences comprehensively.   In the same
year in the field of physics the Halbmonatliches Literaturverzeichnis der Fortschritte der Physik began publication.

Indexes to the periodical literature were also developing in the applied sciences and in technology.

As early as 1856 the Repertorium der technischen
Journal-Literatur had appeared, being an alphabetical subject
index to some 400 engineering periodicals.   Through 1876
the Repertorium was published under the auspices of the
Prussian Ministry of Business, Industry, and Public Works;
from 1877 through 1908 under the auspices of the German
Patent Office.   Its work was taken up by the International
Institute of Technical Bibliography from 1909 through 1913
(with an English edition published as Engineering Abstracts)
covering the various branches of engineering.

The next major index in this area was Wilson's Industrial Arts Index which began publication in 1913 providing a
monthly alphabetical subject index to the periodical literature.

The social sciences and humanities were not without
their indexes, though they seem to have come on the scene
later than those in other fields and to appear with less frequency.   Also, they generally indexed the monographic as
well as the periodical literature.   Important examples are
the Bibliographie der Sozialwissenschaft (Göttingen, 1905-   )
and the Annual Bibliography of English Language and Literature (Cambridge, Eng., 1920-   ).   There were of course
periodical indexes in these fields similar to those in the
sciences and technology, notably the Public Affairs Information Service (New York, 1915-   ) and the Index to Legal
Periodicals (New York, 1908-   ).

The first two decades of the twentieth century were
a period of astounding growth both in the number of periodicals published and in the number of indexing publications
which developed in response to the increased demand for
more specialized coverage.

b.   The Review Journal.

By the term review journal we mean here to refer to

that type of periodical bibliography sometimes called the collective synthesis or Jahresbericht type, i.e., a journal giving a critical survey of progress within a given subject field
in a given period of time in a classified bibliographic essay.
Examples are the "Annual Review of ...," "Advances in ...,"
and "Progress in ...."

Like the abstract and the index journals, the review
journal is also a logical extension of current serial bibliography from the journal-dependent form to independent form.

Vickery[72] states that the first review journal was published in 1795 as a new retrieval tool to deal with the growth
of the literature. It seems to have become a common form
by the middle of the nineteenth century especially in Germany
where it formed, along with the abstract journal, one of the
principal elements of bibliographic control of the periodical
literature.[73]

It is beyond the scope of this present study to examine
in detail the history of the review journal. Rather, here we
ought to note its role in the overall bibliographic control of
the periodical literature, especially in Germany where it
came, by the early twentieth century, to have the dual role
of current critical survey as well as retrospective index to
the Zentralblätter. Take, for example, the firm of Julius
Springer[74] of Berlin which was probably the major medical
publisher of the period. In addition to publishing primary
medical journals, the firm also published numerous Zentralblätter presenting abstracts of every aspect of the world's
medical literature, and compiled by the firm's own abstrac-
tors. In addition, Springer also published a series of Jahresberichte presenting both a critical survey of each year's primary literature and an index to the abstracts in their Zentralblätter. This arrangement seems to have been indicative
of a trend in Germany of publishers assuming responsibility
for bibliographic control of the periodical literature. Unfor-
tunately this interesting development appears not to have been
sustained.

The review has come to play an increasingly important
role in systematic bibliography.

c.   Monographic Bibliography of Periodical Articles.

Since this study is confined to current bibliography of
periodical literature we will only mention here the monographic form of bibliography of the contents of periodicals.

Monographic bibliography was, of course, the earliest form of printed bibliography and remains to this day an important one. Such works as Arthur Black's Index to the Periodical Dental Literature Published in the English Language, 1839-1938 (Buffalo, 1921-39) form an important part of the total complex of devices which provide effective bibliographic organization.

The foregoing exposition, of course, says nothing about the relationships among these devices, or any interactive effects, and little about their patterns of development. The purpose here has been to show the nature of the bibliographic setting in which abstract journals developed, not as the lone bibliographic tool providing access to the periodical literature, but as one of a complex of devices designed for that purpose, all sharing common origins and developmental characteristics.

Let us now examine in detail the development of the abstract journal in an effort more clearly to understand the rise of this one element of the complex and, perhaps, bibliographic organization as a whole.

Notes

1. Theodore Besterman, The Beginnings of Systematic Bibliography (London: Oxford University Press, 1936).
2. Georg Schneider, Theory and History of Bibliography, trans. Ralph R. Shaw (New York: Columbia University Press, 1934).
3. Louise N. Malclès, Bibliography, trans. Theodore C. Hines (New York: Scarecrow Press, 1961).
4. Encyclopedia Americana, 1974 ed., s.v. "Bibliography," by Verner W. Clapp.
5. Besterman, pp. 2-3.
6. Barbara M. Hale, The Subject Bibliography of the Social Sciences and Humanities (New York: Pergamon Press, 1970), p. 6.
7. Malclès, p. 84.
8. Hale, p. 7.
9. Ibid., p. 9. Louise N. Malclès, Les Sources du travail bibliographique, 3 vols. (Geneva: Droz, 1950-58), 1:265.
10. This point is further developed below, pp. 55-56.
11. Malclès, Les Sources du travail bibliographique, 1:266.
12. Malclès, Bibliography, p. 83.
13. Bradford, p. 18.

14.   Ibid., pp. 84-85.
15.   Collison, The Annals of Abstracting, 1665-1970, p. iv.
16.   Ibid.; Malclès, Bibliography, p. 84; Hale, p. 21.
17.   Discussion of this complex issue is clearly beyond the
      scope of this present work. Interested readers are
      referred to Shera, Documentation and the Organiza-
      tion of Knowledge (London: Lockwood, 1966), pp.
      25-27; Maria Dembowska, Documentation and Scien-
      tific Information, trans. Halina Dunin (Warsaw:
      Scientific Publications Foreign Cooperation Center
      of the Central Institute for Scientific, Technical, and
      Economic Information, 1968), p. 25; and Loosjes,
      pp. 15-17.
18.   Dembowska, p. 25. Hale, pp. 11-13.
19.   Malclès, Bibliography, p. 84.
20.   Collison, The Annals of Abstracting, 1665-1970, p. iv.
21.   Ibid.
22.   Katherine O. Murra, "Notes on the Development of the
      Concept of Current Complete National Bibliography,"
      published as an appendix to Unesco/Library of Con-
      gress Bibliographical Survey (Washington: U.S.
      Govt. Print. Off., 1950), p. 5.
23.   William W. Bishop, "Historic Developments in Library
      Buildings," in Library Buildings for Library Service,
      ed: Herman H. Fussler (Chicago: American Library
      Association, 1947), p. 2. William F. Ogburn, "Re-
      cent Social Trends--Their Implications for Libraries,"
      in Library Trends, ed: Louis R. Wilson (Chicago:
      University of Chicago Press, 1940), p. 2.
24.   Murra, "Notes on the Concept of Current Complete Na-
      tional Bibliography," p. 8.
25.   Ibid.
26.   For a detailed account of these activities the interested
      reader is referred to Katherine O. Murra, "History
      of Some Attempts to Organize Bibliography Interna-
      tionally," in Bibliographic Organization, ed: Jesse
      H. Shera (Chicago: University of Chicago Press,
      1951), pp. 24-53.
27.   Malclès, Bibliography, pp. 107-108.
28.   Ibid., pp. 109-110. Hale, p. 14.
29.   Shera, Documentation and the Organization of Knowledge,
      p. 8.
30.   See below, pp. 55-63.
31.   Shera, Documentation and the Organization of Knowledge,
      p. 25.
32.   Malclès, Bibliography, p. 94; Mayer, in Guide to His-
      tory of Science. George Sarton, ed. pp. 105-106.

33. Archer Taylor, General Subject-Indexes Since 1548 (Philadelphia: University of Pennsylvania Press, 1966), pp. 174-175.

34. Clapp, "Indexing and Abstracting Services for Serial Literature," Library Trends 2 (April 1954): 509-510.

35. Collison, Abstracts and Abstracting Services, p. 64.

36. Frank L. Mott, History of American Magazines, 5 vols. (Cambridge, Mass.: Harvard University Press, 1938-68), 1:120.

37. Brodman, p. 131. Malclès, Bibliography, p. 94.

38. Archer Taylor, A History of Bibliographies of Bibliographies (New Brunswick, N.J.: Scarecrow Press, 1955): p. 34.

39. Kronick, pp. 219-33.

40. Malclès, Les Sources du travail bibliographique, 1: 265-76.

41. New York Public Library, A Check List of Cumulative Indexes to Individual Periodicals in the New York Public Library, comp. Daniel C. Haskell (New York: New York Public Library, 1942).

42. Kronick, pp. 226-27.

43. Ernst H. Lehmann, Einführung in die Zeitschriftenkunde (Leipzig: Hiersemann, 1936), p. 202.

44. Verner W. Clapp, "Indexing and Abstracting Services for Serial Literature," p. 511.

45. Ibid., pp. 511-512.

46. Dictionary of American Biography, s.v. "Griswold, William McC."

47. American Library Association, "Proceedings of the First Annual Meeting," Library Journal 1 (November 30, 1876): pp. 113-121.

48. Clapp, "Indexing and Abstracting Services for Serial Literature," p. 512.

49. Ibid.

50. Annual Library Index 1 (1905): iii.

51. Clapp, "Indexing and Abstracting Services for Serial Literature," p. 512.

52. Annual Library Index 1 (1905): iii.

53. Clapp, "Indexing and Abstracting Services for Serial Literature," p. 512.

54. American Library Association, "Proceedings of the Annual Meeting," Library Journal 20 (December 1895): 870-880.

55. Cumulative Index to a Selected List of Periodicals 1 (1896): iii.

56. Clapp, "Indexing and Abstracting Services for Serial Literature," p. 512.

57. John Lawler, <u>The H. W. Wilson Company</u> (Minneapolis:
     University of Minnesota Press, 1950), pp. 39-41.
58. <u>Ibid.</u>
59. Clapp, "Indexing and Abstracting Services for Serial
     Literature," p. 513.
60. Thomas Coulson, <u>Joseph Henry, His Life and Work</u>
     (Princeton: Princeton University Press, 1950),
     p. 203.
61. Smithsonian Institution, <u>Sixth Annual Report</u> (Washing-
     ton: U.S. Govt. Print. Off., 1852), p. 22.
62. Coulson, pp. 203-05.
63. British Association for the Advancement of Science,
     <u>Report of the Twenty Fifth Meeting ... Glasgow,</u>
     <u>1855</u> (London: John Murray, 1856), p. lxvi.
64. Clapp, "Indexing and Abstracting Services for Serial
     Literature," p. 514.
65. American Association for the Advancement of Science,
     <u>Proceedings ... 1882</u> (Washington: American Asso-
     ciation for the Advancement of Science, 1883),
     p. 627.
66. <u>Idem</u>, <u>Proceedings ... 1883</u> (Washington: American
     Association for the Advancement of Science, 1884),
     pp. 147-48.
67. Henry C. Bolton, "An International Index to Chemical
     Literature," <u>Journal of the American Chemical So-</u>
     <u>ciety</u> 15 (October 1893): 577-579.
68. American Association for the Advancement of Science,
     <u>Proceedings ... 1894</u> (Washington: American Asso-
     ciation for the Advancement of Science, 1895),
     p. 172.
69. American Association for the Advancement of Science,
     Committee on Indexing the Chemical Literature,
     <u>Report ... 1894</u> (Washington: American Association
     for the Advancement of Science, 1895), p. 172.
70. H. Van Laer, "Des measures destinées à faciliter aux
     chimistes et techniciens l'accès rapide de toutes les
     publications qui les intéressant," in Congres inter-
     national de chimie appliquée, <u>compte-rendu</u> (Brussels:
     Deprey, 1894), pp. 1-6.
71. Katherine O. Murra, "History of Some Attempts to Or-
     ganize Bibliography Internationally," p. 37.
72. Brian C. Vickery, <u>Techniques of Information Retrieval</u>
     (Hamden, Conn.: Archon Books, 1970), p. 5.
73. E. Wyndham Hulme and C. Kinzbrunner, "On Current
     Serial Digests and Indexes of the Literature of Sci-
     ence and Some Problems Connected Therewith,"
     <u>Library Association Record</u> 15 (January 1913): 23.

74.   "Purpose and Organization of the Medical Reference
         Journals of the firm of Julius Springer in Berlin,"
         <u>Bulletin of the Medical Library Association</u> 20
         (1932): 172-74.

CHAPTER III

ORIGINS AND DEVELOPMENT BEFORE 1790

The Practice of Abstracting

     The practice of abstracting, as mentioned above,
dates from the earliest periods of recorded history. As
understood today, abstracting appears to be an outgrowth of
the ancient art of annotation--an art highly varied in form
and function. Chief among the forms of annotation that had
developed by the time of the invention of printing were: annotation of manuscripts, library catalogs, and bibliographies;
calendaring; and legal digesting and reporting.

     Annotation of manuscripts before the invention of
printing generally took the form of marginalia, or side notes,
which provided a gloss of the text by way of explanation,
definition, or translation of textual words or expressions.
Annotations served the additional purpose in many cases of
summarizing the text by providing a running commentary.
This summarizing function of marginalia is referred to by
Harrod when he points out that "... if read with continuity,
side notes give an abstract of the whole work,"[1] while Dane,
referring to the earliest law digests, defines them as "an
alphabetical arrangement of marginal notes."[2]

     The annotations, or notes, of early library catalogs
and bibliographies summarized, described, elucidated, or,
somewhat less often, evaluated the works listed. The earliest
attempts at describing works in library catalogs and bibliographies, especially in the manuscript era, were limited primarily to biographical matters rather than description being
essentially bio-bibliographical dictionaries as mentioned above.
By the sixteenth century, however, the practice of considering the work for its own sake had become well established
and a system of description and collation began to evolve.[3]
Tritheim, Gesner, and other early bibliographers practiced
the art and provided such annotations and collations in their

bibliographies. [4] In the book trade, it should also be noted, the art of annotation was being practiced in the compilation of booksellers' catalogs. [5] Here annotations, like the side notes just mentioned, seem generally to have been a mixture of summary, description, elucidation, and sometimes, though rarely, evaluation. The subsequent evolution of the annotation is characterized by increased emphasis on the descriptive and explanatory functions.

The two forms of annotation, the marginalia and notes of library catalogs and bibliographies, may be viewed, then, as "internal," in the former case, and "external," in the latter case with reference to the document annotated, both with essentially the same function, viz., summary, description, elucidation, and evaluation. It is here suggested that the "internal" annotation evolved into the homotopic abstract, for summary purposes, and the footnote, for descriptive, elucidative, and evaluative purposes. The "external" annotation evolved into the abstract, for summary purposes, the descriptive and elucidative annotation, and the evaluative review. That all three of these elements of bibliography were well developed in early times is borne out by Malclès'[6] observations regarding the state of enumerative bibliography in the sixteenth century.

Referring to the apparent evolution of the abstract from the early annotations, Robinson states that:

> Abstracting, i.e., the summarizing of books and periodical articles so as to give the researcher or specialist a clear idea of their possible value to him, is an extension of annotation but not really within the field of bibliography. The handling and arrangement of the finished abstract, however, is. [7]

Chandler observes that "Abstracting is itself an extension of the art of annotation which has long been accepted as part of the craft of cataloging books"[8]; while Foskett notes that "... annotation is an art that has been practiced by libraries since antiquity. "[9]

Calendaring is an aspect of archival practice concerned with listing, usually chronologically, documents in a given collection, e.g., charters, rolls, and state papers, giving the date and an annotation indicating the nature of or summarizing the contents of each. Documents of this type

do not have distinguishing authors or subjects and there is a
need, therefore, to provide with each citation a brief summary of the document's contents. Calendaring may be said
to be an application of the art of annotation closely akin to
annotation as practiced by librarians and compilers of bibliographies. Its function was, and still is, primarily inventorial and concerned with documents. It is, therefore, a
separate, parallel evolvement to that of the abstract journal.

The practice of law reporting and digesting is a venerable form of bibliography extant since the middle ages.[10]
As such it represents one of the earliest forms of compilation or consolidation of abstracts from a number of sources
as opposed to monographic abridgements designed to enable
the scholar to have access to the literature.

Law reporting, Moran writes, is "... the production
of an adequate record of a judicial decision on a point of law,
in a case heard in open court, for the subsequent citation as
a precedent."[11] It commonly contains, among other things,
a summary of the essential facts of the case.

Hicks defines law digesting as "... compilation of
paragraphs containing concise summaries of points in cases,
grouped under appropriate headings, the chief of which are
alphabetically arranged. The digest is not conceived, exe-
cuted, or properly announced as a substitute for law reports,
but as an elaborate subject index to them."[12] The digest
developed, according to Dane, as "the product of the system
of commonplacing which was in vogue in the childhood of
English common law, among lawyers as well as students."[13]

The flexibility and hospitality of this system of reports
and digests in effecting bibliographic control of legal literature is attested to by its continuity from the middle ages to
the present.

Legal reporting and digesting, then, seems to be an
outgrowth of the annotation of legal works with emphasis on
the compilation of points of law for the benefit of practitioners; calendaring seems to have evolved from early annotations
of state documents for inventorial purposes; while the abstract, as used in this study, seems to have evolved as an
extension of the art of annotation adopted as a technique of
bibliography with the purpose of providing scholars with a
summary of a book or other publication. These three practices represent separate, yet collateral, lines of development.

The Abstract Journal, 1665-1790

Very little scholarly investigation of the abstract journal in the period from 1665 through 1790 exists, with the principal exception of Kronick's study of the origins and development of the scientific and technological periodical press during this period in which he investigated the abstract journal as an aspect of derivative publication. It would perhaps be best to examine the abstract journal of this period here similarly in the context of the learned journal and its development.

The period from the invention of printing to the invention of the learned journal was a period in which the scholars of the day were handicapped by inadequate facilities for communication and publicity. When one considers the growth of knowledge and the increase in authorship in this period it is not surprising that the system of learned letters, with its defects of time lag, irregularity, and privacy, which had held sway for centuries began to prove inadequate for scholarly communication. [14] These factors, along with a concomitant rise of the sciences and intellectual curiosity in general, combined to produce the learned society and the learned journal as solutions to the problem. [15] The Journal des sçavans, founded in Paris in 1665, and the Philosophical Transactions of the Royal Society of London, founded in the same year, are generally considered to be the first such journals. These publications were so successful that they were soon followed by a host of imitators throughout Europe. Barnes[16] points out that 330 periodicals were founded in seven countries of Europe between 1665 and 1730, with Germany leading in production. The rapid growth of the learned journal suggests that it was the answer to the scholars' need for a rapid, public, and dependable means of communication.

In addition to presenting original contributions discussing discoveries, experiments, and observations, learned journals included from the beginning three major components[17]: abstracts or extracts from other journals or from books, book reviews, and news reports. The former two elements providing as they did a bibliographical function found immediate acceptance among the savants of the age who were anxious to learn of the existence and nature of new materials of interest to them. Many were especially interested to learn of foreign experiences because of the difficulty of provision of foreign language materials since the book trade was, at this point, not yet well developed.

An additional reason for the rapid acceptance by
scholars of the bibliographic function of the learned journal
was the advantage it afforded in speed and convenience over
the alternative bibliographic devices in use up to this time,
the encyclopedias, handbooks, etc., which were in common
use in the late seventeenth and eighteenth centuries.[18] These
guides, such as Müllern's Einleitung in die oekonomische-
physikalische Bücherkunde, surveyed retrospectively the literature of a field, often providing abstracts of the works listed.
It was only natural, then, that the learned journal should
adopt such a device as the abstract, already in common use
in the field of bibliography, to meet the needs of its readers,
particularly given the bibliographic consciousness of early
journal editors.[19]

A word should be inserted here about the nature of
this bibliographic content of these early learned journals.
As already mentioned, the character of these contributions
was not critical or evaluative as the review journals of today
are, nor can their contents be categorized strictly as abstracts, extracts, or reviews as we think of those devices
today; rather, they partook equally of the nature of the abstract, the extract, and the review, combining the form and
function of all three. Further, what review character there
was to these devices was far from the critical review we
know today. Learned opinion at the time, as well as the
anxiety of editors to avoid offending authors and the public
alike, dictated an impartial description of materials.

In addition to the bibliographic guides and handbooks
mentioned above which had to this point traditionally provided
bibliographic access for the scholar, there was also in the
late seventeenth and eighteenth centuries an alternative mechanism which should perhaps be noted here, viz., the serially
issued surveys of the past literature, hybrid between the
handbooks issued monographically and the learned journals
which had carried abstracts from their beginnings. An example of this comparatively rare device is Hager's Geographisches Büchersaal issued in thirty parts from 1764 through
1768 at Chemnitz.

Kronick,[20] in his study of the origins and development
of the scientific and technological periodical press from 1665
through 1790 categorizes the learned journals of the period
as follows:

   I.   Original publication
       A.   The substantive journal
       B.   The society proceedings
  II.   Derivative publication
       A.   The abstract journal
       B.   The review journal
       C.   The collection

Original publication comprises that group of periodicals whose contents are devoted primarily to original contributions. Substantive journals are those independent of society and learned academy sponsorship.

Derivative publication comprises that group of periodicals whose contents are devoted primarily to contributions from other periodicals, usually in the form of abstracts, extracts, translations, or reviews. Collections comprise that group of journals whose entire contents consist of reprints from other journals.

Because of the difficulty in distinguishing the abstract, from the extract, from the review there is a corresponding difficulty in insisting upon any rigid classification of the learned periodical press of the period into such categories as abstract journals and review journals. Further, we are not concerned here with the substantive journals carrying sections of abstracts/reviews covering the monographic literature, or the marginal forms of the abstract journal, the serially issued literature guides surveying past literature in the form of subject bibliography accompanied by abstracts. We are concerned with the journals which were occupied with abstracting the contents of other periodicals and which had developed as a response to the growth of the periodical literature.

Kronick, recognizing these problems, differentiates the abstract journal from the review journal and defines it as follows:

> A broad distinction ... can be made between the
> two categories on the basis that, on the whole, the
> review journals devoted themselves to surveying the
> entire literature, while the abstract ... journals,
> as here defined, concerned themselves predominantly
> with the literature appearing in other periodicals.[21]

He further defines the review journal as being principally concerned with the monographic literature.

The Journal des sçavans is often cited by writers as the first abstract journal because it included among its contents notices of periodical articles. The Journal, while included in this study, is a marginal case at best since notices of books usually predominated over notices of articles. Too, following the appearance of the Philosophical Transactions, the Journal seems to have modified its format to include more original material and fewer abstracts. [22]

Kronick identifies as the first authentic abstract journal devoted exclusively to abstracts and about which we have any knowledge the Aufrichtige und unpartheyische Gedancken über die Journale, Extracte und Monaths-Schriften, worrinen dieselben extrahiret, wann es nutzisch suppliret oder wo es nothig, emediret werden; nebst einer Vorrede von der Annehmlichkeit, Nutzen und Fehlern gedachter Schriften. It was edited by Christian Gottfried Hoffman (1692-1735) who states in the first issue the purpose of the work:

> In the first place I will spare you the task of purchasing and reading all the monthly publications. Secondly, when it is necessary and possible I will include a collation of the reviews along with a list of the books which have been reviewed. And thirdly, you will have an adequate report and an extract of those extracts. [23]

Two volumes of twelve issues each of the Aufrichtige were published between 1714 and 1717 abstracting about forty different titles.

As mentioned earlier, many journals of this period carried sections of abstracts/extracts/reviews covering articles appearing elsewhere. The Vollständige Einleitung in die Monaths-Schriften der Deutschen (Erlangen, 1747) consisted of a list of the contents as well as extracts of some of the articles of a number of learned and belletristic journals published in 1746; the Allgemeines Magazin der Natur, Kunst und Wissenschaft (Leipzig, 1753) similarly contained abstracts of the periodical literature, especially the foreign periodical press, as did the Neue Auszüge aus den Besten ausländischen Wochen- und Monatsschriften (Frankfurt, 1756-1769). Probably the best known of the journals of this type during the period under review was the Esprit des journaux

français et étrangers (Liège; etc., 1772-1818), similar in
content and style to the Neue Auszüge.

English examples of this genre are the Universal Magazine of Knowledge and Pleasure (London, 1747-1815) and the
Monthly Review (London, 1749-1844) both containing reprints,
extracts, condensations and reviews of articles from learned
journals as well as books.

As the eighteenth century progressed the nature of the
literary review periodical changed slowly. It began to assume more of the critical style of the modern review journal,[24] the Monthly Review especially becoming the prototype
of the modern critical review journal. Throughout its existence the Monthly Review attempted in some manner to review all publications of the month. From its beginnings in
1749 it carried extensive reviews, chiefly of books, but also
of articles from other literary journals. With 1764, the
Monthly Review began to carry an appendix entitled "Foreign
Articles," devoted primarily to reviews of foreign books.
With 1778 this section began to carry abstracts of foreign
academy proceedings, expanding quickly to cover the French,
Belgian, and other royal academies and scientific societies
as well as the Philosophical Transactions of the Royal Society.
This section grew to prominence with the turn of the century
and continued through May 1825 when, with a change of editorship, the Monthly Review changed in nature, becoming a
critical literary review journal and adopting lengthy, critical
reviews of books and dropping altogether notices of journal
articles.

The Monthly Review had many imitators, foreign and
domestic, including among their contents abstracts of journal
articles, generally with no attempt at critical review. The
character of the Monthly Review was very strongly reflected
in the other review journals of the day. In fact, Ralph
Griffith (1720-1803), founder and editor of the Monthly Review, is credited with creating what was to be for a hundred
years the standard type of periodical criticism.[25]

The major English imitator of the Monthly Review was
the Analytical Review (London, 1788-1799). The Analytical
Review similarly tried to comment in some way on every important book published. It also attempted coverage of periodical articles. In addition to abstracts from the Philosophical
Transactions, in a section entitled "Literary Intelligence" arranged by broad subject categories, the Analytical Review

carried abstracts of selected journal articles but covered
mainly books.

Another imitator of the <u>Monthly Review</u>, and to a certain extent of the <u>Spectator</u>, was the French <u>Journal encyclopédique ou universel</u> (Liège; Brussels, 1756-1793) which
Kronick describes as "one of the outstanding journals of the
Enlightenment, [26] and which was itself widely imitated on the
continent.

Beyond the abstracts carried in sections of general
literary periodicals like the <u>Monthly Review</u>, there were already specialized journals carrying abstracts, particularly in
the sciences. Here the nature of the abstract was more like
the abstract we are familiar with today--a concise, non-eval-
uative summary. This was probably due to the nature of the
subject and its data.

As early as 1764 Georg Hager (1701-1777) was issuing
his <u>Geographisches Büchersaal zum Nutzen und Vergnügen
eröffnet</u> (Chemnitz, 1764-1778), a periodically issued handbook
in the area of geography containing abstracts of retrospective
works in that field.

The German chemist Lorenz Florenz Friedrich von
Crell (1745-1816), motivated by a desire to promote German
chemical leadership and a wish to spread information about
chemistry, was the founder of several journals of interest to
this study. [27] His first journal was the <u>Chemisches Journal
für die Freunde der Naturlehre, Arzneygelahrtheit, Haushaltungskunst und Manufacturen</u> which appeared from 1778 until
1781 when it was continued by his <u>Die neuesten Entdeckungen
in der Chemie</u> which appeared through 1786. Both of these
journals contained original articles as well as translations,
extracts, and abstracts of articles from foreign scientific society publications as well as from other scientific journals.
His <u>Neues chemisches Archiv</u> (Leipzig, 1783-1791) (1783 as
<u>Chemisches Archiv</u>) fulfilled his desire to make known the
publications of chemical interest in society and other journal
publications. Arranged by society, publication title and issue, the <u>Neues chemisches Archiv</u> comprises a retrospective
bibliography of such publications accompanied by abstracts.
His <u>Chemische Annalen für die Freunde der Naturlehre,
Arzneygelahrtheit, Haushaltungskunst und Manufacturen</u> (Helmstaedt; Leipzig, 1784-1804) and its <u>Beiträge</u> (Helmstaedt;
Leipzig, 1785-1799), while devoted primarily to original articles, also contained abstracts of current work. The <u>Annalen</u>

contained a section through 1797 entitled "Notices of Chemical Literature," noting books of interest and a section entitled "Abstracts of the Chemical Literature of the (year)"
in which were presented abstracts of the contents of the proceedings of the various scientific societies. The Beiträge
contained a similar section called "Abstracts of the Literature of (year)."

Crell's journals were important in that they created
a forum where German chemists exchanged their findings and
views, thus aiding in the development of German chemical
preeminence. His journals were equally important as models
for other scientific and technical periodicals at home and
abroad. Crell's belief in the importance of the abstract as
a bibliographic device and his use of it in his journals undoubtedly influenced its widespread adoption of other learned
journals in the nineteenth century.[28]

Among the journals devoted exclusively to abstracts
from the scientific literature was the Natuur- en Genees-
kundige Bibliothek (Lausanne, 1783-1784) edited by Edouard
Sandifort (1742-1814) and issued in three parts covering medicine, natural history, and chemistry.

Very few of the abstract journals of the period from
1665 through 1790 could be classified exclusively as abstract
journals since many of them contained other materials, such
as original contributions, translations, and excerpts from
other journals.

Kronick has derived data relating to the growth, duration, subject distribution and country of origin of abstract
journals in the period from 1665 through 1790. Table 1
shows growth by subject and decade or origin. Table 2 shows
these same abstract journals tabulated by subject and country
of origin.

As can be seen from Tables 1 and 2, during the entire period from 1665 through 1790 only 42 abstract journals
appeared, the bulk of these being classified by Kronick as
general with medical abstract journals comprising most of
the remainder. Table 1 shows a considerable spurt in growth
in the period 1740-1790. Table 2 indicates a high proportion
of German abstract journals for all subject categories. Regarding duration, Kronick states that "the abstract journals
as a whole were of relatively short duration; only 14 lasting
10 years or longer, and 24 did not continue their existence
beyond a single year."[29]

TABLE 1

ABSTRACT JOURNALS ISSUED 1665-1790 BY SUBJECT AND DECADE OF ORIGIN

	1660-69	1670-79	1680-89	1690-99	1700-09	1710-19	1720-29	1730-39	1740-49	1750-59	1760-69	1770-79	1780-90	Total
General	--	-	-	1	2	-	1	1	9	1	3	4	2	24
Medical	--	-	-	-	-	-	-	1	-	4	1	7	-	13
Other	--	-	-	-	-	-	-	-	1	1	-	1	2	5
Total	--	-	-	1	2	-	1	2	10	6	4	12	4	42

SOURCE: Kronick, p. 156.

TABLE 2

ABSTRACT JOURNALS ISSUED 1665-1790 BY SUBJECT AND COUNTRY OF ORIGIN

	Germany	France	Holland	England	Other	Total
General	13	4	4	1	2	24
Medical	8	2	3	-	-	13
Other	4	-	1	-	-	5
Total	25	6	8	1	2	42

SOURCE: Kronick, p. 157.

In summarizing his findings Kronick states:

> The journals which had their origins in the period
> 1665-1790 can be divided into two major groups,
> which can be designated by several groups of oppos-
> ing terms, e.g., primary and secondary, original
> and derivative, the literature of record and the lit-
> erature of dissemination; these terms reflect the
> two roles of the medium as a repository and as a
> vehicle. These two roles have never been clearly
> differentiated either in the long history of the scien-
> tific periodical or in our current publication prac-
> tices. [30]

Speaking of the abstract journal in particular he stated:

> A large proportion of the early journals devoted a
> considerable portion of their space to extracts and
> reprints from other journals, but journals devoted
> exclusively to abstracts of journal articles did not
> appear in any number until the middle of the eigh-
> teenth century. The necessity for abstract journals
> was reduced to some extent by the existence of
> bibliographic handbooks and by the fact that many
> of the substantive journals as well as many of the
> general literary journals devoted a considerable
> portion of their space to this type of material. [31]

After 1790, and especially in the first quarter of the
nineteenth century, the function of bibliography, as we have
seen, was to change significantly. Rather than a preoccupation with saving the texts of the past from oblivion, bibliography was soon to be concerned with the dissemination of
current advances of learning, i.e., current bibliographical
control. This new role called for a new form of bibliographic device. It is here that the modern abstract journal
emerges.

Notes

1. Harrod, p. 590.
2. Nathan Dane, <u>A General Abridgment and Digest of
   American Law</u>, 9 vols. (Boston: Cummings, Hilliard & Co., 1823-1829), 1:iv.
3. Besterman, p. 26-27
4. <u>Ibid.</u>, p. 18.
5. <u>Ibid.</u>, p. 6.

6.   Malclès, Bibliography, p. 18.
7.   Antony Robinson, Systematic Bibliography, 3d ed.
     (Hamden, Conn.: Linnet Books, 1971), pp. 26-27.
8.   Chandler, p. 6.
9.   D. J. Foskett, Science, Humanism and Libraries (New
     York: Hafner, 1964), p. 38.
10. A good discussion of the history of law reporting and
     digesting is presented in Frederick G. Hicks, Ma-
     terials and Methods of Legal Research, 3d ed.
     (Rochester, N.Y.: Lawyers' Cooperative Pub. Co.,
     1942), pp. 97-155.
11. Clarence G. Moran, The Heralds of the Law (London:
     Stevens, 1948), p. 3.
12. Hicks, p. 128.
13. Dane, p. 282.
14. Sherman B. Barnes, "The Beginnings of Learned Jour-
     nalism," Scientific Monthly (March 1934): 257.
15. Douglas McKie, "The Scientific Periodical from 1665-
     1798," Philosophical Magazine (July 1948): 128-30.
     Martha Ornstein, The Role of Scientific Societies in
     the Seventeenth Century (Chicago: University of
     Chicago Press, 1928), pp. 67-69. Fielding Garrison,
     "The Medical and the Scientific Periodicals of the
     Seventeenth and Eighteenth Centuries," Bulletin of
     the Institute of the History of Medicine 2 (July 1934):
     287.
16. Barnes, p. 257.
17. Kronick, p. 235.
18. Hale, pp. 7-11.
19. Taylor, A History of Bibliographies of Bibliographies,
     p. 34.
20. Kronick, p. 11.
21. Ibid., p. 153.
22. Roger P. McCutcheon, "The Journal des sçavans and
     the Philosophical Transactions of the Royal Society,"
     Studies in Philology 21 (October 1924): pp. 626-628.
23. Aufrichtige und unpartheyische Gedancken über die
     Journale 1 (1714), quoted in Kronick, p. 152.
24. Encyclopaedia Britannica, 11th ed. s.v., "Periodicals,"
     by Henry R. Tedder.
25. Walter J. Graham, English Literary Periodicals (New
     York: T. Nelson, 1930), p. 209.
26. Kronick, p. 41.
27. Joachim Kirchner, Das deutsche Zeitschriftenwesen,
     seine Geschichte und seine Probleme, 2d ed., 2
     vols. (Wiesbaden: Harrasowitz, 1958-62), 1:265.
28. Ibid.

29. Kronick, p. 156.
30. Ibid., p. 235.
31. Ibid., p. 237.

CHAPTER IV

CHRONICLE OF THE ABSTRACT JOURNAL, 1790-1920

It is proposed in this chapter to chronicle the development of the abstract journal in the period from 1790 through 1920 in five broad time divisions, each subdivided into the following subject categories: pure sciences (the Universal Decimal Classification (UDC) class 500); medicine (the UDC classes 610-619); applied sciences and technology (the UDC 600 class exclusive of medicine); social sciences (the UDC classes 159-199; 300's, and 900's); the humanities (the UDC classes 100-158, 200's, 400's, 700's, and 800's); and generalities (the UDC class 000-099). Within each broad subject category titles are arranged further by UDC classification and subarranged chronologically.

The Period 1790-1799

No new abstract journals began in the period from 1790 through 1799. However, several of the prototypes begun earlier and discussed above were still being published in this last decade of the eighteenth century.

Pure Sciences

In the area of the pure sciences the specialized Neues chemische Archiv (Leipzig, 1783-1791); the Chemische Annalen für die Freunde der Naturlehre, Arzneygelahrtheit, Haushaltungskunst und Manufacturen (Helmstaedt; Leipzig, 1784-1804); and the latter's Beiträge (Helmstaedt: Leipzig, 1785-1799) were extant. Each of these titles was discussed above. [1]

Generalities

Among the many periodicals of general interest, the following literary periodicals containing abstracts flourished in the decade under review: the Journal des sçavans; the Universal Magazine of Knowledge and Pleasure (London, 1747-1815); the Monthly Review (London, 1749-1844); the Journal encyclopédique ou universel (Liège; Brussels, 1756-1793); and the Analytical Review (London, 1788-1799). These journals also have been discussed above. [2]

No abstract journals in the fields of medicine, applied sciences and technology, the social sciences, and the humanities were encountered in this time period.

The Period 1800-1819

Pure Sciences

The only abstract journal in the pure sciences which was active at the beginning of this period was Crell's Chemische Annalen, surviving until 1804. The first new abstract journal to appear was the Retrospect of Philosophical, Mechanical, Chemical, and Agricultural Discoveries (London, 1805-1813). The Retrospect was subtitled "... an abridgment of the periodical and other publications, English and foreign, relative to the arts, chemistry, manufactures, agriculture, and natural philosophy; accompanied occasionally with remarks on the merit or defects of the respective papers...." This publication appeared three times in 1805 and quarterly thereafter, presenting abstracts of periodical articles mainly in the area of applied chemistry, randomly arranged under the following subject categories: "Chemistry and Mineralogy," "Natural Philosophy, Arts, and Manufactures," "Agriculture," "Review of Specifications of Patents Published in the 'Repertory of Arts, etc.' in the Months of ...." An annual combined author and subject index to the abstracts was issued.

Speaking in the preface of volume one, the editors remark on the problems of control of the scientific journal literature:

> ... at length the number and variety of scientific journals are become so great as to require, for the conveniency of most readers, a separate work, to serve as a digested index to the whole. This volume is the fruit of an attempt to that end, wherein the Editors believe will be found, in an abridged form, every article contained in those several publications. [3]

Typical of so much of British journal authorship of the period, the Retrospect was edited anonymously. A thorough
search of the entire run of this journal reveals no clue as to
the identity of the editors nor does a search of secondary
bibliographic sources. Again from the preface to volume
one, the editors make the following statement: "It would be
grateful to the proprietors to announce the names of the
gentlemen who assist in the execution of this work, but the
reader will doubtless see an obvious impropriety in it.[4]

A reviewer commenting on the Retrospect in the Critical Review states:

> This work is of a periodical description, and three
> times in the year announces the various occurrences
> which have taken place in the departments of philos-
> ophy and the arts, in the manner stated in its most
> copious title. Great diligence has been used to
> collect much information in little room, and not
> without success. The performance is likely to be
> useful to many whose leisure, whose circumstances,
> or whose inclination do not permit the perusal of
> more diffuse or accurate works. This may be con-
> sidered as a kind of newspaper of science, and we
> are ready to admit that no single periodical work
> can supply all the information here contained.[5]

Interestingly, Callisen[6] comments on the Retrospect
as being an imitation of the Almanach der Fortschritte,
neuesten Erfindungen und Entdeckungen in Wissenschaften,
Künsten, Manufakturen und Handwerken (Erfurt, 1795-1810),
edited by Gabriel Christoph Benjamin Busch (1759-1823) and
constituting a continuation of his dictionary of inventions and
discoveries, the Versuch eines Handbuchs der Erfindungen
(Eisenach, 1790-1798). The Almanach was not seen by the
author and, indeed, is not even listed in the Union List of
Serials or the National Union Catalog, Pre-1956 Imprints.

During 1813 the Retrospect ceased publication without
explanation.

The appearance of the Retrospect was soon followed
by another abstract journal in the pure sciences, the Taschenbuch für die gesamte Mineralogie (Frankfurt, a. M.;
Heidelberg, 1807-1829). The Taschenbuch, founded and
edited by the German mineralogist Karl Cäsar von Leonhard
(1779-1862), was issued once a year from 1807 through 1812;

twice a year from 1813 through 1820; three times a year
from 1821 through 1822; and four times a year from 1823
through 1825. With 1826 it became monthly. Each issue of
the Taschenbuch was comprised of two sections: the "Transactions," containing original contributions, and the "Review
of Latest Discoveries," which contained abstracts of journal
articles as well as correspondence and news notes. From
1825 through 1829 this latter section was called simply "Miscellany."

The abstracts in the Taschenbuch were grouped alphabetically by the geological topic with which each abstract
dealt. Author indexes to the abstracts were provided annually from the beginning.

Leonhard, commenting in the preface to volume one
of the Taschenbuch made the following statement about its
purpose:

> The Taschenbuch will be a presentation as complete
> as possible, of all that has been carried out in the
> year in the field of mineralogy. The repertorium
> shall not be without use to the researcher in nat-
> ural history. It will facilitate his keeping abreast,
> without effort, of the progress in his field, enabl-
> ing him to learn of new discoveries and experi-
> ments. [7]

The Taschenbuch, which according to Zittel[8] soon
came to occupy a high place among the journals of its field,
was superseded in 1830 by the Jahrbuch für Mineralogie,
discussed below.

Applied Sciences and Technology

At the beginning of the period 1800 through 1819
there was no abstract journal covering the area of applied
sciences and technology, principally because these areas were
only beginning to evolve. The first title encountered in this
study in these areas began in 1809, the Bulletin des Neuesten und Wissenwürdigsten aus der Naturwissenschaft (Berlin,
1809-1813), founded and edited by the German physician and
industrial chemist Sigismund Friederich Hermbstädt (1760-
1833). In an earlier period, Hermbstädt had published his
Bibliothek der neuesten physisch-chemischen, metallurgis-
chen, technologischen und pharmaceutischen Literatur (Berlin,
1788-1795), which, like many of the other Bibliotheken of the

time, had as its primary function the review of new developments in the literature. [9] Upon suspension in 1795 of the
Bibliothek due to the vicissitudes of the war, it was Hermbstädt's intention to resume publication on an enlarged plan
with the re-establishment of peace. [10] This he did with the
founding of his monthly Bulletin which contained, especially
in its early numbers (and unlike his Bibliothek), many abstracts of journal articles along with excerpts, reviews and
original articles, all dealing with the newest developments
applicable to industry. The abstracts in the Bulletin were
quite parochial in coverage as were those of the Retrospect
discussed above, being essentially confined to domestic publications. Further, they were scattered throughout the issues,
never constituting a separate section. With the passage of
time these abstracts gave way increasingly to the ever-ex-
panding number of original contributions, and their ephemeral
nature is underscored by the fact that they were never indexed in any way. In 1814 the Museum des Neuesten und
Wissenwürdigsten aus dem Gebiete der Naturwissenschaft,
der Künste, der Fabriken (Berlin, 1814-1818) superseded the
Bulletin. The Museum contained only original contributions.

No abstract journals were being published in this period covering the fields of medicine, the social sciences, and
the humanities.

The Period 1820-1849

Pure Sciences

In 1820 the pioneer American scientific journal American Journal of Science (New Haven, Conn., 1818-   ), begun
under the editorship of the distinguished American mineralogist Benjamin Silliman (1779-1864), began to include a section of abstracts of journal articles called "Intelligence and
Miscellanies," covering primarily selected foreign articles
in a random arrangement. With 1826 this section was subdivided into "Foreign" and "Domestic." From 1830 through
1831 this section was called "Scientific Intelligence" and the
abstracts, now were grouped into subject categories. From
1832 to 1840 the name of the section was "Miscellanies--
Foreign and Domestic" and from 1840 to 1846 simply "Bibliographical Notices." With 1840 the Journal dropped news
items which had been included with the abstracts. With the
beginning of its second series in 1846 the name of the abstract section reverted to "Scientific Intelligence," which

continued through 1920. Material in the abstract section was
included from the beginning in the Journal's author and subject indexes. The frequency of the Journal was irregular
throughout this period, being generally quarterly through 1845,
bimonthly through 1870, and monthly from 1871.

While the Journal was founded and edited for many
year's by a geologist, Silliman, it continued to reflect the
sciences in the broadest sense and its abstract section, similarly, covered science broadly. About the turn of the twentieth century, however, after the Journal had come under the
editorship of Edward S. Dana (1849-1935), also a geologist,
an increasing geological slant in the Journal's articles could
be detected. The abstract section continued through 1920 to
cover science broadly, though, especially the areas of chemistry, physics, geology, and natural history.

The Journal was a major outlet for the publication of
original work by American scientists as well as a model of
scientific journalism. [11] We can only assume that its format,
including a prominent section of abstracts, served as a standard for other American scientific journals.

André Etienne Just Paschal François d'Audebard,
Baron de Ferussac (1786-1836), French military officer and
naturalist, was keenly aware of the need to establish a forum
for keeping the world's scholars in touch by means of regular reports, particularly after the isolation caused by the
Napoleonic Wars. [12] In 1823 he founded the monthly Bulletin
générale et universel des annonces et des nouvelles scientifiques (Paris, 1823) in an effort to achieve this goal. The
Bulletin générale attempted to cover new developments in the
pure sciences, presenting abstracts in a subject classified
arrangement. In 1824 the Bulletin générale was superseded
on an expanded basis[13] by the Bulletin universel des sciences
et de l'industrie (Paris, 1824-1831). Published under the
direction of the Baron de Ferussac and, from 1827, under
the aegis of the Société pour la Propagation des Connaissances Scientifiques et Industrielles, [14] the Bulletin universel
appeared monthly in eight separate, and separately available
sections, each under the editorial direction of a group of experts in the field. The sections were: 1) Bulletin des
sciences mathématiques, astronomiques, physiques et chimiques; 2) Bulletin des sciences naturelles et de géologie;
3) Bulletin des sciences médicales; 4) Bulletin des sciences
agricoles et économiques; 5) Bulletin des sciences technologiques; 6) Bulletin des sciences géographiques; 7) Bulletin des

sciences historiques, antiquités, philologie; and 8) Bulletin des sciences militaires. The first two sections fall into the pure sciences category.

Each of the sections of the Bulletin universel was arranged by broad subject classification and contained abstracts of books but primarily of journal articles. A classified table of contents was provided with each number beginning with 1826, otherwise there were no indexes to the abstracts. The Baron de Ferussac himself contributed many of the abstracts in geology, natural history, geography, and statistics. [15]

A reviewer commenting on the Bulletin universel stated:

> No periodical work was ever commenced on so magnificent a plan, or engaged such weight of talent, as seems pledged for the support of this journal. For the information of those who may consider as visionary the plan of supporting a periodical journal, amounting annually to seventeen octavo volumes, it may be remarked, that the plan has already gone into successful operation. The Bulletin is divided into eight sections, which may be considered entirely independent of each other--each section constituting a distinct monthly journal. Each section is under the immediate charge of one principal editor, or more, and of a number of associates. The Baron de Ferussac has the general superintendence of the work. The plan of conducting this journal, it is thought, must very happily combine the advantages of individual responsibility, and of associated labor.
> It is intended that the work shall be a Methodical Repertory of facts relative to the subjects of which it treats, and a Monthly Review of the successive labours of the human mind throughout the world. [16]

The Bulletin universel ceased in 1831 without explanation.

In physics, the year 1845 marked the establishment of the Physikalische Gesellschaft zu Berlin, from 1899 the Deutsche Physikalische Gesellschaft. The members of the newly-formed society saw as one of their most pressing problems the need to supply German physicists as quickly

as possible with complete information on new developments.[17]
This need they attempted to meet in part by founding the
Fortschritte der Physik (Berlin; Brunswick, 1845-1918). This
important journal presented semi-monthly abstracts from the
international periodical literature in six subdivisions: (1)
General Physics; (2) Acoustics; (3) Optics; (4) Thermody-
namics; (5) Electricity; and (6) Applied Physics. The Fortschritte was edited initially by Gustav Karsten (1820-1900),
professor of physics at Kiel. Author and classified subject
indexes were supplied annually. In 1918 the Fortschritte
merged with the Society's Halbmonatliches Literaturverzeichnis, an unannotated index to current physics literature issued in conjunction with the Fortschritte since 1902, and the
Annalen der Physik Beiblätter, an abstract journal begun in
1877, to form Physikalische Berichte.

In the field of chemistry, the period under review witnessed the birth of a major abstract journal, the Chemisches
Zentralblatt (Leipzig; Berlin, 1830-1969). Founded as Pharmaceutisches Centralblatt, the name was changed in 1850 to
Chemisch-pharmaceutisches Centralblatt; in 1856 to Chemisches Centralblatt and in 1907 to Chemisches Zentralblatt.
The Zentralblatt was founded and edited anonymously by the
eminent experimental psychologist Gustav Theodor Fechner
(1801-1887).

In the statement of purpose prefacing volume one,
Fechner comments:

> The purpose of this undertaking ... is to provide
> for pharmacy a service similar to that provided
> for medicine by Kleinert's Repertorium and Klose's
> Summarium, i.e., a complete and rapid communi-
> cation of all new data important to and of interest
> to the pharmacist appearing in domestic and foreign
> works in such a form that the pharmacist can easily
> obtain the results without a concern for extraneous
> details.[18]

Appearing semi-monthly from January 14 through
October 31, 1830, and weekly thereafter, the Zentralblatt
was at first, as the title implies, restricted primarily to
coverage of the literature of pharmacy. Following 1850 its
coverage soon expanded to the entire literature of pure chemistry as reflected in the title changes from that date. The
Zentralblatt continued to restrict its coverage, however, to
the literature of pure chemistry until 1919 when it took

over the abstract section of the Zeitschrift für angewandte Chemie, from which time it covered both pure and applied chemistry.

Regarding arrangement, the abstracts were apparently in random order, with title entry and with a short table of contents, from 1830 through 1871. With 1872 a more rigorous arrangement was introduced, when the abstracts were numbered and arrayed in a detailed subject classification. Entry was now changed to author-title. Author and subject indexes were issued annually, 1830-1888; semi-annually from 1889 onwards. An annual systematic index was added in 1870, also becoming semi-annual in 1889.

The importance of Chemisches Zentralblatt as an abstract journal lies not only in its broad subject coverage but in the length of time it covered. Further, its style, format, and good abstracts served as a model[19] for other abstract journals which followed. In 1897 the Zentralblatt, previously the product of individual initiative, was taken over by the Deutsche Chemische Gesellschaft, which continued to sponsor it throughout its long existence (jointly with the Verein Deutscher Chemiker from 1919 through June 1923).

In the rather voluminous literature by and about Fechner there is little indication, other than that stated in the introduction to the Zentralblatt cited above, of his motivation in starting this publication.

In 1830 the Neues Jahrbuch für Mineralogie, Geologie und Paläontologie (Heidelberg; Stuttgart, 1830-1949) superseded the Taschenbuch für die gesamte Mineralogie discussed earlier. Edited jointly by Karl Cäsar von Leonhard and Heinrich Georg Bronn (1800-1862), the Jahrbuch fulfilled Leonhard's wish to establish a journal providing a forum for mineralogy, geology, and related subjects expanded from that previously provided from the Taschenbuch.[20] Appearing quarterly, the Neues Jahrbuch contained three sections: (1) "Contributions"; (2) "Correspondence"; and (3) "Abstracts." The latter section comprised a continuously paged section of abstracts arranged by broad subject categories. The title of this section, Auszüge in the original, was changed to Referate in 1880. No indexes were provided to the abstracts before 1885 (except for a systematic table of contents) when an author index was instituted; in 1882 a subject index was added.

Medicine

Besides the Bulletin des sciences médicales (section 3 of the Bulletin universel), discussed above, the period under review witnessed the beginnings of the modern abstract journal in medicine. Several began, covering the literature of medicine generally.

In 1821 the Notizen aus dem Gebiete der Natur- und Heilkunde (Erfurt; Weimar, 1821-1849) appeared. Edited by the physician Ludwig Friedrich von Froriep (1779-1862) and appearing six to ten times per month in a newspaper format, the Notizen carried abstracts from the general medical literature in three rubrics: (1) "Natural Science"; (2) "Medicine"; and (3) "Miscellaneous." No indexes were provided other than a systematic table of contents in each issue. Curiously, in many instances no citation to original materials was made or such citations as were made were usually incomplete, citing only a vague journal title and nothing else.

In 1850 the Notizen was superseded by the Tagsberichte über die Fortschritte der Natur- und Heilkunde* (Weimar, 1850-1852), not examined by the author, but which apparently retained the format of the Notizen.

The next abstract journal to appear in the medical sciences was the Allgemeines Repertorium der gesamten deutschen medizinisch-chirurgischen Journalistik (Leipzig, 1827-1847), edited by Carl Ferdinand Kleinert (1795-1839). The Repertorium appeared irregularly throughout its existence, though it was usually monthly. It was comprised of rather long abstracts of selected medical and surgical articles from current journals, covering until 1840 only the German literature but thereafter expanding its scope to international coverage. Abstracts were arranged under the title of the journals from which they were taken. With the introduction of foreign material in 1840, this section was arranged in subject categories, the entire journal adopting this format in 1845, although the foreign abstracts were still kept separate from the domestic. Fechner, in his introduction to Chemisches Zentralblatt in 1830, refers to the Repertorium, along with Klose's Summarium, as a model for other fields to follow. For the period 1827 to 1828 there were only annual subject indexes, from 1829 to 1847, annual author and subject indexes, published to the Repertorium.

---

*Asterisk in text (not Appendices) means title was not examined.

The Summarium des Neuesten aus der gesamten Medicin (Leipzig, 1828-1843) was similar in format and coverage
to the Repertorium just discussed. It also similarly reflected a growing interest in foreign literature when in 1832
it increased its scope and changed its title to Summarium
des Neuesten der in- und ausländischen Medicin. Edited by
the German physicians Ludolph Hermann Unger (1793-18??)
and Friedrich August Klose (1795-1850) the Summarium appeared monthly subtitling itself "A systematically arranged
review of all literature in the medical arts and sciences, in
abstracts from the journals, critical reviews, newsletters,
clinical yearbooks, and similar periodicals." Its lengthy abstracts were entered by title in broad subject categories, and
author and subject indexes were provided annually for 1828
and the years 1831 through 1843.

In this same period Blake[21] mentions the Bolletino
delle scienze mediche* (Bologna, 1829-1937) as having carried
abstracts of books and journal articles from 1829 through
1835. This publication was not seen by this author but Callisen[22] describes it as being almost exclusively abstracts,
though no range of years for its having carried abstracts is
given.

The German physician Carl Christian Schmidt (1792-
1855) founded in the year 1834 and edited the next in this
series of abstract journals devoted to the general medical
sciences, Schmidts Jahrbücher der in- und ausländischen
Medicin (Bonn; Leipzig, 1834-1922). This journal seems to
have been a response to the growing desire on the part of
German physicians to know more about foreign advances in
medicine. [23] In his forward, Schmidt states: "The intention
of these yearbooks is to make available as quickly as possible to the medical audience the progress and advances of the
medical sciences in the learned world."[24]

The monthly issues of the Jahrbücher were subdivided
into five categories, the first, "Abstracts," containing subject
classified abstracts from foreign and domestic journals.
Other divisions were devoted to original articles, reviews,
and news notes. A final section contained a subject classified bibliography (unannotated) of journal articles and books.

The abstract section of the Jahrbücher presented its
material from 1851 in a subject classification more rigorous
than the previous loose one. An annual author index was
added annually beginning with 1849. Brodman[25] cites

Schmidts Jahrbücher as the first medical abstract journal,
and, further describes it as being inspired by the example
of the Pharmaceutisches Zentralblatt.

Mott[26] describes the 1830's as a time of expansion in
the United States and in each of the two fields of science
most cultivated by the early American journals--medicine and
agriculture--there was considerable activity.   Much of American medical periodical publishing of this era was centered
in Philadelphia where as many as a dozen medical periodicals,
admittedly many short-lived and eclectic, were extant.   Among
these was the American Medical Intelligencer (Philadelphia,
1837-1842).   The Intelligencer was founded by the British-
born medical educator and historian of medicine Robly Dunglison (1788-1869).   Radbill[27] speaks of Dunglison's importance to American medical history because of his extraor-
dinary success in sifting from the world literature information of importance to medical students and physicians and in
his ability to present information effectively.   This ability
was evidenced in Dunglison's semimonthly Intelligencer, a
curious mixture of excerpts, translations and abstracts of
journal articles, letters, news, and notes.   The abstracts
were interspersed among the other contents and followed no
particular arrangement, nor were they indexed in any way.
In 1842 the Intelligencer was superseded by the Medical News
in which the abstracts came to occupy an important part.

In 1840 William Braithwaite (1807-1885), an English
physician, founded the Retrospect of Medicine (New York;
London, 1840-1901).   Half-titled Braithwaite's Retrospect,
simultaneous English and American editions were published
in London and New York.   Braithwaite's Retrospect, which
appeared semi-annually, presented numbered abstracts from
the general medical literature arranged in broad subject
categories with entry by title and author.   From 1840 through
1844 there were annual systematic indexes to the abstracts;
from 1845, author and subject indexes annually.

In 1842 Alfred Charlemagne Lartigue (1817-1883), a
French physician, began his Encyclographie médicale* (Paris,
1842-1846).   The Encyclographie bore the subtitle "An analytical and complete summary of all the medical and pharmaceutical journals published in France."   Although not examined by the author the Encyclographie would seem, judging
from secondary sources[28] and its subtitle, to have been comprised principally of abstracts from the French medical literature.   Lartigue had abandoned the medical profession in

1841 to dedicate his life to the theater. [29]   Adopting the
pseudonym "Delacour" he went on to become an eminent play-
wright, apparently supporting himself initially by means of
the Encyclographie and other publishing ventures.

Isaac Hays, physician and editor of the American
Journal of Medical Sciences, a well established medical journal, undertook in 1843 a monthly in the same field called
Medical News (Philadelphia; New York, 1843-1905).   This
journal superseded Dunglison's American Medical Intelligencer
discussed earlier.   The Medical News, which bore the cap-
tion title Medical News and Abstract from 1843 through 1881,
contained sections entitled "Domestic Intelligencer," primarily
consisting of news notes, and "Foreign Intelligencer," consisting of abstracts from a half dozen or so foreign medical
journals, and randomly arranged.   Subject indexes were provided annually to these abstracts.   In the late 1850's the
"Domestic Intelligencer" began to be given over increasingly
to abstracts of domestic articles until eventually both sections provided abstract coverage of the medical literature,
foreign and domestic.

In 1880 the Medical News absorbed the Monthly Abstract of Medical Science and the abstracts appeared through
1881 as a continuously paged and subject classified section
with author and subject indexes.   In 1882 the Medical News,
formerly monthly, became weekly and adopted a newspaper
format.   Abstracts were included under the section called
"Medical Progress" in a subject classified arrangement.   In
1905 Medical News was absorbed by the New York Medical
Journal.

The English physician William Harcourt Ranking (1814-
1867) founded in 1845 the Half-Yearly Abstract of the Medical Sciences (London, 1845-1873).   This journal consisted
of abstracts from the general medical literature arranged in
a subject classification.   Author and subject indexes were
provided with each issue.

In the preface to volume one of the Half-Yearly Abstract, the editor cites the precedence of the German Jahrbücher and the French and Belgian encyclographies. [30]   Each
issue contained a section entitled "Report on the Progress
of ...," presenting an extensive narrative review of the current state of a particular aspect of medicine.   An American
edition was published in Philadelphia from 1845 through 1873,
this latter edition being superseded by the Monthly Abstract
of Medical Science in 1874.

Various medical specialties began now to be covered
by abstract journals.

In the area of mental health, the Annales médico-
psycholgiques (Paris, 1843-   ) began to appear. Issued eight
to ten times per year, the Annales was edited by the pioneer-
ing French physicians Jules Gabriel François Baillarger
(1806-1890), François Achille Longet (1811-1871), and Laur-
ent Alexis Philibert Cerise (1809-1869).   In it was contained
a section of abstracts entitled "French and Foreign Review,"
later called "Review of Medical Journals." The abstracts
were arranged by country, under country by journal title,
and entered by the title of the article abstracted.   No indexes
were issued to the abstracts.

Pharmacy, in addition to being the principal area of
coverage in this period of the Pharmaceutisches Zentralblatt
was represented by the Archiv der Pharmazie (Berlin, 1822-
).   Rudolph Brandes (1795-1842), who had edited the Archiv
since its inception, died in 1842 to be succeeded as editor by
Heinrich Wackenroder (1798-1854).   In 1843 the monthly issues of the Archiv began to include a section of abstracts of
the literature of pharmacy entitled "Monthly Report." These
unnumbered abstracts were randomly arranged by article
title, and an author and subject index were issued annually.
The section grew rapidly in size until 1868 when the journal
was divided into three parts as follows: Part A--Original
Contributions; Part B--Monthly Report; and Part C--Litera-
ture and Criticism.   The "Monthly Report" was now subject
classified. In 1890 the abstracts were dropped co-incidental
with a change of editorship from Eduard Reichardt (1827-
1891), professor of chemistry at the University of Jena, to
Ernst Schmidt (1845-1921) and Heinrich Beckurts (1855-1929)
and initiation of a new series.   From 1822 until 1850 the
Archiv was the organ of the Apotheker-Verein in Norddeutschland; from 1850 until 1872 of the northern division of the
Allgemeiner Deutscher Apotheker-Verein; and from 1872
through 1932 of the Deutscher Apotheker Verein.

Two years following the introduction of abstracts in
the Archiv, the Journal de pharmacie et de chimie (Paris,
1809-1942) began in 1845 carrying a section of abstracts entitled "Reports on Chemical Works." Arrangement of the abstracts was random and entry was by article title.   With
1849 this section divided into "Medical Review" (which abstracted domestic articles) and "Review of Chemical Works
Published Abroad" (varies), retaining its previous format.

The abstracts were now included in the Table des Matières,
or systematic table of contents, characteristic of French
journals. With 1875 the latter section divided into "Review
of Pharmaceutical Works Published Abroad" and "Review of
Chemical Works Published Abroad"; consolidated in 1889 into
"Review of Chemical and Pharmaceutical Works Published
Abroad." With 1891 a subject classification was adopted for
the abstracts; and with 1900 all abstracts, domestic and foreign, were combined into one section called "Medical Review,"
from 1905 simply "Review of Journals." No indexes were
ever issued to these abstracts.

Applied Sciences and Technology

In the area of applied sciences and technology, in addition to the sections 4 and 5 of the Bulletin universel (covering agriculture and technology, respectively), the period
1820-1849 saw the emergence of an annual devoted to review-
ing new developments in these areas, the Arcana of Science
and Art (London, 1828-1838).

The Arcana was edited by the English author and an-
tiquary John Timbs (1801-1875) and bore the subtitle "An
annual register of useful inventions and improvements, discoveries and facts, in mechanics, chemistry, natural history,
and social economy, abridged from all the scientific journals,
British and foreign, of the past year." The Arcana included
the following sections: "Mechanical Inventions and Improvements," "Chemical Science," "Natural History," and "Useful
and Ornamental Arts." Under these classifications abstracts
were entered by article title and an author-subject index was
included. In 1838 the Arcana was superseded by the Yearbook of Facts in Science and Art (London, 1838-1879/81),
still edited by John Timbs. The Yearbook resembled the
Arcana in scope and format except that the former had subject but no author indexes while the latter did.

Timbs was a curious man who devoted his life to col-
lecting facts from all sources on all subjects. He edited a
number of periodicals, including, from 1827 through 1838,
the Mirror of Literature where his column "Arcana of Science and Art" appeared from October 6, 1827 through June
28, 1828, preceding the issuance of the first volume of the
Arcana.

The Arcana was a hybrid of the annual review and the
abstract journal, serving the purpose of the former with a

format more nearly like that of the latter. It was comprised of abstracts of journal articles, household hints, home remedies, etc. Kronick,[31] referring to the annuals of an earlier period, describes them as being addressed to an audience of laymen, being predominantly popular in their appeal, and not as frequently used as general periodicals as a medium for the primary communication of scientific communication. The Arcana is in keeping with this tradition. Further, its many inaccuracies and poor editing, also marring its successor, the Yearbook, combined with its popular appeal, detracted seriously from its usefulness.

Of greater significance in this area was the Chemisch-technische Mitteilungen der neuesten Zeit (Berlin, 1849-1887), covering broadly the literature of chemical technology. The Mitteilungen was founded and edited initially by Franz Karl Leonhard Elsner (1802-1874), chemist at the Royal Industrial Institute and later arcanist at the royal procelain factory in Berlin.

Volume one of the Mitteilungen (published in 1849) covered the years 1846 through 1848 in a systematically arranged classification; volume two covered the years 1848 through 1850 and adopted an alphabetical subject arrangement which was retained throughout the remainder of the publication's existence. Coverage was by three-year periods until the issue for 1856/57, when intervals of two years were adopted. Subject indexing was begun with the volume for 1874/75 (when the editing function was taken over on the death of Elsner by Otto Dammer (1839-1916). From 1876/77 onward the Mitteilungen was edited by Elsner's son Franz Friedrich Elsner (1842-19??).

In volume one of the Mitteilungen Elsner states:

> I have become convinced through many years of experience of the need for a publication which presents in condensed form the contents of recent chemical and technical periodicals and that such a publication would satisfy the wishes of technical chemists, who lack the time or opportunity to follow the rapid progress of technical chemistry. Provision of such information is unqualifiedly bound up in the advancement of chemical and technical production.
> I have, therefore, attempted through this little work, which I hereby submit for publication, to

fill a gap in that aspect of the chemical and technical literature. [32]

Social Sciences

The social sciences were represented in the period under study only by sections 6, 7, and 8 of the Bulletin universel, devoted respectively to geography, history, and military science. No new abstract journal appeared in this area until the Jahrbücher für Nationalökonomie und Statistik in 1863.

Humanities

No abstract journal in the area of the humanities appeared in the time period here reviewed.

The Period 1850-1869

Pure Sciences

In this period no abstract journal attempted to cover the pure sciences in general, except for the abstract section of the American Journal of Science noted above, which even in this early period was beginning to restrict its coverage as increasingly specialized areas of the pure sciences came to be covered by their own abstract journals.

In 1868 began the oldest abstracting service in the field of mathematics, the Jahrbuch über die Fortschritte der Mathematik (Berlin, 1868-1944), edited by Carl Ohrtmann (1831-1883) and Felix Müller (1843-1928), with the assistance of numerous collaborators. The Jahrbuch appeared annually and covered, with brief, signed abstracts, the literature of mathematics in twelve subject categories. Only author indexes were supplied to the Jahrbuch.

In the area of chemistry and physics, the Annales de chimie et de physique (Paris, 1789-1913), a pioneer journal in these two fields, came in 1852 under the editorship of the noted French physicist and astronomer Dominique François Jean Arago (1786-1853). Arago, whose eyesight was failing him in his last years, discharged his duties as Perpetual Secretary of the Academy of Sciences by writing abstracts for the Annales, apparently being instrumental in the establishment of its abstract section which had begun in 1852. [33]

The Annales had since its inception included original articles (increasing in proportion after 1800), articles from other journals, translated if necessary and often excerpted, and correspondence. Apparently feeling that their readers' domestic interests were satisfied entirely by the Annales, the editors began in 1852 to include abstracts of works published in the foreign periodical press in their now monthly publication. These abstracts were presented in two sections: "Reports on Chemistry Published Abroad," and "Reports on Physics Published Abroad," the contents of the "Reports" being very lenghy abstracts bordering on excerpts, and often four to six pages in length. These abstracts were randomly arranged and entered by title with the customary Table des matières serving as a classified index. The abstracts became increasingly shorter with time until 1864 when the two sections were retitled "Review of Chemical Works Published Abroad" and "Review of Physical Works Published Abroad," with the earlier format retained although the abstracts were now considerably shortened, being on the average several paragraphs in length. The "Reviews" continued until 1873 when the sections were dropped without explanation. Again it is to be noted that the dropping or initiation of an abstract section coincides with a change of editorship. The French chemists Michel Eugène Chevreul (1786-1889) and Jean Baptiste Boussingault (1802-1887) had been joint editors from 1854 through 1873. With 1874 editing of the Annales was taken over by the distinguished chemist Pierre Eugène Marcellin Berthelot (1827-1907) and the physicist Eleuthère Elie Nicolas Mascart (1837-1908). Another factor which undoubtedly contributed to the decision to drop the abstract sections was the success now enjoyed by the abstract sections of the Bulletin of the Société Chimique de Paris and the Journal de physique et le radium.

The Société Chimique de Paris, from 1907 the Société Chimique de France, set to work soon after its founding in 1857 to provide abstract coverage of the literature of chemistry in the nature of that provided by Chemisches Zentralblatt. In 1858 it published two monthly journals attempting to do this: the Répertoire de chimie pure and the Répertoire de chimie appliquée, the latter discussed below under "Applied Sciences and Technology."

The Répertoire de chimie pure (Paris, 1858-1863) was edited by Charles Adolphe Wurtz (1817-1884), a noted French chemist who also edited the "Reports on Chemistry Published Abroad" in the Annales de chimie et physique. The

Répertoire, a cover-to-cover abstract journal, contained unnumbered abstracts arranged in broad subject categories and
entered by title. Annual author and subject indexes were included. In 1863 the Répertoire de chimie pure merged into
the Société's Bulletin followed in 1864 by its companion the
Répertoire de chimie appliquée.

This successor to the two Répertoires, the abstracting
section of the Bulletin, proved to be one of the major abstracting services of the last part of the nineteenth century.
The Bulletin of the Société Chimique de France (Paris, 1858-)
had not previously contained abstracts when in 1863-64 the
Répertoires merged into it. The new abstract section constituted one continuously paged subject classified section covering the literature of pure and applied chemistry, and was
entitled "Abstracts of Reports of Pure and Applied Chemistry
Published in France and Abroad." Author and subject indexes
were provided annually. In 1892 this section divided into two
separately paged sections: "Abstracts of French Works"
(varies) and "Abstracts of Foreign Works." This division
lasted until 1933.

Two abstracting publications in the area of botany
made their appearance in the time period under study, the
Bulletin of the Société Botanique de France and Hedwigia.

In 1854 the Société Botanique de France issued as its
official organ the first number of its monthly Bulletin (Paris,
1854-). From the beginning the publication included a continuously paged section entitled "Bibliographic Review," a
subject grouping of abstracts covering comprehensively the
botanical literature. With 1864 this section was paged separately and the author index, appearing from the first, was
now supplemented with a subject index. The abstracts were
now randomly arranged with no formal subject classification
apparent (although the subject arrangement was restored in
1920). With 1894 consecutive paging of the section was resumed. The Bulletin seems to be the earliest example of an
abstract journal devoted exclusively to the field of botany.

Hedwigia (Dresden, 1852-1944), previously devoted
solely to original articles, began in May 1863 a continuously
paged section of abstracts entitled "Repertorium," arranged
randomly by journal title and with indexes by author and plant
names. With 1888 this section was retitled "Literature" and
subject classified. With 1894 it was called "Repertorium for
Cryptogamic Literature" (varies) and issued as a separately

paged supplement to <u>Hedwigia</u>. Its arrangement was subject
classified. The "Repertorium" was expanded in scope and
formatted from 1897 as follows: "Part A. Short Communications"; "Part B. Repertorium" (1901-1944 as "Abstracts
and Critical Review"); "Part C. New Literature." This
latter section, which had begun in 1901, was an extensively
annotated, classified bibliography of periodical articles from
the literature of botany.

Medicine

     Several more abstract journals covering general medi-
cine appeared in the period 1850-1869. The weekly <u>British</u>
<u>Medical Journal</u> (London, 1857-), the official organ of the
British Medical Association, from its beginnings under the
editorship of Ernest Abraham Hart (1835-1898), physician and
medical journalist, included a section of abstracts entitled
"Periscopic Review." Arrangement was random and entry
was by title of article abstracted. For the period 1861 to
1867 this section was called "Progress of Medical Science,"
and from 1868 the abstracts were subject grouped. Author
and subject indexes to these abstracts were provided in the
<u>Journal</u>'s annual indexes. After 1867 there appeared selec-
tive abstracts called "Selections from the Journals," which
lasted for only a few years after which no abstracts were
contained in the <u>Journal</u>.

     A number of weekly general medical journals were
being published in Germany and Austria after the middle of
the nineteenth century. The <u>Wiener medizinische Wochen-</u>
<u>schrift</u> and the <u>Berliner klinische Wochenschrift</u> were typical
examples. These journals usually carried notices of new
literature, primarily the monographic literature, but such
coverage was not usually extensive and almost entirely confined to unannotated listings. The <u>Münchener medizinische</u>
<u>Wochenschrift</u> (Munich, 1854-), however, was an exception
to this pattern. The <u>Wochenschrift</u> which appeared through
1885 as the <u>Aerztliches Intelligenz-Blatt</u>, while under the
editorship of Aloys Martin (1818-1891) began to include in
1859 a section called "Abstracts and Book Notices," with a
sub-section "New Journal Articles," an unannotated list of
recent articles. Abstracts were arranged by journal title
and then entered by author and title. Author indexes were
published annually.

     Also providing coverage of the general medical liter-
ature was the <u>Zentralblatt für die medizinischen Wissen-</u>

schaften (Berlin, 1863-1915). This cover-to-cover abstract
journal was randomly arranged and entry was by author of
the article cited.   There were author and subject indexes
with each issue. The Zentralblatt, a weekly, attempted to
cover all fields of medicine, practical and theoretical, with
the cooperation of native and foreign experts.[34] Its first
editor was Ludimar Hermann (1838-1914).   While the number of articles covered in each issue of the Zentralblatt was
generally small, the abstracts were extensive in length, often
with emphasis on interpretation and criticism.

        The New York Medical Journal (New York, 1865-1923)
soon after its inauguration came to occupy a high position
among American medical journals.[35] Publication was monthly,
1865-1882, and weekly from 1883.   From the beginning it
contained a continuously paged section called "Reports on the
Progress of Medicine" (varies) with a subject classified arrangement and a subject index.   From April 1899 through
1915 this was retitled "Pith of Current Literature," 1916
through 1919 "Modern Treatment and Preventive Medicine; a
Compendium of Therapeutics," and from 1920 "Practical
Therapeutics and Preventive Medicine." Arrangement varied
from subject classified to random and back.   In 1905 the
New York Medical Journal absorbed Medical News.

        While there were several abstract publications in the
field of general medicine the trend now was to increasing
specialization as abstract journals in sub-fields began to appear in modest numbers.

        In the field of pharmacy, abstracts began to appear
in 1856 in the pioneer American pharmaceutical journal the
American Journal of Pharmacy (Philadelphia, 1825-   ).
While the Journal had, since its beginnings, carried brief
notices of selected journal articles, until 1850 these were
not significant in number being included in a section titled
"Miscellany," (later "Varieties").   In 1856, however, these
notices became organized into a section called variously
"Gleanings from the European Journals," "Gleanings from the
Foreign Journals," etc.   Arrangement was random and entry
was by catchword. No indexes were provided to these abstracts.   Shorter notices continued to be carried in the
"Varieties" and "Notes." In 1871 the Journal, which had
been bi-monthly, became monthly. With 1892 the abstract
section was retitled "Abstracts from the German Journals,"
etc., used alternately after the turn of the century with the
title "Recent Literature Relating to Pharmacy." From 1903

to 1914 this section was retitled "Progress in Pharmacy" and arranged by title in paragraph form.   With 1915 the title be- came "Current Literature--Scientific and Technical Abstracts," retaining its previous format without indexes.

Also covering the literature of pharmacy broadly was the abstract section of the Yearbook of Pharmacy (London, 1864-1927).   The Yearbook bore the subtitle "Comprising ab- stracts of papers relating to pharmacy, materia medica, and chemistry contributed to British and foreign journals ... With the Transactions of the British Pharmaceutical Confer- ence."   The abstract section was broadly subject classified and contained numerous abstracts entered by title.   Subject indexes were supplied but no author indexes.

In the preface to volume one of the Yearbook the edi- tors state that "It has been the earnest wish of the British Pharmaceutical Conference to bring together, with some de- gree of systematic arrangement, various ideas, French, Ger- man, American, and English, bearing on our common mis- tress, pharmacy."[36]

Abstract journals emerged in this period in several medical specialties which previously were not covered by their own journals.

In pediatrics, the Jahrbuch für Kinderheilkunde (Ber- lin, 1858-), edited by the Austrian physician Franz Mayr (1814-1863), began to appear in two sections: (1) "Original Articles," and (2) "Analects," the latter a section of abstracts arranged by journal title.   Each section was separately paged, and a systematic index was provided.   With 1863 other sections, e. g. , "Review," and "Necrology" were added. For the period 1868 to 1882 the format assumed something of the nature of a Jahresbericht with the articles numbered at the head of a discursive review section within broad sub- ject categories.   From 1883 through 1886 the abstracts were arranged by nationality and author, and from 1887 onward, classified by subject with author entry.   In 1900 this section changed its name to "Literature Report" and retained its subject classified form.   Author and subject indexes were issued from 1880.

Dentistry had, until this point, not been covered by its own abstracting service.   In 1860 Dental Cosmos (Phila- delphia, 1860-1936), published by the S. S. White Dental Manufacturing Company and one of the chief among a series

of dental journals representing local and state dental societies
and dental supply houses, began publication, superseding
Dental News Letter. From the beginning the monthly issues
of Dental Cosmos included a section of abstracts entitled
"Periscope of Medical and General Science in Their Relation
to Dentistry" (later simply "Periscope"). Abstracts were
randomly arranged with title entry. In 1903 the "Review of
Current Dental Literature," a section of highly selective abstracts arranged by journal title, was added. Both continued
through 1920.

        Two French language medical specialty journals pro-
vided abstract coverage of their respective fields, ophthalmology and dermatology, beginning in this period, the Annales d'oculistique and the Annales de dermatologie et syphilographie.

        The Annales d'oculistique (Paris, 1838-   ) began
carrying with 1867 a continuously paged section entitled "Review of the Journals of Ophthalmology" in its monthly issues.
Generally each issue presented selected abstracts from one
journal.

        The Annales de dermatologie et syphilographie (Paris,
1868-   ) carried from 1868 through 1879 a "Review of Journals," randomly arranged with abstracts entered by article
title. From 1880 to 1881 this section was divided into two
sub-sections: "French Review" and "Foreign Review." From
1882 to 1889 and from 1894 to 1901 these abstracts appeared
intermittently and were entitled "Review of Dermatology,"
"Review of Syphilography," "Review of Venereology," etc.
An author index was added in 1882. In the period from 1890
to 1893 the abstracts appeared in a subject classified order,
with author entry, in a section entitled simply "Review of
Periodicals." Author and subject indexes were now provided.
From 1902 onward the abstracts appeared in subject groupings
under the heading "Review of Periodical Publications."

Applied Sciences and Technology

        In the period under review abstract coverage of the
literature of the applied sciences and technology was still
meager.

        In the area of plant sciences, the Société Nationale
d'Horticulture de France (founded in 1827) began to include
in 1855 in its monthly Journal (Paris, 1827-   ) a section

entitled "Bibliographic Review," subtitled "New plants described in the horticultural journals published abroad." With
1859 this section was divided into "French Bibliographic Review," and "Foreign Bibliographic Review." With 1867 the
arrangement, which had been previously random, was changed
to journal title arrangement, i.e., arrangement by title of
journal from which the abstracts were taken. From 1895
this section was given the overall name "Review of French
and Foreign Publications," and subdivided into French publications and foreign publications. The number of entries
diminished progressively after the outbreak of World War I
and none appears after 1918.

The now fast growing field of chemical technology is
represented by two abstract journals in this time period, the
Répertoire de chimie appliquée and the Chemisch-technisches
Repertorium.

The Répertoire de chimie appliquée (Paris, 1858-
1864) covered the periodical literature of applied chemistry
and, along with its companion publication the Répertoire de
chimie pure discussed above, attempted to provide comprehensive coverage for all of chemistry. A cover-to-cover
abstract journal, the Répertoire de chimie appliquée was
edited by the French industrial chemist Charles Louis Barreswil (1817-1870) and contained unnumbered abstracts in a
subject classified format, entered by title. Author and subject indexes were provided. The Répertoires merged into
the Bulletin of the Société Chimique de France in 1864.

The Chemisch-technisches Repertorium (Berlin, 1862-
1901) edited by Emil Jacobsen (18??-1901), was a cover-to-
cover abstract journal covering the literature of chemical
technology. Author and subject indexes were included in the
monthly issues of this subject classified abstract journal.

Social Sciences

In the area of the social sciences the only abstract
journal in this period to provide coverage was the Jahrbücher
für Nationalökonomie und Statistik (Jena, 1863-   ), covering
the literature of economics and statistics. From 1863 through
1870 the Jahrbücher contained a continuously paged section
entitled "The National Economic Literature in the Periodical
Press." This section presented abstracts arranged by
country, then by journal title. No indexes were provided.
With 1878 this section was reconstituted with the following

divisions: (1) "The Foreign Periodical Press" and (2) "The German Periodical Press." It contained, however, no abstracts. The Jahrbücher, which appeared monthly, was an important early force in the development of the field of economics,[37] and was edited by Bruno Hildebrand (1812-1878), a professor at the University of Jena for many years.

Humanities

Abstract coverage in the humanities is represented in this period only briefly. In 1861 the Numismatic Chronicle (London, 1838-), a quarterly, began a series which included a section entitled "Notice of Recent Numismatic Publications," containing abstracts of periodical articles, arranged under journal title. This section ceased to carry abstracts with 1897, consisting from this time onward solely of book reviews.

The Period 1870-1889

From 1870 onward the growth rate of abstract journals rises significantly. For this reason only selected titles will be enumerated from this point onward and only major services will be discussed.

Pure Sciences

The two decades under study witnessed a dramatic growth in the number of abstract services in the pure sciences.

General science was covered by: the abstract section of the Revue des questions scientifiques (Louvain, 1877-), sponsored by the Société Scientifique de Bruxelles; Science (New York; etc., 1883-); and Naturwissenschaftliche Rundschau (Brunswick, 1886-1912). It is interesting to note that Science, one of America's leading scientific periodicals, carried abstracts for its first year of existence only, 1883. These appeared in a section called "Weekly Summary of the Progress of Science," subject arranged and entered by title. No reason is given for their cessation. Naturwissenschaftliche Rundschau presented weekly reviews of articles and books of general scientific interest along with original articles. Its successor Naturwissenschaften devoted itself primarily to book reviews.

Mathematics was now being covered by a section of the Bulletin des sciences mathématiques (Paris, 1870-), originally entitled Bulletin des sciences mathématiques et astronomiques. The abstract section of the Bulletin was issued separately as its Part 2 from 1877.

Physics was now covered by a section of abstracts in the Journal de physique et le radium (Paris, 1872-), the section being divided into foreign and domestic literature. The Journal, published by private enterprise from 1872 was taken over in 1911 by the Société Française de Physique.

The Annalen der Physik, Beiblätter (Halle; Leipzig, 1877-1919) was an effort on the part of German physicists to provide comprehensive coverage of the literature of physics. The Beiblätter, a cover-to-cover abstract journal, was issued twelve times a year through 1903 and twenty four times a year thereafter, and as a supplement to Annalen der Physik. Initially the Beiblätter were edited by Johann Christian Poggendorff (1796-1877), who since 1824 had also edited the Annalen der Physik. After 1919 the Beiblätter merged with the Fortschritte der Physik, discussed above, and the Halbmonatliches Literaturverzeichnis to form Physikalische Berichte.

Chemistry was now being covered by three new abstract journals: the Journal of the Chemical Society, the Repertorium der analytischen Chemie, and Analyst.

The Journal of the Chemical Society (London, 1847-) began to include in 1871 a continuously paged section of subject classified abstracts covering the literature of pure chemistry. The semi-monthly Journal presented one of the most comprehensive set of abstracts in English before the founding of Chemical Abstracts in 1907.[38] With 1878 the abstract section was paged separately from the original papers (the Transactions) and given separate volume numbering so that they could be bound separately. Annual author and subject indexes were issued. Coverage of the literature of applied chemistry in English was supplied by the Journal of the Society of Chemical Industry, discussed below.

The Repertorium der analytischen Chemie (Hamburg, 1881-1887) was issued in two parts: "Original Contributions" and "News from the Literature," this latter a section of abstracts. The weekly Repertorium was the official organ of the Verein Analytischer Chemiker. It merged in 1888 with

the Zeitschrift für die chemischen Industrie to form Zeitschrift für angewandte Chemie.

The Analyst (London, 1877-), a monthly published
by the Society of Public Analysts and Other Analytical Chemists, contained an abstract section from 1884 variously titled.

Mineralogy and crystallography were represented by
Mineralogical Magazine and the Zeitschrift für Kristallographie. Mineralogical Magazine (London, 1876-), published
by the Mineralogical Society, contained a section of abstracts
which ran through 1903, to be revived and reconstituted as
Mineralogical Abstracts in 1920. The bimonthly issues of
the Zeitschrift für Kristallographie contained a small section
of abstracts relating to crystallography.

In this period geology was covered by the annual
Geological Record (London, 1874-1880/84). This cover-to-
cover, subject classified abstract publication, edited by the
British geologist William Whitaker (1836-1925), began to lag
in its coverage soon after its initial appearance and abstracts
ceased to be included with the volume for 1879. The single
volume covering the years 1880 through 1884 (published in
1889) contained unannotated citations only.

In the area of the life sciences four journals contained
sections of abstracts: the Annales of the Institut Pasteur
(Paris, 1887-) (though only for the period 1887 through
1888); the Zentralblatt für Bakteriologie und Parasitenkunde
(Jena, 1887-); the Journal of the Royal Microscopical Society (London, 1878-); and the Zeitschrift für wissenschaftliche Mikroskopie und für mikroskopische Technik (Stuttgart,
1884-).

Botany is covered in this period by several titles,
chief among them are Botanischer Jahresbericht (Berlin;
Leipzig, 1873-), conducted by the eminent German botanist
Leopold Just (1841-1891), and Botanisches Zentralblatt
(Kassel; Jena, 1880-1945), the organ of several botanical
societies, notably the Botanischer Verein in Munich, the Bo-
tanska Sällskepet in Stockholm, and the Gesellschaft für
Botanik in Hamburg. Together the two cover-to-cover abstract publications constituted until the appearance of Botanical Abstracts in 1918 the major abstract services in the
field. Botanisches Zentralblatt, not unlike many other German abstract journals of the time, contained occasional
original articles.

Also appearing in this same period and providing coverage of the literature of botany were the Botanische Jahrbücher für Systematik, Pflanzengeschichte und Pflanzengeo-
graphie (Leipzig, 1880-) and the Revue bryologique (Caen;
Paris, 1874-), the former containing abstracts from 1884,
the latter from 1882.

Medicine

The period under study here reflects great growth in
the area of coverage of general medicine and especially the
medical specialties.

General medicine was now well represented by the
newly begun cover-to-cover abstracts journals: the American
Monthly Abstract of Medical Science (Philadelphia, 1874-1879);
Epitome; a Monthly Retrospect (New York, 1880-1889); the
English Medical Chronicle (Manchester, Eng., 1884-1916);
the French Revue des sciences médicales en France et à
l'étranger (Paris, 1873-1898); and the German Zentralblatt
für innere Medizin (Leipzig, 1880-1943).

The Monthly Abstract of Medical Science superseded
the American edition of the Half-Yearly Abstract of the Medical Sciences and was in turn absorbed by Medical News.
The Epitome, published from 1880 to 1885 as the Quarterly
Epitome of Practical Medicine and Surgery, was an American
supplement to Braithwaite's Retrospect. In 1890 it merged
into Medical Analectic which became Epitome of Medicine
(New York, 1884-1893). Medical Chronicle, subtitled "A
monthly record of the progress of medical science," contained
occasional review articles as well as abstracts, which were
arranged according to a subject classification. Author and
subject indexes were provided.

In addition to the above-mentioned cover-to-cover abstract journals several abstract sections of primary journals
began in this period, notably those of the Journal of the
American Medical Association (Chicago, 1883-), Fortschritte
der Medizin (Berlin, 1883-1943), and Brasil-medico (Rio de
Janeiro, 1887-). The Journal of the American Medical
Association carried a section of abstracts from the journal
literature from its earliest numbers variously titled "Medical
Progress," "Practical Notes," and "Current Medical Literature," subarranged by American and foreign articles. From
1917 the American Medical Association provided bibliographic
coverage of the medical periodical literature by means of its

Quarterly Cumulative Index to Current Medical Literature,
prepared by its library staff. In 1927 this publication merged
with Index Medicus to form the Quarterly Cumulative Index
Medicus. The Fortschritte, containing a subject classified
section of abstracts, became in 1920 the organ of the Vereinigung für Ärztlichen Meinungsaustausch and the Gesellschaft
für Mechanotherapie.

Abstract sections of primary journals in the medical
specialties now began to emerge: in physiology, the Zentralblatt für Physiologie (Leipzig, 1887-1921); in public health,
the Annales d'hygiêne publique (Paris, 1828-1950) from 1872;
the Revue d'hygiêne et de police sanitaire (Paris, 1879-1939);
and the Zentralblatt für allgemeine Gesundheitspflege (Bonn,
1882-1919) (though abstracts were dropped from this latter
title with 1915). Pharmacy and therapeutics were now being
covered by the abstract section of the Zentralblatt für die
gesamte Therapie (Vienna; Berlin, 1883-1917).

Medical journals devoted to diseases began to contain
sections of abstracts. Mental health was represented by abstract sections in the Journal of Nervous and Mental Disease
(Chicago, 1874-   ) and Zentralblatt für Nervenheilkunde und
Psychiatrie (Leipzig, 1878-1910); otorhinolaryngology was
represented by Annales des maladies de l'oreille, du larynx,
du nez et du pharynx (Paris, 1875-1930), Monatsschrift für
Ohrenheilkunde und Laryngo-Rhinologie (Berlin, 1867-   ) from
1877, Revue de laryngologie, d'otologie et de rhinologie
(Paris, 1880-   ), Internationales Zentralblatt für Laryngologie, Rhinologie und verwandte Wissenschaften (Berlin, 1884-
1922), and Journal of Laryngology, Rhinology and Otology
(London, 1887-   ).

Pediatrics was represented by abstract sections in
Archiv für Kinderheilkunde (Stuttgart, 1880-   ) and the Archives of Pediatrics (New York; etc. , 1884-   ). Dentistry
was covered by the abstract section of the British Dental
Journal (London, 1872-   ) from 1881; dermatology by Dermatologische Wochenschrift (Leipzig, 1882-   ) and the British
Journal of Dermatology and Syphilis (London, 1888-   ).
Veterinary medicine was represented by the Journal de
médecine vétérinaire et de zootechnie (Lyons, 1845-1926)
from 1876, the Revue vétérinaire (Toulouse, 1876-   ), and
the Journal of the American Veterinary Medical Association
(New York, 1877-   ) from 1889.

Other specialties were represented by such titles as

the Zentralblatt für die Krankheiten der Harn- und Sexualor-
gane (Hamburg; Leipzig, 1889-1906), which merged with the
Monatsblatt für Urologie in 1907 to form the Zeitschrift für
Urologie (Berlin; Leipzig, 1907-); by the Zentralblatt für
Chirurgie (Leipzig, 1874-); the Zentralblatt für praktische
Augenheilkunde (Leipzig, 1877-1919), which later was superseded by the Zentralblatt für die gesamte Ophthalmologie und
ihre Grenzgebiete (Berlin, 1914-); and by the Zentralblatt
für Gynäkologie (Leipzig, 1877-).

Applied Sciences and Technology

In the area of applied sciences and technology generally, the period saw the emergence of two major cover-to-
cover abstract publications: the Abstracts of Papers of the
Institution of Civil Engineers (London, 1875-) and the Engineering Index (New York, 1884-).

The Abstracts of Papers of the Institution of Civil
Engineers first appeared in the quarterly issues of the Institution's Minutes of Proceedings, constituting its Section
III.   These abstracts were subject classified and entered by
title and author and subject indexes were included.   With
October 1919 the Abstracts were reconstituted as the Abstracts of Papers in Scientific Transactions and Periodicals
and now issued separately, with format and indexing identical
to its predecessor.   With January 1921 these became Engineering Abstracts.

The abstracts constituting Engineering Index originated
with a section of abstracts devoted to the engineering periodical literature which was begun in 1884 in the Journal of the
Association of Engineering Societies by John Butler Johnson
(1850-1902), professor of civil engineering at Washington University.   This section was entitled "Index Notes" and was a
subject arrangement of abstracts.   These "Index Notes,"
which had been also available separately, were issued in a
cumulative volume for the years 1884 through 1891, arranged
in alphabetical subject order and entitled Descriptive Index
of Current Engineering Literature.   With 1892 the abstracts
were published in the monthly numbers of Engineering Magazine (successor to the Journal).   These abstracts were re-
issued in three cumulations covering the years 1892-1895,
1896-1900, and 1901-1905.   From 1906 the Engineering Index
Annual was issued, being a compilation of the abstracts published monthly in the Engineering Magazine and its successor
Industrial Management.   In 1918 the responsibility for the

Engineering Index was taken over by the American Society of
Mechanical Engineers, which combined it with the "Selected
Titles of Engineering Articles" section of the Society's
monthly journal Mechanical Engineering and increased its
scope threefold. With 1919 the Annual was restored to its
alphabetical subject format to replace the format of eight
broad subject classifications which had prevailed since 1906.
No indexes were published to the Engineering Index in the
period under study. Coverage was primarily in the areas of
mechanical, electrical, and civil engineering.

In agriculture two major abstracting services emerged
in this period: Biedermann's Zentralblatt für Agrikulturchemie und rationellen Landwirtschaftsbetrieb (Leipzig, 1872-
1932) and Experiment Station Record (Washington, 1889-1946).

Biedermann's Zentralblatt was a monthly, cover-to-
cover subject classified abstract journal covering the broad
field of agriculture. The Experiment Station Record, issued
by the United States Department of Agriculture, in addition
to providing coverage of the publications issuing from United
States agricultural experiment stations, provided international
coverage of the literature of agriculture.

Chemical technology is represented in this period by
three major abstracting services: the Journal of the Society
of Chemical Industry (London, 1882-1950), Chemisch-technische Übersicht (Cothen; etc., 1885-1945), and the Zeitschrift
für angewandte Chemie (Berlin; Leipzig, 1888-   ).

From its beginnings in 1881 the Journal of the Society
of Chemical Industry had included a section of abstracts covering all phases of applied chemistry. With volume 37,
1918, the Journal was issued in three separately paged sections: (1) "Review," (2) "Transactions," and (3) "Abstracts."
Annual author, subject and patent number indexes were issued
to the abstract section.

Chemisch-technische Übersicht was a cover-to-cover
abstract journal originally entitled Chemisches Repertorium
and issued as a supplement to Chemiker Zeitung. It was especially useful in that it supplemented Chemisches Zentralblatt by providing coverage for industrial and applied chemistry before the adoption by Chemisches Zentralblatt of the
abstract section of the Zeitschirft für angewandte Chemie in
1919. Annual author and subject indexes were supplied.

The Zeitschrift für angewandte Chemie, formed by the
merger of the Zeitschrift für die chemische Industrie and the
Repertorium der analytischen Chemie, was issued every three
of four days and included an important "Abstracts" section,
which was also issued separately from 1913.   From 1888 to
1895 the Zeitschrift was the organ of the Gesellschaft für
Angwandte Chemie; from 1896, the Verein Deutscher Chemiker.
An important abstract journal for applied chemistry, the
Zeitschrift contained extensive abstracts in the field and, with
the Chemisch-technische Übersicht, supplemented Chemisches
Zentralblatt.

Social Sciences

One abstract journal in the area of geography and
three in the area of history represent the extent of abstract
journal coverage in the field of the social sciences.

In geography, Petermann's Mitteilungen aus Justus
Perthes' Geographischer Anstalt (Gotha, 1855-) began, with
1885, to carry abstracts of periodical articles and books in
a section entitled "Literature Report" (later "Geographic
Literature Report").   Abstracts were arranged geographically
and an author index was included.   This section was also issued separately from 1886 through 1909 as a supplement to
the Mitteilungen.

In history, three journals began with sections of abstracts of the periodical literature: Revue historique (Paris,
1876-), Historisches Jahrbuch of the Goerres-Gesellschaft
zur Pflege der Wissenschaft im katholischen Deutschland
(Bonn, 1882-), and the American Journal of Archaeology
(Concord, N.H.; etc., 1885-).

The Revue historique, still today a major journal in
the field, contained a section of abstracts from current journals arranged by journal title and with no indexes.   The Historisches Jahrbuch contained from its beginning a section of
abstracts arranged by journal title to which an author index
was added in 1885.   The American Journal of Archaeology,
begun under the aegis of the Archaeological Institute of America, consisted mainly of reports to its members and technical notes but did include a subject classified section of abstracts called "Summaries of Articles in Recent Periodicals"
(varies).   Publication was suspended from 1892 through 1896.

Humanities

Mind; a Quarterly Review of Psychology and Philosophy (London, 1876-) included abstracts in a section called
"Reports" from 1876 through 1888. This section degenerated
from 1889 to 1891 into a list of journal titles and articles
while a section called "Foreign Periodicals" provided abstracts
for these journals. When a new editor was installed and a
new series begun in 1892 a section was introduced called
"Philosophical Periodicals" which abstracted the contents of
selected foreign and American periodicals; arrangement was
by journal title and there were no indexes to the abstracts.

In the area of religion, the Revue de l'histoire des
religions (Paris, 1880-) carried a section of abstracts at
first randomly arranged, then from 1897 subject categorized.
With the death in 1901 of one of its founding editors (Léon
Marillier [1842-1901]) the abstracts ceased to appear. The
Berliner philologische Wochenschrift (Berlin; Leipzig, 1881-
1944) carried abstracts arranged by journal title and with no
indexes.

The Period 1890-1920

Pure Sciences

The number of abstract journals increased significantly
in all areas, but especially in the sciences, in this period.
In the area of general science, the Revue générale des sciences pures et appliquées (Paris, 1890-) contained a section of abstracts from 1890 through 1891. After 1891 this
section was devoted almost exclusively to book reviews. The
Mitteilungen zur Geschichte der Medizin und der Naturwissenschaften (Hamburg; etc., 1902-1941/42), published by the
Deutsche Gesellschaft für Geschichte der Medizin und der
Naturwissenschaften, contained a subject classified section of
abstracts relating to the history of medicine and the natural
sciences with author and subject indexes.

The Revue semestrielle des publications mathématiques
(Amsterdam, 1893-1934), a publication sponsored by the Société Mathématique d'Amsterdam, provided cover-to-cover
abstracts in the field of mathematics.

Astronomy, previously unrepresented, was now being
covered by the Astronomischer Jahresbericht (Berlin, 1899-),

a cover-to-cover abstract journal issued by the Astronomische
Gesellschaft, and the abstract section of the Revue générale
des travaux astronomiques (Paris, 1920-1926/27) issued by
the Observatiore de Paris for the International Astronomical
Union.

Physics is now well represented by abstract journals.
In 1895 the Physical Society of London issued its Abstracts
of Physical Papers From Foreign Sources (London, 1895-
1897), providing monthly a subject classified presentation of
abstracts.   The Abstracts was superseded in 1898 by Science
Abstracts (London, 1898-) with a greatly expanded coverage.
Science Abstracts was sponsored from 1898 until 1902 jointly
by the Institution of Electrical Engineers and the Physical
Society and provided coverage primarily of the literature of
physics and electrical engineering.   With 1903 Science Abstracts was issued in two sections: (A) "Physics" and (B)
"Electrical Engineering." In the same year the sponsorship
statement on the title page was changed to read "with the co-
operation of the American Physical Society, the American
Institute of Electrical Engineers, and the American Electro-
Chemical Society (through 1906); in 1907 the Associazione
Elettrotecnica Italiana was added as a sponsor.

The literature of physics was now being covered by
the German Physikalische Berichte (Brunswick, 1920-),
formed by the merger of the Fortschritte der Physik, the
Annalen der Physik Beiblätter and the Halbmonatliches Literaturverzeichnis der Fortschritte der Physik.   The Berichte,
a semi-monthly subject classified cover-to-cover abstract
journal with annual author and subject indexes, was under
the joint sponsorship of the Deutsche Physikalische Gesellschaft and the Deutsche Gesellschaft für Technische Physik.

In this same period the Anales of the Sociedad Española de Física y Química (Madrid, 1903-1947) carried from
1912 a small section of abstracts from the foreign literature.

It was in this period that the earliest abstract journals
with industrial sponsorship began to emerge.   Among these
was the Abstract Bulletin (Cleveland, 1913-1941) issued by
the Lamp Development Laboratory of the General Electric
Company.   The Abstract Bulletin contained abstracts of papers
published in the professional literature by staff members with
citations to the originals.   Also in the field of electricity,
the Electrical World (New York, 1883-) from 1894 carried
a section entitled "Digest of Electrical Literature" (varies)

presenting abstracts in a broad subject classification with author and subject indexes. This McGraw-Hill publication, one of the many electrical journals that had begun in the last decades of the nineteenth century, is an early example of commercial sponsorship of abstracting.

Chemistry saw the development of its major abstracting publication in this period. Staff members of the Massachusetts Institute of Technology, dissatisfied with European coverage of the American chemical literature, undertook the Review of American Chemical Research (Cambridge, Mass.; Easton, Pa., 1895-1906) which was issued both as a section of Technology Quarterly and separately. In 1907 this publication was superseded by the American Chemical Society's Chemical Abstracts (Columbus, 1907-   ), the most comprehensive abstract journal in the field of chemistry. [39] Until Chemisches Zentralblatt took over the abstract section of the Zeitschrift für angewandte Chemie in 1919, Chemical Abstracts provided the only coverage of both pure and applied chemistry. It was the only one in English until the establishment of British Chemical Abstracts in 1926. [40]

General chemistry was also covered by the abstract sections of the Journal de chimie physique et de physicochimie biologique (Geneva, 1903-   ) for the period 1903-1905 only; the abstract section of Kolloid-Zeitschrift (Dresden; Leipzig, 1906-   ), which contained a large number of abstracts of both pure and applied chemistry. Physical chemistry was covered briefly by the Physikalisch-chemisches Zentralblatt (Leipzig, 1904-1909). Analytical chemistry was covered by the Annales de chimie analytique et de chimie appliquée (Paris, 1896-   ) in its sections: "Review of French Publications" and "Review of Foreign Publications." The Annales was the publication of the Centre de Documentation Chimique and the Société des Chemistes Français.

Mineralogical Magazine, mentioned earlier as having contained a section of abstracts until 1903, reinstituted them and from 1920 issued then as a supplement entitled Mineralogical Abstracts (London, 1920-   ).

Geology is represented in this period by two cover-to-cover abstract journals, the Geologisches Zentralblatt (Leipzig; Berlin, 1901-1931) and the Revue de géologie et des sciences connexes (Liège, 1920-1970), sponsored by the Société Géologique de Belgique and the Société Géologique de France. In the introduction to the Revue the editor speaks of the need to replace the German beginnings in geological documentation. [41]

Economic Geology (Lancaster, Pa. , 1905-) carried a section of abstracts from 1908 through 1918.

The life sciences also experienced the development of a significant number of abstract journals, both cover-to-cover and sections of primary journals. Among the former were the Année biologique (Paris, 1895-) (though now almost completely a book review medium), sponsored from 1920 by the Federation des Sociétés des Sciences Naturelles and previously the product of individual enterprise; Biochemisches Zentralblatt (Berlin; Leipzig, 1902-1909), which united with the Biophysikalisches Zentralblatt to form Zentralblatt für Biochemie und Biophysik (Leipzig, 1910-1921); the Review of Bacteriology (London, 1911-1919); Abstracts of Bacteriology (Baltimore, 1917-1925); and the Berichte über die gesamte Physiologie und experimentelle Pharmakologie (Berlin, 1920-), sponsored by the Deutsche Physiologische Gesellschaft. In the introduction to volume one of the Abstracts of Bacteriology the editor speaks of the need for that publication because of the growth of the literature and the cut off of foreign reviews due to the war. He further exhorts other American professional societies to emulate their action, stressing the responsibilities of such societies to advance scientific information. [42]

The major development in botany in this period is the emergence of Botanical Abstracts (Baltimore, 1918-1926), which later was to merge with Abstracts of Bacteriology to form Biological Abstracts. [43]

Zoology was represented by such abstract journals as the Zentralblatt für Zoologie (Leipzig, 1912-1918), formed by the merger of Zoologisches Zentralblatt and Zentralblatt für allgemeine und experimentelle Biologie; and Physiological Abstracts (London, 1916-1937), issued by the Physiological Society with the cooperation of the American Physiological Society and other associated groups, including abstracts taken from Chemical Abstracts and the Journal of the Chemical Society. The Review of Applied Entomology (London, 1913-) covered the literature of that field and was issued by the Imperial Bureau of Entomology.

Medicine

The number of titles now appearing in medicine and

the medical specialties precludes the discussion of all but a
few, major titles.   Others are included with the complete
lists in Appendixes I through III.

General medicine was covered by such cover-to-cover
abstract journals as the Epitome of Current Medical Literature (London, 1890-   ); the Zentralblatt für die Grenzgebiete
der Medizin und Chirurgie Jena, 1897-1917); International
Medical and Surgical Survey (New York, 1920-1925), prepared
by the library staff of the American Institute of Medicine;
International Medical Digest (New York, 1920-   ); and Excerpta Medica (Leipzig, 1891-1927).

Physiology, hygiene, public health and pharmacy and
therapeutics were well represented by abstract sections of
primary journals in this period.

Medical specialties now being covered are represented
by such titles as: Zentralblatt für Kinderheilkunde (Leipzig,
1896-1917); Folia Haematologica (Berlin; Leipzig, 1904-   );
Zentralblatt für die gesamte Tuberkuloseforschung (Berlin;
Wurzburg, 1906-   ); and Tropical Diseases Bulletin (London,
1912-   ).   Many other primary journals contained sections of
abstracts, such as Abstracts of Tuberculosis (Baltimore,
1917-1959), a section of the American Review of Tuberculosis and Pulmonary Diseases sponsored by the National Tuberculosis Association.

Surgery was represented by such titles as the International Abstract of Surgery (Chicago, 1913-   ), published as
a supplement to Surgery, Gynecology and Obstetrics, and
through mid 1918 by a collaboration between the Journal de
chirurgie de Paris, the Zentralblatt für die gesamte Chirurgie, and the Zentralblatt für die gesamte Gynäkologie und
Geburtshilfe; and the Zentralorgan für die gesamte Chirurgie
(Berlin; Leipzig, 1913-   ) of the Deutsche Gesellschaft für
Chirurgie.

Pediatrics and veterinary medicine were also covered
by abstract services in this time period.

Applied Sciences and Technology

In 1856 under the auspices of the Prussian Ministry
of Business, Industry, and Public Works, Dr. Ernst Ludwig
Schubarth (1797-1868) issued the first retrospective volume
covering the years 1823 through 1853 of his Repertorium der

technischen Journal-Literatur (Berlin; Leipzig, 1856-1909).
A second and third volume covering the years 1854 through
1868 and 1869 through 1873 were issued under the editorship
of Georg Heinz Bruno Kerl (1824-1905), professor of chemical
technology at the Bergakademie in Berlin. Following these,
Kerl produced annual volumes for the years 1874 through
1881 which were continued under a succession of editors until 1909. With the annual for 1899 the Repertorium, now
covering some 400 technical periodicals in various languages,
began to include abstracts of the articles cited and continued
to do so through the remainder of its existence. The Repertorium was superseded in 1909 by the Fortschritte der Technik (Berlin, 1909-1910) sponsored by the International Institute for Technical Bibliography. The monthly issues of the
Fortschritte were issued under the title Technische Auskunft
(Berlin, 1909-1913) and an English language version, one of
several foreign language equivalent editions of the monthly,
was published as Engineering Abstracts (London, 1910-1913).
The Institute, with branches in France, Italy, Germany,
England, and Russia, employed specialists to collect, abstract, index, and classify articles from the technical literature. As such it was a prototype of the modern abstract
service. [44]

From 1910 through 1919 the Association Internationale
du Froid published its Bulletin mensuel covering the literature of refrigeration. This was also available in an English
language edition as Monthly Bulletin. With 1920 a new series
was begun by the reconstituted International Institute of Refrigeration as the Monthly Bulletin of Information on Refrigeration (Paris, 1920-   ).

In the area of agriculture the principal journal to appear in the period under review is the International Review
of the Science and Practice of Agriculture (Rome, 1910-
1926), sponsored by the International Institute of Agriculture
in Rome.

Chemical technology was well covered in this period.
Chimie et industrie (Paris, 1918-   ) covered the literature
of applied chemistry with considerable thoroughness, being
issued in three sections, each also bearing its own numbering: (1) "Technology," (2) "Documentation," and (3) "Economic Organization," the "Documentation" section containing
the abstracts. The Société de Chimie Industrielle sponsored
the journal.

In 1907 the American Gas Association began to issue
its Bulletin of Abstracts (Easton, Pa. , 1907-1930). These
abstracts were published in loose-leaf form, each sheet containing one abstract and being subject classified. The British
Ceramic Society, or rather its predecessor the North Staf-
fordshire Ceramic Society, carried a section called "Abstracts
from Foreign Journals" in volume one of its Transactions
(Stoke-on-Trent, 1901-) but they did not appear again until
1906 when a section called "Abstracts from Pottery Journals"
was initiated. - Suspended during the War from 1915 through
1916, they resumed simply as "Abstracts," separately paged
and covering an extensive area of the literature.

The Journal of the Society of Glass Technology (London, 1917-1959) included a section of abstracts from its beginnings, separately paged, covering comprehensively the
literature of that field.

In June 1919 abstracts were included for the first time
as a section of the monthly Journal of the American Ceramic
Society (Easton, Pa. , 1918-). These continued through
December 1921, after which they were reconstituted as Ceramic Abstracts with separate paging and an independent title
page and volume numbering but still issued in the Journal.

In metallurgy the Journal of the Institute of Metals
(London, 1909-) with volume two, 1909, introduced as
Section II its "Abstracts of Papers Relating to the Non-Fer-
rous Metals and the Industries Connected Therewith" while
the Revue de métallurgie (Paris; 1904-1959), sponsored by
the Société d'Encouragement pour l'Industrie Nationale and
the Comité des Forges de France, included an abstract section as its Part II.

The Journal of the Textile Institute (Manchester, Eng. ,
1910-), official organ of the British Cotton Industry Research Association and several allied groups, began to include a section of abstracts in its monthly publication in 1918.

Social Sciences

The field of psychology had undergone considerable
maturing as an academic discipline in the period under review. This fact was reflected in abstracting in the field.

From 1894 the Psychological Review (Lancaster, Pa. ,
1894-) contained selected abstracts of periodical articles

mingled with reviews of books in a section entitled "Psychological Literature." The material was indexed annually in Psychological Index (New York; etc., 1894-1935). With 1904 the "Literature" section of the Review was transferred to the new Psychological Bulletin (Lancaster, Pa.; etc., 1904-) where periodical articles continued to be abstracted along with critical reviews of books. With 1927 this section became Psychological Abstracts. The Année psychologique (Paris, 1894-) covered periodical literature from 1897 in its section entitled "Bibliographic Abstracts."

Sociology, political science, economics, education, folklore and history were some of the other areas of the social sciences which now came to be covered by abstracting services, in almost every case by selective abstract sections of primary journals.

Humanities

In the humanities, similarly, abstract sections of such journals as Journal of Philosophy, Psychology, and Scientific Method (New York, 1904-); Archiv für Reformations-Geschichte (Leipzig; Berlin, 1903-); and Rocznik slawistyczny (Krakow, 1908-) were published. In 1915 the Eastman Kodak Company Research Laboratory began publication of its Monthly Abstract Bulletin (Rochester, N.Y., 1915-1961) covering all phases of the chemistry of photography. [45]

Generalities

In this last period two abstract publications began which can be classed as generalia, the Times Official Index (London, 1906-) and the New York Times Index (New York, 1913-). The latter index was actually maintained from 1851 but not published until 1913. The years from 1851 through 1912 have now been published.

Notes

1. See pp. 60-61.
2. See pp. 59-60.
3. Retrospect of Philosophical, Mechanical, Chemical, and Agricultural Discoveries 1 (1805): iii.
4. Ibid., p. iv.
5. Critical Review, 3d series, 3 (1806): 443.
6. Adolph C. Callisen, Medicinisches Schriftsteller-Lexicon

der jetzt lebenden Aerzte, Wundärzte, Geburtshelfer,
Apotheker, und Naturforscher aller gebildeten Völker,
33 vols. (Copenhagen: 1830-45), 25:329.

7.   Taschenbuch für die gesamte Mineralogie 1 (1807): v.

8.   Karl von Zittel, History of Geology and Palaeontology
     to the End of the Nineteenth Century, trans. Maria
     Ogilvie-Gordon (London: W. Scott, 1901), p. 49.

9.   On this point see especially Kirchner, 1:157-158.

10. National Union Catalog; Pre-1956 Imprints, s.v. "Bib-
     liothek der neuesten physisch-chemischen, metallur-
     gischen, technologischen und pharmaceutischen Liter-
     atur."

11. Mott, 1:151.

12. Le Moniteur universel, 19 March 1836, p. 492.

13. Cf. Callisen, 23:424.

14. A thorough search of sources reveals nothing about the
     nature of the Société.

15. Le Moniteur universel, 19 March 1836, p. 492.

16. American Journal of Science 8 (August 1824): 386.

17. Kirchner, 2:114.

18. Chemisches Zentralblatt 1 (1830): 1-2.

19. Evan J. Crane, Austin M. Patterson, and Eleanor B.
     Marr, A Guide to the Literature of Chemistry, 2d
     ed. (New York: Wiley, 1957), p. 133.

20. Kirchner, 2:41-42.

21. John B. Blake and Charles Roos, eds., Medical Refer-
     ence Works, 1679-1966; a Selected Bibliography
     (Chicago: Medical Library Association, 1967), p. 11.

22. Callisen, 33:580.

23. Kirchner, 2:120.

24. Schmidts Jahrbücher der in- und ausländischen Medicin
     1 (1834): i.

25. Brodman, p. 128.

26. Mott, 1:438.

27. Dictionary of Scientific Biography, s.v. "Dunglison,
     Robley," by Samuel X. Radbill.

28. Half-Yearly Abstract of the Medical Sciences 1 (1845):
     iii.

29. Dictionnaire de biographie française, s.v. "Delacour,"
     by Roman d'Amat.

30. Half-Yearly Abstract of the Medical Sciences 1 (1845):
     iii.

31. Kronick, p. 238.

32. Chemisch-technische Mitteilungen der neuesten Zeit
     1 (1849): 1-2.

33. Dictionary of Scientific Biography, s.v. "Arago, Dom-
     inique," by Roger Hahn.

34. Kirchner, 2:199.
35. Mott, 1:140.
36. Yearbook of Pharmacy 1 (1864): 1.
37. Kirchner, 2:182.
38. Crane and Patterson, p. 129.
39. For a detailed treatment of the beginnings of Chemical
    Abstracts see Charles A. Browne and Mary E. Weeks,
    A History of the American Chemical Society (Wash-
    ington: American Chemical Society, 1952), pp. 336-
    67.
40. Crane and Patterson, p. 129.
41. Revue de géologie et des sciences connexes 1 (1920): ii.
42. Abstracts of Bacteriology 1 (1917): i.
43. For more on this see John E. Flynn, A History of
    Biological Abstracts (Philadelphia: 1951).
44. Wyndham and Kinzbrunner, p. 25.
45. The Monthly Abstract Bulletin is here classed as a
    journal in the humanities since the Universal Decimal
    Classification has been followed.

CHAPTER V

ANALYSIS AND INTERPRETATION

It is the purpose of this chapter to discuss such aspects of abstract journal development as growth, sponsorship, subject diffusion, and geographic diffusion along with the development of certain associated bibliographic characteristics, based upon the literature review phase of this study and examination of the pieces themselves, as presented in the preceding chronology.

Growth

Examination of the preceding chapter has already suggested to the reader that continued growth of the number of abstract journals has occurred in the period under review corresponding to the growth in the periodical literature in that same period. Data on the growth of abstract journals, both cumulative and active titles, are presented in Table 3 and displayed as a line graph in Fig. 1.

The growth rate for the cumulative total is fairly steady as can be seen from the figure. As calculated from Table 3 the average decennial percentage growth rate here is 37.6 percent for the period 1800-1849; 36.5 percent for the period 1850-1899; and 33 percent for the period 1900-1920. Overall the average decennial percentage growth rate is 36.4 percent.

The growth rate of the active titles is more erratic, especially in the first half of the nineteenth century. As calculated from Table 3 the average decennial percentage growth rate of abstract journals here is 26.8 percent for the period 1800-1849; 52.4 percent for the period 1850-1899; and 35.5 percent for the period 1900-1920. The overall average decennial percentage growth rate for active abstract journals is 38.9 percent.

TABLE 3

CUMULATIVE AND ACTIVE ABSTRACT JOURNALS BY DECADE, 1790-1920

		1790–99	1800–09	1810–19	1820–29	1830–39	1840–49	1850–59	1860–69	1870–79	1880–89	1890–99	1900–09	1910–20	End '20
Cumul.	Number	9	12	12	25	30	38	47	59	86	127	176	230	310	310
	% change	–	33	–	108	20	27	24	26	46	48	39	31	35	–
Active	Number	9	7	6	15	18	17	22	34	58	94	136	185	249	209
	% change	–	-22	-14	150	20	–	29	55	71	62	45	36	35	-16
	% of total	100	58	50	60	60	45	47	58	67	74	77	80	80	68

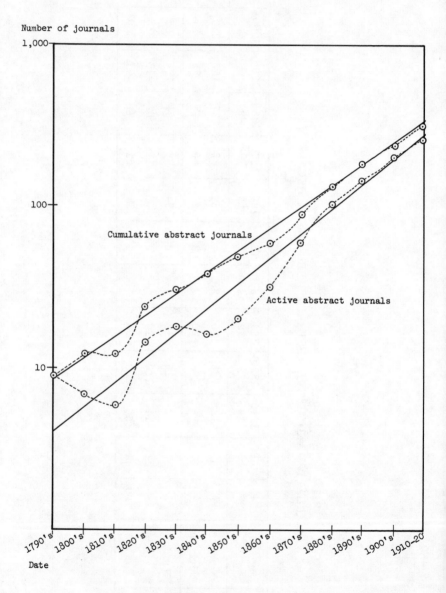

Number of journals

Fig. 1. Cumulative and Active Abstract Journals, 1790-1920

A significant change can be seen in the percentage of the total which are active, increasing with time, from the greater slope of the line representing active journals as compared with that representing the cumulative total. While the average percentage of active to cumulative titles is around 60 percent, this figure, except for anomalies in the early decades where small sample size prevails,[1] was continuing to rise at the end of the period.

The continued rate of growth and the rising percentage of active titles suggest that the abstract journal was fulfilling the role that it had set for itself and enjoying wide support.

The final column of Table 3 indicates a total of 209 active abstract journals at the end of 1920 compared with 249 in 1910. This major reversal of all previous trends in the growth of the abstract journal since the middle of the nineteenth century can only be attributed to the economic, social, and political effects of World War I, masked in the foregoing presentation of data by decades. For this reason, data for the individual years 1910 through 1920 are presented in Table 4 and Figure 2 showing growth of abstract journals, both cumulative and active, for these years.

These data show the annual percentage growth rate dropping during the war but rising after it, while the growth rate for active abstract journals, behaving more erratically, drops sharply during the war also and rises, again sharply, afterwards. The percentage of active abstract journals declines to 63 percent in 1918 and only begins to rise[2] in 1920, suggesting the effects of the war.

Certain writers, notably Price,[3] have suggested that the abstract journal developed in response to the periodical literature as a mechanism to provide bibliographic control. More precisely, Price observed that the emergence and growth of the abstract journal is primarily, if not entirely, a function of the size of the "information base," i.e., the volume of the journal literature as measured by the number of journal titles. Price maintains that the number of scientific journals increases exponentially with time, the constant factor being a doubling of the number of titles every fifteen years. He further maintains that when the amount of information in the "archive" becomes larger than some "critical" quantity it becomes necessary to introduce a new method for accessing the "archive." For scientific journals, Price continues, the point seems to have been reached with the

TABLE 4

CUMULATIVE AND ACTIVE ABSTRACT JOURNALS, 1910-1920

		1910	1911	1912	1913	1914	1915	1916	1917	1918	1919	1920
Cumul.	Number	238	246	258	267	276	277	279	287	292	298	310
	% change	-	3	5	4	3	-	1	3	2	2	4
Active	Number	177	185	192	196	202	188	186	192	184	189	209
	% change	-	5	4	2	3	-7	-1	4	-4	3	11
	% of total	74	75	74	73	73	68	67	67	63	63	67

existence of about 300 periodicals about 1830 and the abstract journal was "born." He goes on to discuss the growth of the number of abstract journals with time saying that it, like total journal growth, is exponential and growing at a rate of 5 percent per year. These data are shown in Figure 3. Price's hypothesis does not define such terms as "abstract journal" or the terms "scientific" and "technical;" nor does it state whether he is speaking of cumulative or active abstract and primary journal growth. [4]

Suspecting, nonetheless, that there is a correlation between journal growth in general, the growth of scientific and technical journals, and the emergence and growth of the abstract journal, and realizing at the same time that the matter is fraught with substantive problems of definition and lack of reliable data, it might be useful here to examine this relationship in the light of growth figures for abstract journals as developed in the present study.

Data from Iwinski[5] on active periodical growth have been tabulated in Table 5, while Table 6 represents a composite of data on journal growth in science and technology, taken from the works of Kronick, Grogan, Gottschalk and Desmond, Bourne, and Price. These data, along with figures on active abstract journal growth, are presented in Fig. 4 as a semi-logarithmic plot of growth versus time.

Examination of Fig. 4 shows abstract journal growth, after an initially uncertain period, to be exponential. The doubling period as shown here, compared with Price's observation of fifteen years, varies in length but averages, as calculated from the figures in Table 3, at around twenty eight years, a period nearly twice that which might have been expected on the basis of Price's hypothesis.

From Table 5 it is possible to calculate the annual growth rate for the general periodical literature for the period 1800-1908 as 4.1 percent; while the annual growth rate for scientific and technical periodicals for the period 1790-1900 can similarly be calculated from Table 6 as 2.3 percent. Using the figures from Table 3 the annual growth rate of active abstract journals can be seen to vary from 0.25 in the first half of the nineteenth century, to 4.25 percent for the last half of the century, to 3.1 percent for the period 1900-1920, for an overall annual growth rate of 2.6 percent (compared with Price's observation of 5 percent). It can be seen from these data and from Fig. 4 that the annual growth

(cont. on p. 116)

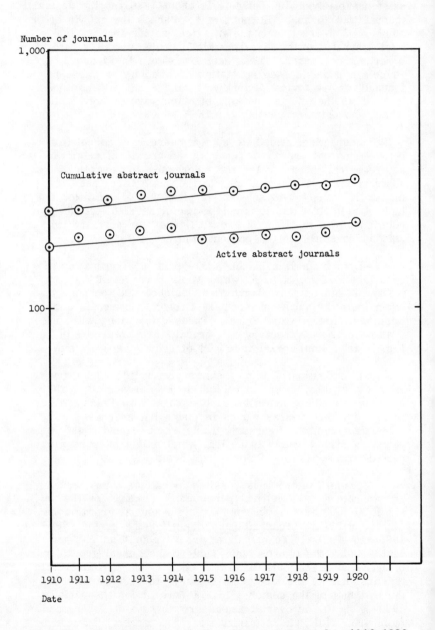

Fig. 2.   Cumulative and Active Abstract Journals, 1910-1920

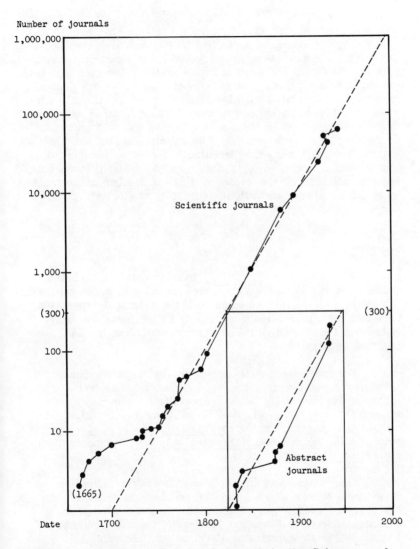

Fig. 3.   Correlation of Journal Growth in the Sciences and
Abstract Journal Emergence and Growth.   Reproduced by per-
mission from Derek de Solla Price, Science Since Babylon,
enlg. ed.   New Haven: Yale Univ. Press, 1975, p. 166.

rate of the general journal literature exceeds that of the scientific and technical journal literature which is very close to that for active abstract journals.

We see, then, that abstract journal growth is exponential and positively correlated with overall journal growth and essentially the same as scientific and technical journal growth, and doubling every twenty-eight years with an overall annual rate of growth of 2.6 percent. (Of course, the fact that both scientific and technical journal growth and abstract journal growth are correlated in this manner is not sufficiently persuasive evidence to suggest a causal effect. Much more detailed evidence beyond the scope of the present study would be required for such proof.) The hypothesis that the abstract journal emerged when the "archive," i.e., the number of journal titles, reached a "critical" point of 300 titles seems not be sustained by the evidence since a number of abstract journals have been identified as existing before this point in time.

Sponsorship

The preceding chronology has indicated that abstract journals in the period under review have been produced under the aegis of a variety of sponsors, the principal types being: personal enterprise, learned society or professional body, industrial research institution, governmental body, and commercial enterprise.

Personal enterprise refers to that type of sponsorship in which an individual, or a group of individuals working collaboratively, generally subject specialists, assume full responsibility for the production of an abstract journal. Examples are Leonhard's Taschenbuch für die gesamte Mineralogie, Just's Botanischer Jahresbericht, and Fechner's Pharmaceutisches Centralblatt.

Learned society or professional body sponsorship, as is evident, involves production of an abstract journal under the aegis of such a body. Examples are the American Chemical Society's Chemical Abstracts and the Deutsche Physikalische Gesellschaft's Physikalische Berichte.

Sponsorship by an industrial research institution is exemplified by the Monthly Abstract Bulletin of the Eastman Kodak Research Laboratory. Here production is often in

(cont. on p. 119)

TABLE 5

GROWTH OF PERIODICAL LITERATURE, 1800-1908
(ACTIVE TITLES)

Year	No. of Titles	Year	No. of Titles
1800	910	1892	46,678
1826	3,179	1898	53,249
1866	14,240	1901	59,057
1872	20,882	1904	67,319
1880	25,901	1908	71,248
1882	35,296		

SOURCE: Iwinski, p. 6, Table 1

TABLE 6

GROWTH OF SCIENTIFIC AND TECHNICAL PERIODICAL
LITERATURE, 1665-1966 (ACTIVE TITLES)

Year	No. of Titles	Year	No. of Titles
1665	35[a]	1900	5,000[b]
1700	12[a]	1962	30-35,000[c-d]
1750	119[a]	1963	30,000[e]
1790	416[a]	1965	26-35,000[f]

SOURCE: a) Kronick, p. 73; b) Grogan, p. 108; c) Charles M. Gottschalk and W. F. Desmond, "Worldwide Census of Scientific and Technical Serials," American Documentation 14 (July 1963): 190; d) Charles P. Bourne, "The World's Technical Journal Literature," American Documentation 13 (April 1962): 160; e) Price, p. 8; f) K. P. Barr, "Estimates of the Number of Currently Available Scientific & Technical Periodicals," Journal of Documentation 23 (June 1967): 114.

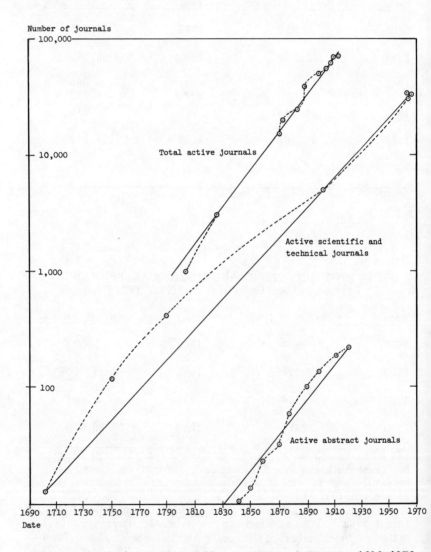

Fig. 4. Journal Growth and Abstract Journal Growth, 1690-1970

the hands of the institution's library staff, designed to serve local needs only, and often with a restricted distribution.

Governmental sponsorship is exemplified by such titles as Abstracts from Recent Medical and Public Health Papers, published by the United States Public Health Service, and Medical Science Abstracts and Reviews, published by the British Medical Research Council. This category also includes abstract journals produced under the sponsorship of international bodies such as the International Review of the Science and Practice of Agriculture, published by the International Institute of Agriculture. Generally sponsorship by governmental bodies is in the hands of a ministry, department, commission or board.

Sponsorship of abstract journals by commercial enterprise is a relatively infrequent occurrence even today, perhaps because of the small profit margin involved, though there are now such proprietary services as Excerpta Medica. Dental Cosmos published by the S. S. White Dental Manufacturing Company is an example of this type of publication. The New York Times Index as well as the Times Index could also be classified in this category.

In addition to these principal types of sponsorship a small minority of miscellaneous types of sponsorship are represented in this study. Comprised almost entirely of educational and research institutions, this category is discussed in more detail below.

Admittedly it is sometimes difficult to ascertain the exact nature of corporate responsibility for a publication, but an attempt has been made to do this, ascribing sponsorship to individuals when the corporate body has functioned solely as publisher.

From the preceding chapter it is apparent that a pattern of changing sponsorship of abstract journals has occurred in the period under review roughly as follows.

Initially abstract journals were the result of personal sponsorship (at first on an individual basis, then increasingly on a collaborative personal basis) in which individuals, generally subject specialists, assumed full responsibility for production. By mid-nineteenth century there was a clear trend, especially in the areas of science and technology, towards sponsorship by professional and learned societies

as these bodies developed and began to assume responsibility
for the bibliographic control of their respective fields. In
the last quarter of the nineteenth century other types of sponsorship began to emerge: governmental and inter-govern-
mental, industrial, and commercial enterprise being the principal types.

Table 7 and Fig. 5 contain data on type of sponsorship
of abstract journals by decade. It can be seen that personal
sponsorship was the earliest form, and, in terms of numbers
at least, continued to be the dominant form throughout the
period under review (though collaborative personal sponsorship had by the twentieth century replaced individual sponsorship). Society sponsorship was the next form to develop,
emerging in the 1820's and soon assuming major proportions.
Governmental sponsorship came to the fore in the last quarter of the nineteenth century accounting for a significant number of titles; while commercial and industrial sponsorship in
this period accounted for only a handful of titles. The miscellaneous category accounts for a small number of titles.

Personal Sponsorship

Personal sponsorship of the individual kind in which a
lone scholar produces an abstract journal because of his own
keen concern for the bibliographic control of the literature of
his field, is manifested by the earliest examples of the abstract journals cited in the chronology preceding this chapter.
Crell's Chemische Annalen, its Beiträge and his Neues chemisches Archiv, as well as Leonhard's Taschenbuch which followed, were the work of subject specialists, in the former
case a chemist, in the latter a mineralogist, motivated by a
concern for the control of the literature of their fields and
a desire to facilitate the growth of the field, especially in
their own country, through the compilation and publication of
these abstracts. Hermbstädt's Bulletin which followed was,
similarly, such a work. Throughout the nineteenth century
we observe, although with increasingly less frequency, the
phenomenon of cover-to-cover abstract journals and abstract
sections of primary journals published by individuals.

If one reads the editorial prefaces to abstract journals of the first half of the nineteenth century it becomes
plain that increasingly the editors, having previously relied
on their own efforts and the voluntary contributions of a
handful of close colleagues, had recourse to solicited contributions of abstracts from practitioners in the field. .

TABLE 7

ACTIVE ABSTRACT JOURNALS BY TYPE OF SPONSORSHIP AND DECADE, 1790-1920

	1790-99	1800-09	1810-19	1820-29	1830-39	1840-49	1850-59	1860-69	1870-79	1880-89	1890-99	1900-09	1910-20	End '20
Personal	9	7	6	7	9	14	13	21	36	55	77	108	121	95
Society	-	-	-	8	9	3	8	11	17	31	47	62	97	86
Industrial	-	-	-	-	-	-	-	-	-	-	1	1	3	3
Governmental	-	-	-	-	-	-	-	-	1	2	3	4	11	11
Commercial	-	-	-	-	-	-	-	-	-	-	-	1	2	2
Other[a]	-	-	-	-	-	-	1	2	4	6	8	10	15	12

[a] Academic (8); Private research institute (6); and manufacturing (1)

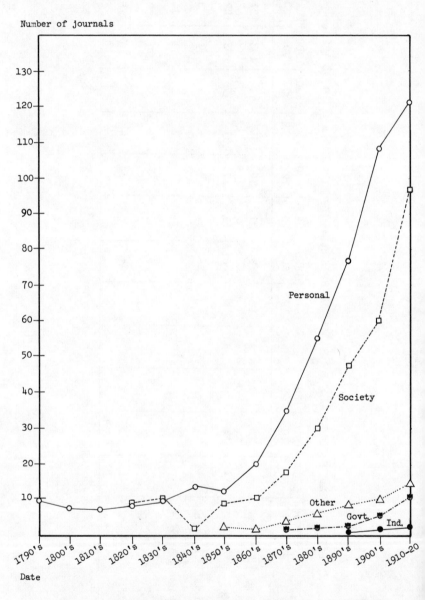

Fig. 5.   Sponsorship of Abstract Journals, 1790-1920
(Active Titles)

Increasingly their efforts reflected such reliance on the voluntary contribution of abstracts, as the volume of literature to be covered continued to grow.

The transition from individual to collaborative personal sponsorship is difficult to pinpoint with any exactness and is, of course, not reflected in Table 7. Ferussac clearly had such an arrangement in his Bulletin universel, which was divided into eight separate sections, each presided over by a panel of subject experts who, along with others in the field, provided the abstracts. In this and other respects, though, Ferussac was ahead of his time. Following the demise of the Bulletin universel the incidence of collaborative sponsorship grew while that of individual sponsorship seems to have declined rapidly. [6]

In the sciences personal sponsorship continued to play an important part in abstract journal production throughout the period under review although the trend clearly was to other forms, notably sponsorship by learned and professional societies. To be sure this personal sponsorship was generally of the collaborative variety. The following are examples of journals thus produced: in mathematics, the Jahrbuch über die Fortschritte der Mathematik; in physics and chemistry, the Annales de chimie et de physique and the Annalen der Physik Beiblätter; in chemistry, the Review of American Chemical Research and the Journal de chimie physique; in mineralogy, the Neues Jahrbuch für Mineralogie, Geological Record, and Geologisches Zentralblatt; in the life sciences, the Zentralblatt für Bakteriologie, Biochemisches Zentralblatt and the Review of Bacteriology; in botany, Hedwigia, Botanischer Jahresbericht, and Botanische Jahrbücher; and in zoology, Zoologisches Zentralblatt.

Medicine seems to have exhibited a good deal less collaborative sponsorship than purely individual. Examples here are Froriep's Notizen, Kleinert's Allgemeines Repertorium, Unger's Summarium, Schmidt's Jahrbücher, and Dunglison's American Medical Intelligencer in the first part of the nineteenth century, followed by publications like Braithwaite's Retrospect, the Annales médico-psychologiques, Medical News, Ranking's Half-Yearly Abstract of the Medical Sciences, the Journal de pharmacie et de chimie, and the Jahrbuch für Kinderheilkunde later in the century, and even to many of the German Zentralblätter of the first decades of the twentieth century.

In agriculture, personal sponsorship produced <u>Bieder-</u>
<u>mann's Zentralblatt</u>; in technology Timbs' <u>Arcana</u> and <u>Year-</u>
<u>book</u>; in psychology, the <u>Zeitschrift für Psychologie</u>, <u>Psycho-</u>
<u>logical Review</u>, and <u>Psychological Bulletin</u>; in philosophy,
<u>Mind</u> and the <u>Journal of Philosophy</u>; in history, the <u>Revue</u>
<u>historique</u>; and in sociology the <u>Année sociologique.</u>

The subject of personal sponsorship should not be left
without examining in a little more detail the relationship between individual sponsorship and the publication of abstract
journals. Without delving deeply into the archives of individual publications and the lives of individual editors it is not
possible to state what motivated these men to sponsor abstract publications or abstract sections of primary journals.
Personal gain in the monetary sense is nowhere suggested.
It may not be unreasonable to assume that their efforts reflected a desire to enhance their status in their respective
fields. The fact that they were carried on by lone and collaborating subject specialists combined with evidence from
such prefatory statements as exist suggests that there is a
strong sense of bibliographic responsibility at work here,
whatever its underlying motivation. Consider the <u>Archiv der</u>
<u>Pharmazie</u> and the <u>Annales de chimie et de physique</u>, for
example, which began to include sections of abstracts with
a change of editorship and dropped them coincidental with a
change of editorship; or the <u>Monthly Review</u>, the <u>Revue de</u>
<u>l'histoire des religions</u>, and <u>Mind</u> all of which dropped sec-
tions of abstracts with the death of their editors.

Most of the results of personal sponsorship as the
nineteenth century progressed were abstract sections of primary journals. As stated above, it is almost impossible to
tell from secondary evidence how these were produced. With
time many of them changed from personal sponsorship to
sponsorship by learned and professional societies, the task
of dealing with the ever-growing volume of literature proving
to be too much for such personal efforts. Only in medicine
does there remain in this period a high degree of personal
sponsorship, the reasons for this not being immediately clear.
It is perhaps a function of the fragmentation of medical societies, especially in Germany where much medical research
was being conducted in this period. In the sciences and
technology, society and government sponsorship had taken the
lead as these bodies were increasingly anxious to exert bibliographic control over the literature, with an added impetus
supplied by economic and political pressures. The literature
of medicine, not being subject to the same pressures, con-

tinued with a rather loose system of bibliographic control.
The literature of the social sciences and humanities was only
beginning to develop and bibliographic control by abstracts or
any other device was a long way off in these areas.

Sponsorship by Learned and Professional Societies

The principal type of abstract journal sponsorship
which evolved after personal sponsorship was that of sponsorship by professional and learned societies.

As the eighteenth century progressed, for a variety of
reasons, scholars and professional men associated themselves
into societies. One of the principal reasons for this was to
effect the improved communication of ideas and developments
of mutual interest.[7] As an aspect of this there developed a
corresponding need to organize and access the written record.
Stated another way, there soon developed a need to exert bibliographic control over the literature.

Aside from the sponsorship of the Bulletin universel
by the Société pour la Propagation de Connaissances Scientifiques et Industrielles from 1827-1831, the earliest abstract
publication to appear under such sponsorship was the abstract
section of the Archiv der Pharmazie which began in 1843.
This was followed in 1845 by the first cover-to-cover abstract
journal sponsored by a learned society, the Fortschritte der
Physik, sponsored by the Physikalische Gesellschaft zu Berlin. Many abstract publications previously personally sponsored changed to society sponsorship and many new ones began under society sponsorship, especially after mid-nineteenth
century. Examples in the pure sciences are the Bulletin of
the Société Chimique de France, the Journal of the Chemical
Society, Mining Magazine, Botanisches Zentralblatt, Repertorium der analytischen Chimie, Analyst, Revue semestrielle
des publications mathématiques, Abstracts of Physical Papers,
Année biologique, Science Abstracts, Astronomischer Jahresbericht, Chemical Abstracts, Abstracts of Bacteriology, Botanical Abstracts, Mineralogical Abstracts, and Physikalische
Berichte.

Examples in the field of medicine of such sponsorship
are the Yearbook of Pharmacy, the Journal of Nervous and
Mental Disease, the Monatsschrift für Ohrenheilkunde, the
Revue d'hygiène, British Dental Journal, Journal of the
American Medical Association, Zentralblatt für Physiologie,
Journal of the American Veterinary Medical Association,

Epitome of Current Medical Literature, Kongresszentralblatt
für die gesamte innere Medizin, Abstracts of Tuberculosis,
Archives of Neurology and Psychiatry, and International Medical and Surgical Survey.

Examples of abstract journals in the field of the applied sciences and technology with society sponsorship are
the Abstracts of Papers of the Institution of Civil Engineers,
the Journal of the Society of Chemical Industry, Engineering
Index, Zeitschrift für angewandte Chemie, Revue de métallurgie, Transactions of the Ceramic Society, Bulletin of Abstracts of the American Gas Association, Fortschritte der
Technik, Journal of the Institute of Metals, Mechanical Engineering, Journal of the Society of Glass Technology, Chimie
et industrie, Journal of the Textile Institute, Ceramic Abstracts, and the Revue universelle des mines.

Examples of society sponsorship in the social sciences
and humanities are comparatively few. In the former case,
examples are the American Journal of Archaeology, the Bibliographie géographique, Economic Journal, the American
Economic Review, the Journal of American Folklore, and
Mental Hygiene. In the latter case examples are Numismatic
Chronicle, Analecta Bollandiana, and the Archiv für Reformations-Geschichte.

The trend towards bibliographic control of the literature of a field by the responsible society, generally within
each country, was definitely established by the turn of the
twentieth century. This was especially true in the pure sciences and in the applied sciences and technology. For example, the literature of chemistry was controlled in each
major country by the responsible chemical society: in England, the Chemical Society (abstract section of the Journal of
the Chemical Society); in France, the Société Chimique de
France (the abstract section of its Bulletin); in Germany, the
Deutsche Chemische Gesellschaft (Chemisches Zentralblatt);
and in the United States, the American Chemical Society
(Chemical Abstracts). In some other subject areas collaborative efforts were apparent as with the American, Italian, and
English participation in Science Abstracts. Few examples of
national control through responsible professional or learned
societies or collaborative efforts are found outside science
and technology, with some exceptions in the field of medicine
such as the Quarterly Cumulative Index to Current Medical
Literature, prepared by the library staff of the American
Medical Association, and the Epitome, prepared under the

auspices of the British Medical Association, though control
here was generally dispersed, as mentioned above, among a
growing number of personally sponsored publications.   No
comprehensive coverage of the literature of the social sciences or the humanities was provided by society sponsorship
of abstract publications at this time.   While there were
scattered and tentative examples in these two fields, what
coverage was provided was generally in a narrow field, and
even then was not significant in terms of degree of coverage
of the literature.

Industrial Sponsorship

Industrial sponsorship of abstract journals is manifested in the period covered by this study in only three titles:
Therapeutic Notes begun in 1894 by Parke, Davis and which
carried a section of selected abstracts from medical journals
concerned with therapy; the Abstract Bulletin of the Lamp
Development Laboratory, General Electric Company, beginning in 1913 and carrying abstracts of articles by staff members appearing in the professional literature; and the Monthly
Abstract Bulletin of the Eastman Kodak Company Research
Laboratory, beginning in 1915 and providing excellent coverage of the literature of the rapidly expanding field of photography.   It is interesting to note that industrial sponsorship
of abstract publications in this period is confined entirely to
the United States and is in highly competitive and fast-grow-
ing fields.

Government Sponsorship

Government sponsorship of abstract journals is a
phenomenon manifested in the last third of the nineteenth
century.   The first such journal encountered in this study
was the Bulletin des sciences mathématiques sponsored from
its inception in 1870 by the French Ministry of National Education and providing extensive abstract coverage of its field.
In 1889 the United States Department of Agriculture began its
Experiment Station Record which provided for many years a
record of current agricultural literature.   Several other government sponsored abstract journals followed with no particular pattern or trend as to country or subject field.   In
1899 the German Patent Office began publication of its Repertorium der technischen Journal-Literatur, covering the field
of engineering; various British government agencies produced
such publications as the Bulletin of the Imperial Institute,
Tropical Diseases Bulletin, the Review of Applied Entomology,

<u>Medical Science Abstracts and Reviews</u>, and <u>Technical Review</u>; the United States Public Health Service began publication in 1920 of <u>Abstracts from Recent Medical and Public Health Papers</u>; and the International Office of Public Hygiene, representing international sponsorship of an abstracting publication, produced from 1909 its <u>Bulletin</u>. One obvious characteristic of all these publications is a concern with matters of interest to governments, viz., agriculture, public health, and technology.

Commercial Sponsorship

Commercial sponsorship in the period studied is represented only by a handful of titles. The <u>Times Official Index</u> and the <u>New York Times</u>, mentioned above as marginal abstract publications, are two examples of such sponsorship. <u>Dental Cosmos</u>, sponsored by the S. S. White Dental Manufacturing Company of Philadelphia furnished abstracts of the dental literature for the practitioner from 1860 and McGraw-Hill's <u>Electrical World</u> carried from 1894 an extensive section of abstracts entitled "Digest of Electrical Literature." Another example is <u>Engineering Index</u> for the period from 1892 through 1919 when it was sponsored by <u>Engineering Magazine</u>. Again, with the exception of the <u>Times Official Index</u>, commercial sponsorship, like industrial, is confined to the United States and in competitive subject areas. Commercial sponsorship seems to have been desultory at best, probably because of the low profit margin associated with such an enterprise. To this day it has not proved a popular form of abstract journal sponsorship.

Miscellaneous Types of Sponsorship

Two types of sponsorship other than those indicated above accounted for a small number of titles: sponsorship by an educational institution and sponsorship by a research institute.

Sponsorship of an abstract journal by an educational institution seems to this writer to be an extension of the collaborative variety of sponsorship described above, since many of these individuals were affiliated with educational institutions. In a few instances abstract journals were produced with the imprimatur of the institutions with which the collaborators, or the principal editors, were affiliated. Examples here are the <u>Abstract of the Literature of Industrial Hygiene and Toxicology</u> produced by staff members at the

Harvard Medical School, and the abstract sections of: the
Bulletin of the Ecole Française d'Extrême-Orient, the _Ameri-
can Journal of Sociology_, produced by staff members of the
Department of Sociology and related departments at the University of Chicago, and the _American Journal of Pharmacy_,
produced at the Philadelphia College of Pharmacy.

Sponsorship by research institutes was manifested in
the _Annales_ and _Bulletin_ of the Pasteur Institut, the _Monthly
Review_ of the International Institute of Refrigeration; the _In-
ternational Review of the Science and Practice of Agriculture_
(the International Institute of Agriculture in Rome), and the
Zentralblatt für Gewerbehygiene (the Institut für Gewerbehygiene, Frankfurt).

Multiple Sponsorship

Multiple sponsorship of abstract journals is tabulated
in Table 8.

As concern with bibliographic organization mounted
throughout the latter half of the nineteenth century and on up
to the outbreak of World War I, there was a corresponding
mutual concern among individuals involved in the production
of abstract journals to rationalize their efforts, these con-
cerns being generally manifested in this period by cooperative or multiple sponsorship of an abstracting enterprise.
This phenomenon seems especially to have been exhibited in
the pure sciences, to a much lesser extent in medicine, and
rarely in the applied sciences and technology.

TABLE 8

MULTIPLE SPONSORSHIP OF ABSTRACT JOURNALS
BY SUBJECT CATEGORY

Subject	Number
Pure Sciences	6
Medicine	4
Applied Science & Technology	2
Social Sciences	-
Humanities	-
Generalities	-
TOTAL	12

Manifestations of this in the pure sciences were such abstract journals as the following: Chemisches Zentralblatt (sponsored from 1897 by the Deutsche Chemische Gesellschaft and from 1919 through June 1923 with the Verein Deutscher Chemiker); the Botanisches Zentralblatt (from 1880 through 1901 the organ of numerous German and foreign botanical societies and from 1902 the organ of the Association Internationale des Botanistes); Science Abstracts (issued through 1902 by the Institution of Electrical Engineers and the Physical Society; and from 1903 by the Institution of Electrical Engineers in association with the Physical Society and various foreign societies, including the American Electrochemical Society, from 1903 through 1906, the American Physical Society and the American Institute of Electrical Engineers (both of the latter from 1903); Physiological Abstracts (sponsored by the Physiological Society in cooperation with the American Physiological Society and numerous other national societies; Physikalische Berichte (sponsored by the Deutsche Physikalische Gesellschaft and the Deutsche Gesellschaft für Technische Physik); and the Revue de géologie et des sciences connexes (sponsored by the Société Géologique de Belgique, the Revue critique de paléozoologie, and the Société Géologique de France).

Examples of such cooperation in the field of medicine were fewer and, interestingly, did not represent international cooperation attempting to solve the problem of bibliographic control as did the examples cited above in the pure sciences, being rather regional in nature. The Journal of Nervous and Mental Disease was sponsored by the American Neurological Association in conjunction with various local neurological associations; Fortschritte der Medizin was sponsored by the Vereinigung für Freien Ärztlichen Meinungsaustausch and the Gesellschaft für Mechanotherapie, both regional groups in Germany; the Zentralblatt für Physiologie was sponsored by the Physiologische Gesellschaft zu Berlin from 1887, briefly with the Morphologisch-Physiologische Gesellschaft zu Wien from 1901 through 1904; and the Hahnemannian Monthly was sponsored by the Homeopathic Medical Societies of the State of Pennsylvania.

The only examples of joint sponsorship in the applied sciences and technology were the Zeitschrift für Pflanzenzüchtung, sponsored by the Gesellschaft zur Förderung Deutsche Pflanzenzüchtung and several Austrian and Bavarian societies in the field; and the Journal of the Textile Institute, official organ of the British Cotton Industry Research Association, the Research Association of the Woolen and Worsted Industry, the Linen Industry Research Association, the British Silk Research Association and other associated bodies.

It can be concluded from the above exposition that multiple sponsorship of abstract publications seems to have been greatest in the area of the pure sciences where it was practiced by cooperating professional and learned societies. The motivation here seems to have been that of providing a rational scheme of bibliographic control of the literature through the cooperation of national societies. Multiples sponsorship in medicine is not significant and seems not concerned with overall control of the literature (most of the examples here are sections of primary journals rather than cover-to-cover abstract journals). Medical bibliography seems not to have come to grips yet with the problems of control of the periodical literature, though one must bear in mind the excellent resource at the time in the Index-Catalogue of the Library of the Surgeon-General's Office.

Multiple sponsorship of abstract publications in the applied sciences and technology was very limited, competition not cooperation being the byword here. Of course, the bibliographic control mechanism in the social sciences and humantities had not yet matured to the point where cooperative sponsorship was manifested.

Change of Sponsorship

From Table 9 it can be seen that the predominant form of change of sponsorship of abstract journals was from personal to society sponsorship. A surprisingly low percentage, 7 percent, changed sponsorship. By the end of 1920 personal sponsorship was giving way to sponsorship by professional and learned societies as well as government and commercial sponsorship. In addition to the significantly diminishing rate of personal sponsorship of active abstract journals, the War seems not at all to have lessened the absolute number of industrial, governmental and commercially sponsored abstract journals, suggesting that society sponsorship was supplanting personal sponsorship while other forms of sponsorship were assuming importance.

A change of sponsorship from personal to society was manifested by Chemisches Zentralblatt when in 1897 it came under the aegis of the Deutsche Chemische Gesellschaft; by the Journal de physique et le radium, which came under the

TABLE 9

CHANGE OF SPONSORSHIP OF ABSTRACT JOURNALS

Type of Change	Number
Personal to society	17
Other[a]	4

[a]Multiple to international society (1); society to personal (1); society to personal and back to society (1); Association of professional groups of varying composition (1)

sponsorship of the Société Française de Physique in 1911; by the Journal of Nervous and Mental Disease, which came under the sponsorship of the American Neurological Association in 1895; Botanisches Zentralblatt, sponsored by the Botanischer Verein in Munich from 1881; Fortschritte der Medizin, which came under the sponsorship of the Gesellschaft für Mechanotherapie and the Vereinigung für Freien... Meinungsaustausch in 1920; and Revue neurologique which came under the sponsorship of the Société de Neurologique de Paris in 1899.

Several anomalous changes of sponsorship occurred. Engineering Index, under personal sponsorship from 1884 through 1891, came under the commercial sponsorship of Engineering Magazine from 1892 through 1919. From 1920 it has been sponsored by the American Society of Mechanical Engineers. The Zentralblatt für allgemeine Gesundheitspflege changed from society sponsorship to collaborative personal sponsorship in 1898.

Sponsorship and Subject Category

Table 10 shows the distribution of sponsorship of abstract journals in the period under review as a function of subject category. Personal and society sponsorship can be seen to be the dominant forms of sponsorship in all categories. In the pure sciences, personal and society sponsorship are about equally divided; in technology, where abstract journals appeared later than in the pure sciences, society sponsorship predominates. In medicine, personal sponsorship predominates by a factor of more than two to one. In the social sciences and humanities the sponsorship is about equally divided between personal and society; in the generalities, sponsorship is predominantly personal.

TABLE 10

CUMULATIVE ABSTRACT JOURNALS BY TYPE
OF SPONSORSHIP AND SUBJECT CATEGORY

	Pure Sciences	Medicine	Applied Science & Technology	Social Sciences	Humanities	Generalities	Total
Personal	40	82	17	11	5	6	161
Society	36	34	29	12	5	-	116
Industrial	1	1	-	-	1	-	3
Governmental	3	5	3	1	-	-	12
Commercial	-	-	-	-	-	2	2
Other	2	4	3	6	1	-	16
TOTAL	82	126	52	30	12	8	310

Industrial sponsorship, slight as it is in this period, is evidenced in the sciences, medicine, and humanities (the Eastman Kodak <u>Monthly Bulletin</u> in the field of photography), while governmental sponsorship is evidenced in medicine, the pure sciences, and technology, with one example in the social sciences.

Sponsorship and Country of Origin

Table 11 shows type of sponsorship as a function of country of origin.   Again we see the dominance of society and personal sponsorship in virtually every country.   In England and Belgium society sponsorship predominates over personal sponsorship; while in France, Germany, and Italy the reverse is true.   In the United States sponsorship is about equally divided between personal and society sponsorship. The figures for the remaining countries are too sparse to permit conclusions in this area.   No reason relative to national characteristics seems apparent to explain this distribution.

Industrial sponsorship is manifested only in the United States, while governmental sponsorship is strongest in England.   Commercial sponsorship is manifested in England and the United States, comprising in each only 2 percent of the total.

Subject Diffusion

Table 12 and Fig. 6 display active abstract journals by subject category and decade of origin.   Fig. 7 is a line graph showing subject distribution of abstract journals by Universal Decimal Classification over time giving some quantitative idea as to continuity and chronological subject distribution.   In terms of broad subject areas, the order of development of abstract journals seems to follow a pattern of earliest appearance in the field of broad, general learning, dying out with the passing of the polymathic journal by 1820; to appearance, almost simultaneously in the pure sciences and medicine; followed by appearance in the applied sciences and technology.   Toward the end of the nineteenth century abstract journals had developed in certain of the fields of the social sciences and, to a much less extent, in certain of the humanities.   This pattern of subject development, not surprisingly, parallels the historical development of these fields of scholarship, especially as measured by the growth of

(cont. on p. 145)

TABLE 11

CUMULATIVE ABSTRACT JOURNALS BY TYPE OF SPONSORSHIP AND COUNTRY OF ORIGIN

		England	France	Germany	U. S.	Italy	Neth.	Poland	Switz.	French Indo-China	Spain	Austria	Belgium	Brazil
Personal	Number	17	32	77	25	6	1	1	1	-	-	2	1	1
	Percent	36	50	70	42	60	25	100	50	-	-	100	17	100
Society	Number	22	25	29	24	3	3	-	1	-	1	-	5	-
	Percent	47	38	26	41	30	75	-	50	-	100	-	83	-
Indus.	Number	-	-	-	3	-	-	-	-	-	-	-	-	-
	Percent	-	-	-	5	-	-	-	-	-	-	-	-	-
Govt.	Number	6	2	2	2	-	-	-	-	-	-	-	-	-
	Percent	13	1	2	3	-	-	-	-	-	-	-	-	-
Comm.	Number	1	-	-	1	-	-	-	-	-	-	-	-	-
	Percent	2	-	-	2	-	-	-	-	-	-	-	-	-
Other	Number	1	7	2	4	1	-	-	-	1	-	-	-	-
	Percent	2	11	2	7	10	-	-	-	100	-	-	-	-
	TOTAL	47	66	110	59	10	4	1	2	1	1	2	6	1

TABLE 12

ACTIVE ABSTRACT JOURNALS BY SUBJECT AND DECADE, 1790-1920

	1790-99	1800-09	1810-19	1820-29	1830-39	1840-49	1850-59	1860-69	1870-79	1880-89	1890-99	1900-09	1910-20	End '20
Pure Sciences	3	3	2	4	5	4	7	10	19	27	37	48	62	51
Medicine	-	-	-	4	6	11	11	17	29	48	65	84	109	92
Appl. Sci., Tech.	-	1	1	3	4	2	4	5	6	11	15	27	43	37
Social Sciences	-	-	-	3	3	-	-	1	2	4	14	16	23	18
Humanities	-	-	-	-	-	-	-	1	2	4	5	9	10	9
Generalities	6	3	3	1	-	-	-	-	-	-	-	1	2	2
TOTAL	9	7	6	15	18	17	22	34	58	94	136	185	249	209

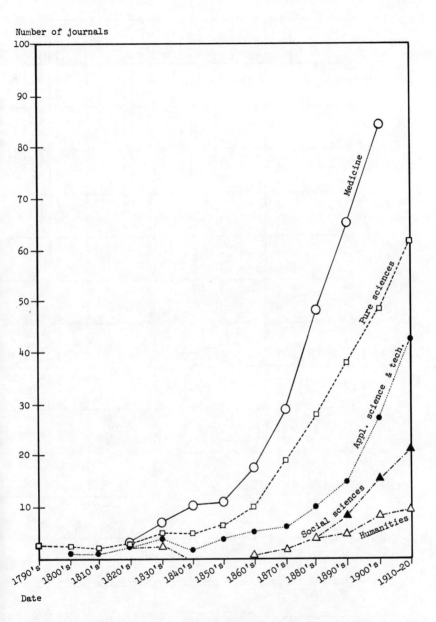

Number of journals

Date

Fig. 6. Abstract Journal Growth by Subject Categories,
1790-1920 (Active Titles). <u>Following seven pages</u> (138-144):
Subject Diffusion of Abstract Journals, 1790-1920. [See also
pp. 228-246.]

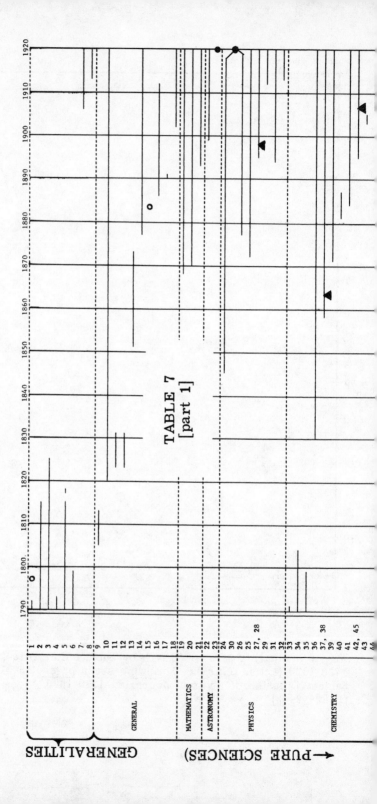

TABLE 7
[part 1]

TABLE 7
[part 1 cont.]

GEOLOGY

LIFE SCIENCES

BOTANY

ZOOLOGY

51
52
53
54
55
56
57
58
59
60
61
62
63
64
65
66, 73
67
68
69
70
71
72
74
75
76
77
78
79
80
81
82
83
84
85, 86
87
88
89
90

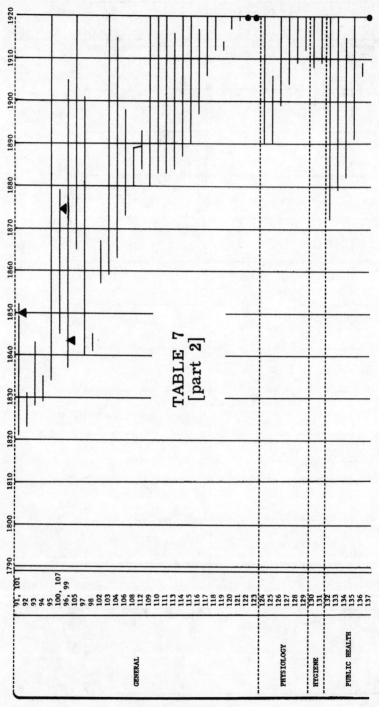

TABLE 7
[part 2]

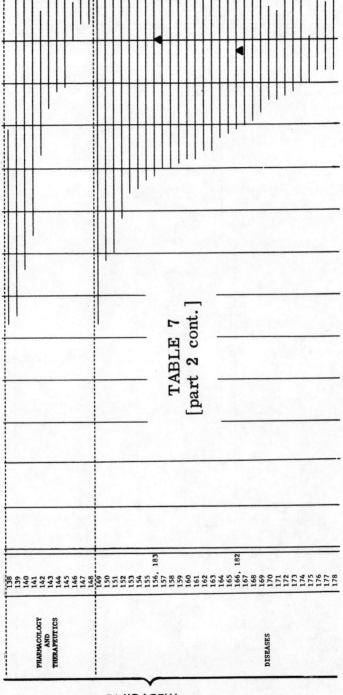

TABLE 7
[part 2 cont.]

TABLE 7
[part 2 concluded]

(MEDICINE)

SURGERY
AND
OPHTHALMOLOGY

GYNECOLOGY
AND
OBSTETRICS

VETERINARY
MEDICINE

179
180
181
184
185
186
187
188
189
190
191
192
193
194
195
196
203
197
198
199
200
201
202
204
205
206
207
208
209
210
211
212
213
214
215
216
217
218
219

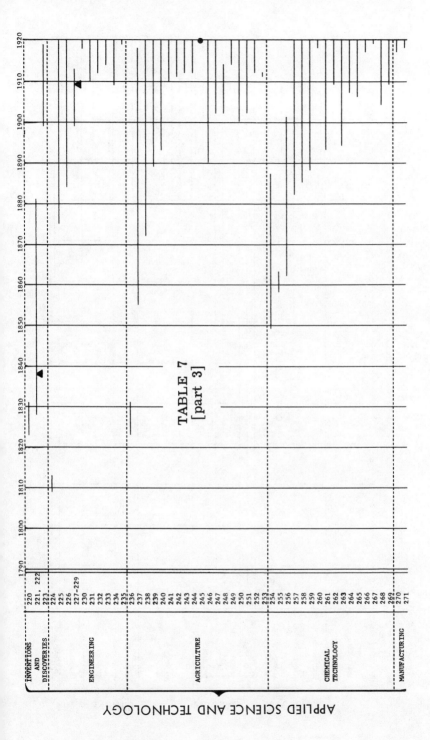

TABLE 7
[part 3]

TABLE 7
[part 3 cont.]

PSYCHOLOGY	272 273 274 275 276 277 278 279
SOCIOLOGY	280 281 282
POLITICAL SCIENCE	
ECONOMICS	283 284 285
MILITARY SCIENCE	286 287
EDUCATION	288 289
COMMERCE, ETC.	290
FOLKLORE	291 292
GEOGRAPHY	293
HISTORY	294 295 296 297 298 299 300 301
PHILOSOPHY	302 303
RELIGION	304 305 306 307
LANGUAGES	308 309 310
NUMISMATICS	311 312
PHOTOGRAPHY	313

SOCIAL SCIENCES

HUMANITIES

literature. The chronology of the development of abstract journals by subfields within each of these fields is another matter. The following discussion is arranged by broad subjects in the order of development of abstract journals and within by subfield in order of appearance.[8]

Generalities

In the area of general scholarship the abstract journal had died out by the first decades of the nineteenth century with the decline of broad scholarship and the polymathic periodical. Most of the abstract publications in this field, never numerous or comprehensive in scope, constituted sections of literary periodicals, and as the literary periodicals, like the French Journal des sçavans and Esprit des journaux and the English Universal Magazine and Monthly Review, changed in nature with the evolution of a critical literary style and as increasingly more specialized periodicals appeared, these abstracts soon ceded the field to the subject abstract journal and abstract sections of specialized primary journals. Only the Times Official Index and the New York Times Index remain today as examples of this kind of abstract publication.

Pure Sciences

As abstracting in the field of general scholarship died out it next emerged in the pure sciences and in the following chronology by subfields: chemistry; general science; mineralogy; geology; physics; botany; mathematics; life sciences; zoology; and astronomy. No major subfield of the pure sciences is unrepresented by an abstract publication of some kind in the period under study.

a. Chemistry

At the beginning of the period covered by this study, 1790, chemistry was represented by three prototype abstract journals: the Neues chemisches Archiv; the Chemische Annalen; and the latter's Beiträge, all three under the editorship of the German chemist Lorenz von Crell. It was not until 1823 with the publication of the Bulletin des sciences mathématiques, astronomiques, physiques et chimiques (section one of the Bulletin universel) that pure chemistry was again covered, this time on a current basis. Following the Bulletin the next abstract publication to appear to provide coverage of the literature of pure chemistry was Fechner's Pharmaceutisches Centralblatt (predecessor of Chemiches Zentralblatt)

in 1830.   The Centralblatt rather strictly limited its coverage
until 1850 to the literature of pharmacy, in that year broaden-
ing its coverage to pure chemistry in general.

In 1851 the venerable Annales de chimie et de physique
began to include a section of abstracts of the literature of
chemistry, edited by the French chemist Dominique Arago.
It was very soon after that the Société Chimique de Paris,
in an attempt to emulate the success of the Chemisches Zentralblatt initiated its Répertoire de chimie pure and Répertoire de chimie appliquée.   Both of these publications, having
begun in 1858, merged in 1863 and 1864 respectively into the
Société's Bulletin.   It was not until 1871 that an English language abstract journal in the field of pure chemistry appeared.
It was in that year that the Chemical Society began to include
an extensive section of abstracts in its semi-monthly Journal.
These were the most comprehensive set of abstracts in English covering pure chemistry before the founding of Chemical
Abstracts in 1907.   The first American entry in the field
came with the publication in 1895 of the Review of American
Chemical Research by staff members at the Massachusetts
Institute of Technology.   This publication, inspired by a need
for domestic bibliographical coverage of the chemical literature, was taken over by the American Chemical Society,
broadened in scope, and continued from 1907 as Chemical Abstracts.

Abstract coverage of the literature of pure chemistry,
begun in the latter half of the eighteenth century, has been
continuous since the founding of Chemiches Zentralblatt in
1830.   The abstracting publications in this field are generally
either cover-to-cover in nature or comprise extensive sections
of primary journals.   By 1920 the coverage of the chemical
literature had essentially resolved itself into the four major
services mentioned above: Chemisches Zentralblatt (Germany);
Bulletin of the Société Chimique de France (France); Journal
of the Chemical Society (England); and Chemical Abstracts
(United States), each sponsored by the principal chemical society in that country.   Beyond these there were a handful of
cover-to-cover abstract journals and abstract sections of primary journals concerned with highly specialized areas of
chemistry, like the abstract sections of Kolloid-Zeitschrift
and the Analyst.

b.   General Science

Abstract coverage of science in general was attempted

on an intermittent basis in the period covered by this study.
The Retrospect of Philosophical, Mechanical, Chemical, and
Agricultural Discoveries, founded in 1805, tried to provide
broad coverage of science generally interpreted. It, however,
was biased in the direction of covering literature of importance to industrial development. The abstract section of
Silliman's American Journal of Science, beginning in 1820,
also tried to cover science generally, albeit not comprehensively. The Bulletin universel during its brief existence from
1823 to 1831 tried with herculean effort to provide comprehensive and broad coverage of science as well as certain non-
science areas of knowledge. The abstract sections of the
Revue des questions scientifiques and the Revue générale des
sciences pures et appliquées were highly selective though covering science broadly. Such coverage as was attempted in
this area, as can be seen, was generally very selective and
often biased towards some specialty.

c. Mineralogy

        When in 1807 Carl von Leonhard founded his Taschen-
buch für die gesamte Mineralogie, continued by his Neues
Jahrbuch für Mineralogie, Geologie, und Paläontologie, he
initiated a pioneer abstract publication in this field, one which
has provided continuous coverage down to the present day.
In fact only the British Mineralogical Abstracts has provided
an alternative source for broad coverage of this field. Abstract coverage of the literature of crystallography, an aspect of mineralogy, was provided from 1877 by the abstract
section of the Zeitschrift für Kristallographie.

d. Geology

        The geological literature was first covered by the
Bulletin des sciences naturelles et de géologie, section two
of the Bulletin universel, from 1823 through 1831, and by
the Neues Jahrbuch für Mineralogie, Geologie, und Paläontologie from 1830. It was not until 1874 with the appearance
of the annual Geological Record that an English language abstract publication appeared in this field, but even this was
short-lived. In 1901 the Geologisches Zentralblatt began its
coverage of the literature, followed in 1908 by the abstract
section of Economic Geology and in 1920 by the Revue de
géologie et des sciences connexes. Coverage of the literature of geology, like that of so many other of the pure sciences before the outbreak of World War I, seems to have
been principally provided by the German abstract services.

e.   Physics

With the exception of the <u>Bulletin des sciences mathé</u>-
<u>matiques, astronomiques, physiques, et chimiques</u> (section
one of the <u>Bulletin universel</u>) which appeared from 1823
through 1831, the earliest coverage of the literature of physics occurred with the publication, beginning in 1845, of the
<u>Fortschritte der Physik</u>, published under the aegis of the
Deutsche Physikalische Gesellschaft.   The <u>Fortschritte</u> was
followed in 1872 by the abstract section of the <u>Journal de</u>
<u>physique et le radium</u>; in 1877 by Poggendorff's <u>Annalen der</u>
<u>Physik Beiblätter</u>; in 1898 by <u>Science abstracts</u>; and in 1920
by the result of the merger of the <u>Fortschritte der Physik</u>,
the <u>Annalen der Physik Beiblätter</u>, and the <u>Halbmonatliches</u>
<u>Literaturverzeichnis</u>, the <u>Physikalische Berichte</u>.

The number of abstract journals covering the literature of physics is few, but their coverage seems, as in the
case of chemistry, to have been comprehensive.   Also like
chemistry, the coverage in the field of physics was provided
by the principal society in the field in each major country:
the <u>Journal de physique et le radium</u> (France); <u>Physikalische</u>
<u>Berichte</u> (Germany); and <u>Science Abstracts</u> (England).   Phy-
sics in the United States seems not to have yet reached the
degree of organization it had in Europe (the American Institute of Physics being founded in 1931) and there was no society sponsored abstract publication in the field here in this
period.

f.   Botany

The field of botany was first covered by an abstract
publication with the appearance in 1854 of the <u>Bulletin</u> of the
Société Botanique de France which carried an extensive section of abstracts, followed in 1863 by the "Repertorium" section of <u>Hedwigia</u>.   In 1873 the distinguished German botanist
Leopold Just began his monumental <u>Botanischer Jahresbericht</u>,
followed in 1880 by <u>Botanisches Zentralblatt</u>.   The latter two
publications comprised the major abstracting services in the
field down to recent times.   English language abstracting in
the field of botany began in 1918 with the publication of <u>Bo</u>-
<u>tanical Abstracts</u>, produced by the collaboration of a number
of subject specialists in the United States.

With botany, we again have a discipline with comparatively few abstract publications but extensive and comprehensive coverage.   German domination down to the outbreak of

World War I is again apparent. Sponsorship of abstract publications in the field was about evenly divided between personal and society.

g. Mathematics

    With the exception of section one of the Bulletin uni-
versel the first coverage of the literature of mathematics by
an abstract publication seems to have been the Jahrbuch über
die Fortschritte der Mathematik which began in 1868 under
the editorship of Carl Müller.   The French Ministry of Public
Instruction began its Bulletin des sciences mathématiques in
1870 which was followed in 1893 by the Revue semestrielle
des publications mathématiques, published by the Société
Mathématique d'Amsterdam.

    In the field of mathematics there were few abstract
publications which appeared in the period studied.   The Jahrbuch seems to have provided the most extensive coverage of
the literature, being international in scope.   Personal, governmental, and society sponsorship are represented by these
three titles.

h. Life Sciences

    Abstract coverage of the literature of the life sciences
resembles that of medicine more closely than it does that of
the pure sciences.   It is characterized by a wide dispersion
of effort and little coordination or centralized control.   Few
were truly comprehensive in their coverage, while much
highly specialized coverage, especially in the form of sections of abstracts in primary journals, was typical.

    The abstract section of the Journal of the Royal Mi-
croscopical Society beginning in 1878 was one of the earliest
in this area.   It was followed by the Zentralblatt für Bakteriologie in 1887; the Année biologique in 1895; the Bulletin of
the Pasteur Institut in 1903; and Abstracts of Bacteriology in
1917, to mention only a few of the titles.   Referring again
to Table 11 it can be seen that personal sponsorship was the
most common type in this field.

i. Zoology

    The abstract section of the Monitore zoologico Italiano,
published from 1890 (from 1900 under the auspices of the
Unione Zoologica Italiana), seems to have been the earliest

abstract journal in the field of zoology. This was followed
in 1894 by the appearance of the Zoologisches Zentralblatt
and its successor Zentralblatt für Zoologie. Essentially only
these two covered the field broadly, though after the turn of
the twentieth century a number of specialized abstract journals, like the Review of Applied Entomology, appeared.

j. Astronomy

Again with the possible exception of section one of the
Bulletin universel, astronomy was first covered by the Astronomischer Jahresbericht beginning in 1899 under the auspices of the Astronomische Gesellschaft. This was followed
in 1920 by the abstract section of the Revue générale des
travaux astronomiques published by the Observatoire de Paris
for the International Astronomical Union.

Medicine

The chronological pattern of subject development of
abstract journals in the field of medicine is roughly as follows: general medicine; pharmacology and therapeutics;
diseases; surgery and ophthalmology; public health; veterinary
medicine; gynecology and obstetrics; physiology; and hygiene.
Much dispersion of coverage among a variety of sponsors is
characteristic in this field with little coordination of control;
rather, highly specialized abstracting, usually as sections of
primary journals, seems to be the rule. For this reason
only a selected number of titles will be enumerated below.

a. General Medicine

The earliest abstract journal identified in this study
as covering the field of medicine generally is the abstract
section of Froriep's Notizen aus dem Gebiete der Natur-
und Heilkunde which appeared from 1821 through 1849. The
Notizen was followed in 1823 by the Bulletin des sciences
médicales (section three of the Bulletin universel) and in
1828 by Unger and Klose's Summarium des Neuesten aus der
gesamten Medicin, and in 1834 by Schmidt's Jahrbücher der
in- und ausländischen Medicin.

Journals covering the field of medicine generally
quickly proliferated after 1850 and many of these journals
contained sections of abstracts from the medical periodical
literature. Notable examples are Dunglison's American Medical Intelligencer, Medical News, the British Medical Journal,

the New York Medical Journal, and Medical Science Abstracts and Reviews. In addition, the tradition of extensive cover-to-cover abstracting in general medicine, begun by men like Unger and Klose, was continued by such publications as Braithwaite's Retrospect of Medicine (published in simultaneous English and American editions); the Half-Yearly Abstract of the Medical Sciences; the Zentralblatt für die medizinischen Wissenschaften; the Revue des sciences médicales; the Monthly Abstract of Medical Science; Epitome (an American supplement to Briathwaite's Retrospect) the Epitome of Current Medical Literature; and International Medical Digest.

By 1920 the field had essentially narrowed down to a handful of titles covering medicine generally. In Germany only five abstract publications remained in existence: Schmidt's Jahrbücher; the Münchener medizinische Wochenschrift; and the Zentralblatt für innere Medizin (all under personal sponsorship); and the Fortschritte der Medizin and Kongresszentralblatt für die gesamte innere Medizin (both under society sponsorship). Only the latter two were cover-to-cover abstract journals. In England only two abstract publications remained: the Medical Science Abstracts and Reviews and the Epitome of Current Medical Literature, the latter being a cover-to-cover abstract publication. Sponsorship in England was divided between the British Medical Association and the Medical Research Council.

The United States was represented by five titles, one having begun in 1919 and two more in 1920, indicating a late entry into the field: the New York Medical Journal; the Journal of the American Medical Association; Hahnemannian Monthly; International Medical and Surgical Survey; and International Medical Digest, the last two being cover-to-cover abstract journals. Society sponsorship accounted for the abstracts in the Journal of American Medical Association, Hahnemannian Monthly, and the International Medical and Surgical Survey.

The Netherlands is represented by the abstract section of the Nederlandsch Tijdschrift voor Geneeskunde (sponsored by the Nederlandsche Maatschappij tot Bevordering der Geneeskunst). France is not represented at all.

While abstract coverage within subfields of the pure sciences came to be achieved by means of a few comprehensive services, generally on a national and subject basis, coverage in medicine evolved differently. In medicine

abstract coverage became increasingly specialized and fragmented, with few comprehensive and many short-lived selective publications providing often duplicate coverage. Primarily these services were of German and English origins, the
United States not entering the area of medical abstract coverage until after World War I. Major medical societies (with
the notable exception of the British Medical Association)
seemed not to have been as concerned as the societies in the
pure sciences with the provision of bibliographic control of
the medical periodical literature.

b.   Pharmacology and Therapeutics

     The literature of pharmacology and therapeutics was
first abstracted by Fechner's Pharmaceutisches Centralblatt
in 1830. With 1850, though, this publication expanded its
coverage to pure chemistry in general. In 1843 the Archiv
der Pharmazie, which had begun in 1822, began to carry a
section of abstracts, followed in 1845 by a similar section in
the Journal de pharmacie et de chimie. The American Journal of Pharmacy followed suit in 1856 by beginning to include
in its monthly issues a section of abstracts from the journal
literature. With 1864 the British Pharmaceutical Conference
began issuing annually with the transactions of its conference
a collection, international in scope, of abstracts of the literature of pharmacy. From 1899 the Bulletin des sciences
pharmacologiques included an important set of abstracts of
the literature of pharmacy.

     By 1920 only a handful of titles covered the literature.
In Germany, the Zeitschrift für physikalische und diätätische
Therapie; in France, the Journal de pharmacie et de chimie
and the Bulletin des sciences pharmacologiques; in England,
the Yearbook of Pharmacy; and in the United States, the
American Journal of Pharmacy. Only the Yearbook provided
cover-to-cover abstracts, and then only annually. This title
also represents the only society sponsorship in the field.
Again we have few titles, scattered, uncoordinated, and usually highly selective coverage, with little concern manifested
by professional organizations in the field.

c.   Diseases

     Abstract control of the literature of diseases and their
treatment is well represented throughout this period, having
proliferated greatly after the mid-nineteenth century. Probably the earliest example in this field is the Annales médico-

psychologiques begun in 1843.   The Annales was followed by
a long succession of titles, notable examples being the Jahrbuch für Kinderheilkunde; Dental Cosmos; Annales de dermatologie et de syphilographie; Journal of Nervous and Mental
Disease; Monatsschrift für Ohrenheilkunde; Zentralblatt für
Nervenheilkunde; Archives of Pediatrics; Journal of Laryngology; Excerpta Medica; Review of Neurology and Psychiatry;
and Abstracts of Tuberculosis.

   Most of the abstracting in the area of disease preven-
tion and control was in the nature of abstract sections, generally highly selective, of specialized journals.   There was
little comprehensive abstracting except for that of Excerpta
Medica.   Also, there seems to have been little mortality in
this field, most of the titles surviving past 1920.   By this
date there were some fifteen titles in this field published in
Germany, five of them cover-to-cover, and three sponsored
by medical societies.   In France at the same time there were
some nine abstract publications, of which none were cover-
to-cover and only one was sponsored by a medical society.
Four abstract publications flourished in England at the end of
1920, two of which were sponsored by the Government.   In
the United States seven abstract publications were extant in
the field, three of them having started during or soon after
the War.   None was cover-to-cover and four of the seven
were sponsored by societies.   Italy was publishing two journals which contained sections of abstracts in the field, one
society sponsored.

d.   Surgery and Ophthalmology

   Probably the earliest abstract journal in the field of
surgery was Kleinert's Allgemeines Repertorium der gesamten deutschen medizinisch-chirurgischen Journalistik which
appeared from 1827 through 1847.   This was followed by the
Zentralblatt für Chirurgie and in 1913 by the International Abstract of Surgery, this latter published until the War as the
result of an international collaboration of journals in the
field.   Ophthalmology was represented by such publications
as the abstract section of Annales d'oculistique, by the Zentralblatt für praktische Augenheilkunde and the Zentralblatt
für die gesamte Ophthalmologie.

   There were few abstracting publications in this field,
and, with one or two exceptions, all were either French or
German.   There seems also to have been a rather low mortality rate in this field, even during the War.

By the end of 1920 there were some four German publications in the field, two of which were cover-to-cover, and
two of which were society sponsored. France accounted for
only two of the publications, none cover-to-cover and none
society sponsored, while the United States accounted for only
two, one of which was a cover-to-cover abstract journal.

e. Public Health

The earliest journal to provide abstract coverage of
the field of public health was the Annales d'hygiène publique
beginning in 1872; this was followed in 1879 by the Revue
d'hygiène and in 1891 by Hygienische Rundschau. In 1920
the United States Public Health Service began its Abstracts
from Recent Medical and Public Health Papers.

By the end of 1920 only three titles (one from Germany, two from France, and one from the United States;
and only one cover-to-cover; and one sponsored by a society)
covered the literature of public health.

f. Veterinary Medicine

The abstract section of the Journal de médicine
vétérinaire et de zootechnie provided the first abstract coverage of veterinary medicine, beginning in 1876. This was
followed in 1889 by the appearance of an abstract section in
the Journal of the American Veterinary Medical Association,
and in 1893 by the Deutsche tierärztliche Wochenschrift.

By 1920 Germany, Belgium, England, the United
States, Austria, and the Netherlands are each represented by
one abstract publication in this field, only one being cover-
to-cover and two being society sponsored.

g. Gynecology and Obstetrics

The Zentralblatt für Gynäkologie, which first appeared
in 1877, seems to have been the earliest abstract journal in
the field of gynecology and obstetrics. Other journals covering the literature of this field by means of abstracts were
Kinderarzt, the Journal of Obstetrics and Gynecology, the
Revue française de gynécologie, the American Journal of
Obstetrics and Gynecology, and Gynécologie et obstétrique.

All of these journals, current at the end of 1920,
covered the literature by means of sections of abstracts,

two were German, two French, one English and one American; only one was sponsored by a society.

h. Physiology

The literature of physiology began to be covered with the appearance in 1887 of the Zentralblatt für Physiologie, followed by such journals as the Journal de physiologie and the Zentralblatt für Herz- und Gefässkrankheiten, and the Bulletin of the Société Scientifique d'Hygiène.

Again by the end of 1920 coverage in this field was limited to the abstract sections of a small number of periodicals, three German and two French, only two of these being under society sponsorship.

i. Hygiene

The field of hygiene was first covered by the abstract section of Igiene moderna in 1908, followed by the Bulletin mensuel of the Office Internationale d'Hygiène Publique in 1909. At the end of 1920 these two were the only publications in the field, and provided only a section of abstracts of the literature.

Applied Sciences and Technology

As the nineteenth century progressed and science began to be applied to the needs of man, applied science and technology came to assume increasing importance. It was only natural that the literature of these fields grew commensurately as did the problems of its bibliographic control. The pattern of chronological appearance of abstract journals by subfields in this area is roughly as follows: inventions and discoveries; chemical technology; agriculture; engineering; and manufacturing.

a. Inventions and Discoveries

At the beginning of the nineteenth century there was quite naturally an intense interest in many quarters in learning of new technical developments. During the first half of the period under study here it was difficult for researchers to learn of new developments, particularly before the development of patent bulletins. As the Industrial Revolution began to spread outward from England to the continent and to America this difficulty became even greater. One of the efforts

to remedy this situation was the issuance of the aforemen-
tioned abstract bulletins by patent offices and the inclusion of
patent information on a more or less systematic basis in
many abstract publications.   Before this latter development,
though, there arose a breed of publication almost wholly pe-
culiar to the late eighteenth century and first half of the nineteenth century, viz. , publications monographic, quasi-serial,
and serial concerned with the new developments of interest
to technology and more especially to industrial development,
often presenting abstracts from the periodical literature.

One of the earliest examples of an abstract publication
devoted to the reporting of new technical developments was
the Retrospect of Philosophical, Mechanical, Chemical, and
Agricultural Discoveries, previously mentioned under "General Science," published in London from 1805 through 1813
and which included a good deal of material of interest to industrial technology.   The Bulletin des sciences technologiques,
section five of the Bulletin universel, published between 1823
and 1831, is another early example of such a publication.
Timbs' Arcana of Science and Art and its successor the
Year-Book of Facts in Science and Art are marginal examples
in this category, mainly because of their semi-popular nature.
The Mois scientifique et industriel published between 1899 and
1919 by the Institut Scientifique et Industriel proved something
of an anachronism as well as a casualty of the War.   By the
end of 1920 no examples of abstract coverage in this category
remained, their function having been largely replaced by the
coverage of the regular abstract journals and the patent bulletins which emerged in the last half of the nineteenth century.

b.   Chemical Technology

Unlike the field of inventions and discoveries, which
as a separate category for abstract journal publication was
essentially replaced, abstracting in the field of chemical
technology grew rapidly following the appearance of Elsner's
Chemisch-technische Mitteilungen, published between 1849
and 1887 and constituting a pioneer work in the field.   In
1858 the Société Chimique de Paris began its Répertoire de
chimie appliquée, covering the literature of chemical technology broadly.   This was followed in 1862 by Jacobsen's
Chemisch-technisches Repertorium.   In 1882 the Society of
Chemical Industry in England began to publish its Journal
which included from the first an extensive and comprehensive
section of abstracts.   This was followed by such journals as

the Zeitschrift für angewandte Chemie and Chimie et industrie. From this point onward (1918) other abstract journals
began to appear in the various specialized areas of chemical
technology, such as the Transactions of the Ceramic Society,
the Journal of the Society of Glass Technology, Ceramic Abstracts, the Revue de métallurgie, and the Journal of the
Institute of Metals.

By the end of the period under review all the titles in
this category, some eighteen, with the exception of the
Chemisch-technische Mitteilungen and the Chemisch-technisches
Repertorium, were flourishing. Germany was responsible for
three of them, two cover-to-cover, and one society sponsored;
France for three, one cover-to-cover and all three society
sponsored; England for five, none cover-to-cover and four
produced under society sponsorship; the United States had only
two abstract publications in this category, one cover-to-cover,
and both sponsored by societies.

We see in this area, then, low mortality, and a high
degree of society sponsorship, with steady growth of the number of titles.

c. Agriculture

With the exception of the Bulletin des sciences agricoles, section four of the Bulletin universel, the earliest abstract publication in the field of agriculture seems to have
been the Journal of the Société Nationale d'Horticulture which
began to carry a section of abstracts in 1855. In 1872 appeared Biedermann's Zentralblatt für Agrikulturchemie.
From 1889 to 1946 the United States Department of Agriculture published abstracts of the publications of its experiment
stations and other agricultural literature in its Experiment
Station Record; and from 1910 the International Institute of
Agriculture in Rome published abstracts in its International
Review of the Science and Practice of Agriculture.

By the end of 1920 the periodical literature of agriculture was covered by four cover-to-cover abstract journals,
three of which were German. The bulk of the coverage of
the literature of agriculture was, in fact German, eight publications in all. France and England had no representation
in this field, while the United States had three titles, one
sponsored by the Government, the rest personally sponsored.
Italy and Belgium each had one title.

d. Engineering

    With the exception of the Bulletin des Neuesten und
Wissenwürdigsten aus den Naturwissenschaften, published
briefly from 1809 to 1813, the earliest abstract coverage in
the field of engineering seems to have been the Abstracts of
Papers of the Institution of Civil Engineers, published from
1875. With 1884 began the publication of Engineering Index,
the first publication devoted to engineering in the broadest
sense. Other abstract publications of note in the field of
engineering which followed are the Repertorium der technischen Journal-Literatur and its successor the Fortschritte der
Technik; the Monthly Bulletin of the International Institute of
Refrigeration and the abstract section of the Revue universelle
des mines.

    By the end of the period under study there were three
English publications covering the literature of engineering,
one American, one German, and one Belgian. Four of the
seven were cover-to-cover publications (the publications covering engineering generally were) and all but two (one government sponsored, one personal) were the result of society
sponsorship.

e. Manufacturing

    Manufacturing in this period is represented by only
two entries: the Journal of the Society of Leather Trades'
Chemists and the Journal of the Textile Institute, both British, and both sponsored by societies. In addition each constituted an extensive section of abstracts in a primary journal.

Social Sciences

    Chronological appearance of abstract journals in the
social sciences according to subfields is as follows: history,
geography, sociology, psychology, commerce, trade, and
communications.

a. History

    With the exception of the Bulletin des sciences his-
toriques, section seven of the Bulletin universel, which appeared from 1823 through 1831, the earliest abstract publication in the field of history was the extensive abstract section
of the Revue historique (still a major abstract publication in

the field), published from 1876. Throughout the remainder
of the period under review this is the only abstract publication covering the periodical literature of history, though specialized ones like the abstract section of Rivista storica
Italiana and the American Journal of Archaeology appeared.

By the end of the period under review there were
some five journals with abstract sections covering the field
of history or some special area of it, one each from France,
Italy, England, Germany, and the United States, two were
the result of personal sponsorship, two of society sponsorship,
and one sponsored by an educational institution.

b.   Geography

Again with the exception of the Bulletin des sciences
géographiques, section six of the Bulletin universel, the
earliest abstract publication to cover the literature of geography was the abstract section of Petermanns Mitteilungen,
beginning in 1885.   This was an extensive section of abstracts
also issued separately from 1886 through 1909 as Geographischer Literaturbericht.   The only other major publication
covering the literature of the field during this period was the
annual Bibliographie géologique, published from 1891, from
1915 by the Association de Géographes Français.

By the end of 1920 these above-mentioned publications
were the only abstract organs in the field, both cover-to-
cover, both society sponsored, and one French and one German.

c.   Economics

Economics is represented only by the abstract sections of the Economic Journal, from 1891, and the American
Economic Review, from 1911.   Both were sponsored by societies, one being English the other American.

d.   Sociology

Sociology generally is represented only by the abstract
sections of the Rivista internazionale di scienze sociali, from
1895, and the American Journal of Sociology, the former society sponsored.   The Année sociologique had contained abstracts from its inception in 1896 but ceased carrying them
following 1912.   This practice was, however, resumed in
1923.

e.   Psychology

The periodical literature of psychology is first represented by abstract coverage by the abstract section of the
Psychological Review from 1894 through 1903.   With 1904 this
coverage was transferred to the "Psychological Literature"
section of Psychological Bulletin, where it continued under
various names through 1926, following which Psychological
Abstracts superseded it.   French coverage was provided from
1897 by the abstract section of Année psychologique.   Coverage of special aspects was provided by the abstract section
of the Journal of Abnormal Psychology from 1906 through
1914, the Journal of Applied Psychology for 1917 only, and
Mental Hygiene from 1917.

By the end of 1920 there were, then, only two publications abstracting the literature of psychology generally, both
sections of journals, one French, one American, the former
sponsored by an educational institution, the latter personally
sponsored.

f.   Commerce, Trade, and Communication

The only entries in this category in the period covered
were the abstract sections of the Bulletin of the Imperial Institute, published from 1911, and the Annales des postes,
télégraphes, et téléphones, from 1910.

Humanities

The pattern of chronological appearance of abstract
journals in the humanities is as follows: philosophy, religion, languages, and photography.

a.   Philosophy

Beginning in 1876 the journal Mind carried a section
of abstracts covering the periodical literature of philosophy
generally, followed in 1904 by the abstract section of the
Journal of Philosophy, and in 1907 by the abstract section of
the Revue des sciences philosophiques; one British, one
American, and all personally sponsored.

b.   Religion

While no abstract publication appeared in this period
to cover the literature generally, the Revue de l'histoire des

religions carried from 1880 through 1901 an extensive section
of abstracts in the field of religion, and abstract sections appeared in several specialized journals such as Moslem World,
Analecta Bollandiana, and the Archiv für Reformations-Geschichte.

c.   Languages

        As with religion there seems to have been no abstract
publication covering the field of languages as a whole; rather
there existed a number of abstract sections of specialized
publications, such as those of the Berliner philologische Wochenschrift, which carried a section from 1881 concerned
with the Germanic languages, Rocznik slawistyczny from 1908
and concerned with Slavic philology, and the Bulletin of the
Ecole Française d'Extrême-Orient from 1901 through 1916.

        Scattered examples of abstracting in the field of the
humanities occurred during the period studied here, such as
the extensive abstract section of the Numismatic Chronicle
which appeared in that journal from 1861 through 1896, and
in the field of photography in the Monthly Abstract Bulletin
of the Eastman Kodak Company Research Laboratory which
began publication in 1915.   This publication might equally
well be considered in the area of the applied sciences and
technology.

Geographic Diffusion

        Table 13 and Fig. 8 display the geographic diffusion
of active abstract journals, showing the country of origin
versus decades.   The data indicate that the abstract journal
had its beginnings in German, France, and England.   In
terms of numbers Germany soon took the lead in the production of abstract journals, a lead which it did not relinquish
in the period covered.   Following Germany are the United
States, which nearly doubled its output in the 1910's, France,
and England.

        As in the treatment of growth above, the effects of
World War I on the geographic diffusion of abstract journals
are masked by cumulating the statistics for the entire decade.
For this reason a breakdown is given in Table 14 and Fig. 9
by country of origin and year for the period 1910-1920.   Examination shows that German output decreased from seventy-
three active titles in 1910 to sixty-six in 1920; France

TABLE 13

ACTIVE ABSTRACT JOURNALS BY COUNTRY AND DECADE, 1790–1920

	1790–99	1800–09	1810–19	1820–29	1830–39	1840–49	1850–59	1860–69	1870–79	1880–89	1890–99	1900–09	1910–20	End '20
Germany	3	3	2	4	6	9	8	13	22	41	55	77	91	67
France	3	1	1	8	8	2	7	10	17	20	32	40	47	43
U.S.	–	–	–	1	2	4	4	6	8	16	20	26	50	44
England	3	3	3	2	2	2	3	5	10	14	17	22	35	32
Italy	–	–	–	–	–	–	–	–	–	–	4	7	10	9
Belgium	–	–	–	–	–	–	–	–	1	1	3	4	6	6
Netherlands	–	–	–	–	–	–	–	–	–	–	3	4	3	3
Austria	–	–	–	–	–	–	–	–	–	1	1	1	2	1
Switzerland	–	–	–	–	–	–	–	–	–	–	–	1	1	1
Spain	–	–	–	–	–	–	–	–	–	–	–	–	1	1
Brazil	–	–	–	–	–	–	–	–	–	1	1	1	1	1
Poland	–	–	–	–	–	–	–	–	–	–	–	1	1	1
Fr. Indo-China	–	–	–	–	–	–	–	–	–	–	–	–	1	–
TOTAL	9	7	6	15	18	17	22	34	58	94	136	185	249	209

Number of journals

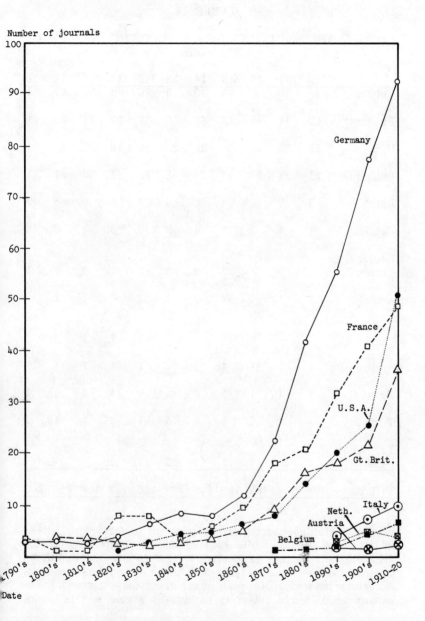

Date

Fig. 8. Geographic Diffusion of Abstract Journals, 1790-1920
(Active Titles)

TABLE 14

ACTIVE ABSTRACT JOURNALS BY COUNTRY AND YEAR, 1910-1920

	'10	'11	'12	'13	'14	'15	'16	'17	'18	'19	'20
Germany	73	75	77	79	80	75	70	69	59	67	66
France	42	44	45	42	42	35	37	37	39	40	44
U.S.	23	25	26	28	29	29	29	36	37	32	44
England	21	23	25	27	28	28	28	28	29	31	32
Italy	7	7	8	8	8	8	9	9	9	5	9
Belgium	4	4	3	3	4	3	3	3	3	6	6
Netherlands	3	3	3	3	3	3	3	3	3	3	3
Austria	1	1	1	2	3	3	3	2	1	1	1
Switzerland	-	-	-	-	1	-	-	1	1	1	1
Spain	1	1	1	1	1	1	1	1	1	1	1
Brazil	1	1	1	1	1	1	1	1	1	1	1
Poland	1	1	1	1	1	1	1	1	1	1	1
Fr. Indo-China	1	1	1	1	1	1	1	1	-	-	-
TOTAL	178	186	192	196	202	188	186	182	184	189	209

remained stable changing from forty-two to forty-four titles in the same period, while England and the United States increased their outputs respectively from twenty-one to thirty-two and twenty-three to forty-four titles. The emergence of American leadership is made clear from these figures. The remainder of world output is essentially stable in this period.

Table 15 shows active abstract journal output tabulated as country of origin and subject category. Examination of

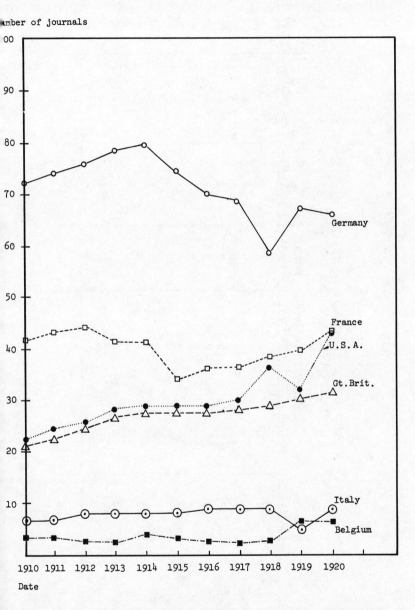

Fig. 9. Geographic Diffusion of Abstract Journals, 1910-1920
(Active Titles)

TABLE 15

CUMULATIVE ABSTRACT JOURNALS BY
SUBJECT CATEGORY AND COUNTRY

	Pure Sciences	Medicine	Applied Sciences & Technology	Social Sciences	Humanities	Generalities	TOTAL
Germany	34	51	19	4	2	–	110
France	16	25	10	10	2	3	66
U.S.	11	27	7	10	3	1	59
England	13	13	12	3	2	4	47
Italy	2	4	2	2	–	–	10
Belgium	2	1	2	–	1	–	6
Netherlands	1	2	–	1	–	–	4
Austria	–	2	–	–	–	–	2
Switzerland	2	–	–	–	–	–	2
Spain	1	–	–	–	–	–	1
Brazil	–	1	–	–	1	–	1
Poland	–	–	–	–	1	–	1
Fr. Indo-China	–	–	–	–	1	–	1
TOTAL	82	126	52	30	12	8	310

Table 15 shows German predominance in medicine and the
pure sciences followed by applied sciences and technology.
France has a similar pattern but with somewhat more emphasis than Germany in the social sciences. The United
States is represented by an emphasis on medicine, followed
by the pure sciences, then the social sciences, the latter re-
ceiving more emphasis than the applied sciences and technology. English output is about evenly divided among the pure
sciences, medicine, and applied sciences and technology, with
some representation in the social sciences, humanities, and
generalities.

It may logically occur to the reader to wonder about
the failure of this study to identify any Russian or Soviet abstract journals. None seems to have been published in the
period covered. This statement is based on the following
evidence: 1) No Russian titles were identified in the initial
culling of a wide range of sources for the establishment of
the "candidate file"; 2) Review guides to the Russian bibliographic literature, such as John Dorosh's Guide to Soviet
Bibliographies, turned up none before 1921; and 3) Karol
Maichel, Slavic Librarian at Columbia University, writing
about Russian abstract journals states:

> The Abstracting journal proper, of the kind familiar
> to us today, began in Russia in 1928, with the pub-
> lication of Indeks nauchnoi literatury (Register of
> Scientific Literature). This journal was intended to
> cover all scientific literature but it was discontinued
> the same year after the publication of a few issues,
> to be replaced by a series of individual abstract
> journals. Each of these was devoted to a scientific
> specialty, and some were devoted to the abstracting
> of foreign scientific literature. [9]

With the exception of several anomalies the overall
picture in each case in terms of numbers of titles at least,
is one of emphasis on medicine, followed by pure sciences
and applied science and technology, with the social sciences,
humanities, and generalities being the balance.

Language Diffusion

Tables 16 and 17 and Fig. 10 and 11 show active abstract journal development as a function of language of publication, with the latter table and figure showing the period
1910 through 1920 in detail.

TABLE 16

ACTIVE ABSTRACT JOURNALS BY LANGUAGE AND DECADE, 1790-1920

	1790-99	1800-09	1810-19	1820-29	1830-39	1840-49	1850-59	1860-69	1870-79	1880-89	1890-99	1900-09	1910-20	End '20
German	3	3	2	4	6	9	8	13	22	42	56	78	93	68
French	3	1	1	8	8	2	7	10	18	22	38	49	56	52
English	3	3	3	3	4	6	7	11	18	30	37	48	87	77
Italian	-	-	-	-	-	-	-	-	-	-	3	6	8	7
Netherlandish	-	-	-	-	-	-	-	-	-	-	2	3	2	2
Polish	-	-	-	-	-	-	-	-	-	-	-	1	1	1
Spanish	-	-	-	-	-	-	-	-	-	-	-	-	1	1
Other[a]	-	-	-	-	-	-	-	-	-	-	-	-	1	1
TOTAL	9	7	6	15	18	17	22	34	58	94	136	185	249	209

[a]English and French.

TABLE 17

ACTIVE ABSTRACT JOURNALS BY LANGUAGE AND YEAR, 1910–20

	1910	1911	1912	1913	1914	1915	1916	1917	1918	1919	1920
German	76	75	78	79	83	75	71	72	61	62	69
French	48	51	52	51	51	44	44	45	45	46	54
English	45	50	52	56	58	59	60	64	66	70	75
Italian	6	6	6	6	6	6	7	7	7	7	7
Netherlandish	1	2	2	2	2	2	2	2	2	2	2
Polish	1	1	1	1	1	1	1	1	1	1	1
Spanish	-	-	1	1	1	1	1	1	1	1	1
Other[a]	-	-	-	-	-	-	-	-	1	-	-
TOTAL	177	185	192	196	202	188	186	192	184	189	209

[a]English and French.

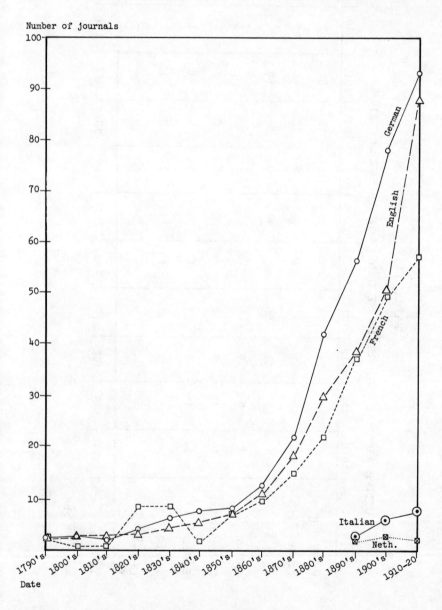

Fig. 10.   Language Diffusion of Abstract Journals, 1790-1920
(Active Titles)

Number of journals

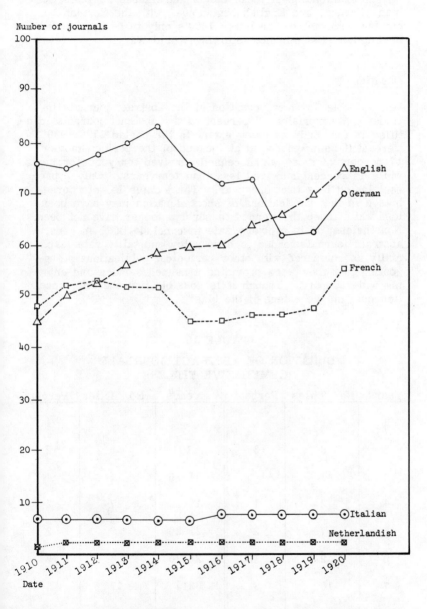

Fig. 11.   Language Diffusion of Abstract Journals, 1910-1920
(Active Titles)

Examination of these tables and figures suggests German, French, and English beginnings, with the German becoming dominant by the latter 1800's only to be superseded by English predominance following World War I.

Duration

Table 18 shows duration of the abstract journals in years. A surprising 70 percent of the abstract journals identified in the study as being extant in the period 1790-1920 were still being published at the end of the period; another 17 percent of those which ceased survived ten years or more, while 14 percent survived less than ten years. Only 2 percent lasted less than one year. The sample is, of course, biased in that publications of short duration may have been lost while those that tended to survive longer have not been. Nonetheless, it is probably safe to conclude that, in general, abstract journals tended to have a low mortality rate (especially as compared with other periodical publications), suggesting that they were providing a needed service and enjoying wide support. Though it is possible that the difference lies only on the extent of the bias.

TABLE 18

DURATION OF ABSTRACT JOURNALS
(CUMULATIVE TITLES)

Years	No. Titles	Percent	Years	No. Titles	Percent
1	6	2	9	3	1
2	8	3	10	6	2
3	1	-	11-15	11	4
4	2	1	16-20	7	2
5	7	2	21-25	7	2
6	2	1	26-30	5	2
7	10	3	31+	17	5
8	4	1	Current at end 1920	214	70

TABLE 19

COMPARISON OF DURATION OF ABSTRACT JOURNALS WITH SPONSORSHIP
(CUMULATIVE TITLES)

	1 yr or less	2 yrs	3 yrs	4 yrs	5 yrs	6 yrs	7 yrs	8 yrs	9 yrs	10 yrs	11-15 yrs	16-20 yrs	21-25 yrs	26-30 yrs	31+ yrs	Current at end of '20	% ceased
Personal	3	4	1	1	5	1	2	3	3	5	8	6	6	4	13	96	40
Society	2	3	-	1	2	1	8	1	-	-	2	-	-	1	4	90	22
Industrial	-	-	-	-	-	-	-	1	-	-	-	-	-	-	-	3	-
Governmental	-	-	-	-	-	-	-	-	-	1	-	-	-	-	-	11	8
Commercial	-	-	-	-	-	-	-	-	-	-	-	-	-	-	-	2	-
Other	1	1	-	-	-	-	-	-	-	-	1	1	-	-	-	12	25

TABLE 20

COMPARISON OF DURATION OF ABSTRACT JOURNALS WITH SUBJECT CATEGORIES

	1 yr or less	2 yrs	3 yrs	4 yrs	5 yrs	6 yrs	7 yrs	8 yrs	9 yrs	10 yrs	11-15 yrs	16-20 yrs	21-25 yrs	26-30 yrs	31+ yrs	Current at end of '20	% ceased
Pure Sci.	2	3	-	-	3	2	3	3	-	3	3	3	3	2	2	50	39
Medicine	1	2	1	-	2	-	1	-	3	1	4	3	3	3	7	95	25
Appl. S. & T.	1	1	-	2	1	-	2	-	-	2	1	1	-	-	3	38	27
Social Sci.	2	2	-	-	1	-	4	1	-	-	1	-	-	-	-	19	37
Humanities	-	-	-	-	-	-	-	-	-	-	1	-	1	-	1	9	25
Generalities	-	-	-	-	-	-	-	-	-	-	1	-	-	-	4	3	63

Table 19 shows duration of abstract journals as a function of type of sponsorship. It can be seen that the highest mortality rate (40 percent) is for those abstract journals under personal sponsorship followed by those under other types of sponsorship (25 percent) (primarily sponsorship by educational institutions and private research institutes), and society sponsorship (22 percent). None of the three industrially sponsored abstract journals in this period ceased and the mortality rate for governmentally sponsored abstract journals is similarly low (8 percent).

Table 20 shows duration of the abstract journals as a function of subject category. The mortality rate is highest in the generalities (63 percent), as might be expected as these early abstract journals gave way to the specialized ones, followed by the pure sciences (39 percent) and the social sciences (37 percent). Mortality is lowest for medicine (25 percent) and the humanities (25 percent).

Type of Publication

Table 21 shows the number of abstract journals as a function of type of publication. Type of publication is about

TABLE 21

CUMULATIVE ABSTRACT JOURNALS BY TYPE AND SUBJECT

	Pure Sci.	Med.	Appl. Sci. & Tech.	Soc. Sci.	Human- ities	Gen.	Total
Cover-to- cover	38	33	24	5	1	2	103
Section[a]	39	91	22	24	10	6	192
Section[b]	3	2	4	1	1	-	11
Other	2	-	2	-	-	-	4
TOTAL	82	126	52	30	12	8	310

[a]continuously paged
[b]separately paged

evenly divided in the pure sciences and in the applied sciences
and technology between cover-to-cover and continuously paged
sections; in other subject areas the continuously paged section predominates. Abstract sections separately paged constitute only a small portion of the total as do a miscellaneous
category of other formats. All the journals studied were in
journal format with the exception of the Bulletin of Abstracts
of the American Gas Association which was issued as an insertion. The abstracts of the Concilium Bibliographicum
were issued on cards as well as in journal format, one edition of which was printed on one side of the page only.

Table 22 shows changes in type of publication. As
might be expected the largest change is from a section of a

TABLE 22

CHANGE OF TYPE OR ABSTRACT JOURNAL

Change	Number
Cover-to-cover (from sect. cont. pgd.)	10
Cover-to-cover (from sect. sep. pgd.)	-
Other[a]	5

[a]Section with continuous pagination to separate
pagination, back to continuous (2); section with
continuous pagination to separate pagination (1);
journal issued in two parts, part one continuously paged, part two cover-to-cover (1); section from continuous to separate pagination (1).

primary publication, and continuously paged, to independent
publication as a cover-to-cover abstract journal.

Relationship to Predecessor and Successor Titles

Thirty-two of the abstract journals included in this
study were related to predecessor titles while twenty-seven
were related to successors. These data are shown in Tables
23 and 24.

TABLE 23

RELATIONSHIP OF ABSTRACT JOURNALS
TO PREDECESSOR TITLES

Relationship	Number
Superseded predecessor	22
Absorbed predecessor	5
Formed by merger	5
Formed by division	–

TABLE 24

RELATIONSHIP OF ABSTRACT JOURNALS
TO SUCCESSOR TITLES

Relationship	Number
Superseded by successor	15
Absorbed by successor	5
Merged with other title(s) to form successor	7
Divided into successor (and other titles)	–

These tables show supersession to be the predominant form of change (assumption of new numbering), though over-all bibliographic change on the part of abstract journal seems not significant (less than 10 percent having changed). (It should be pointed out that the numbers of supersessions in Tables 23 and 24 do not agree because in some instances the predecessor or successor may not have been an abstract journal.)

Other Bibliographic Changes

Other bibliographic changes of abstract journals are tabulated in Table 25. These can be seen to be a variety of changes, including title change; discontinuance; a section of abstracts in a primary journal ceasing, being transferred to another journal, or changing in nature so that it no longer includes abstracts.

TABLE 25

OTHER BIBLIOGRAPHIC CHANGES

	1790-99	1800-09	1810-19	1820-29	1830-39	1840-49	1850-59	1860-69	1870-79	1880-89	1890-99	1900-09	1910-20
Current	-	-	-	1	4	6	10	18	39	69	101	140	209
Changed Title	-	2	2	2	2	4	5	5	6	5	10	13	8
Discontinued	9	5	4	12	12	6	3	5	7	12	13	16	19
Sec. Stops	-	-	-	-	-	1	4	6	6	7	9	13	11
Sec. Transf.	-	-	-	-	-	-	-	-	-	-	2	2	-
Sec. ceases to carry abstracts	-	-	-	-	-	-	-	-	-	1	1	1	2
Total Act.	9	7	6	15	18	17	22	34	58	94	136	185	249

Arrangement

Table 26 shows a breakdown of the arrangement of the abstract journals in this study while Table 27 shows change of arrangement.

TABLE 26

ARRANGEMENT OF ABSTRACT JOURNALS

Arrangement	Number
Subject classified & numbered	52
Subject classified & unnumbered	142
Alphabetical subject & numbered	2
Alphabetical subject & unnumbered	8
Random & numbered	1
Random & unnumbered	62
Journal title	38
Other[a]	5

[a]Geographic (4); alphabetical by author (1);

The predominant form of arrangement by far is subject classified (194 of 310), unnumbered abstracts far outnumbering numbered ones, while random arrangement is significant being used in sixty-three of the journals. Journal title arrangement is also significant.

Change of arrangement, as might be expected, is primarily from random to subject classified with various other changes constituting the remainder.

TABLE 27

CHANGE OF ARRANGEMENT OF ABSTRACT JOURNALS

Change	Number
Random to subject classified	18
Random to journal title	1
Journal title to subject classified	6
Subject classified to alphabetical classified	2
Author to subject	1
Other	17

Indexes

Table 28 presents a breakdown of the types of indexes included in the abstract journals in this study and Table 29 presents data on the change in indexing undergone.

Author and subject indexes had become an established feature of abstract journals by 1920 as indicated in Table 28, though a significant number of abstract journals still had none or only author or subject indexes.

TABLE 28

INDEXES TO ABSTRACT JOURNALS

Index	Number
Author	23
Subject	13
Author & subject	192
None	72
Other[a]	10

[a]Tables des matiêres (6); journal title (1); plant name (1); cumulated and rearranged in Psych. Index (2).

TABLE 29

CHANGE OF INDEXING OF ABSTRACT JOURNALS

Change	Number
None to auth. & subj. index	5
None to author index	5
None to subject index	3
Table des Matières adds author index	2
Author index adds subject index	2
Subject adds author index	1
TOTAL	18

Supplements

A handful of abstract journals were issued as supplements to primary journals. These are shown in Table 30.

TABLE 30

ABSTRACT JOURNALS ISSUED AS SUPPLEMENTS

Abstract Journals	Number
Issued as supplements	14
Formerly issued as supplements	3

Frequency

The frequency of the abstract journals included in this study is tabulated in Table 31. In cases where the frequency varied the latest frequency was used. No attempt was made

TABLE 31

FREQUENCY OF ABSTRACT JOURNALS

Frequency	Number
Annual	18
Biennial	1
Bimonthly	29
Irregular[a]	27
Monthly	146
Quarterly	38
Semi-annual	4
Semi-monthly	20
Weekly	20
Bi-Weekly	7
TOTAL	310

[a]Generally 6-10 issues per year

to evaluate change in frequency, though a general trend was observed of increasing frequency with time.

The predominant frequency can be seen to be monthly, though the range is from weekly to biennially.

Purpose

As stated above, there seems to have been little editorial indication of the intentions of sponsors of abstract journals. In nearly every case editors did not agree with the founder of the Piscataqua Evangelical Magazine who observed, "It may justly be expected that a new periodical work should be introduced to the public by some account of its origin and design, and of the reasons and motives that have induced its publication."[10] What intentions there were stated could be summarized as an attempt to provide a convenient, current digest and index to the periodical literature to enable scholars to keep abreast of new developments. The reasons given for launching a new abstract publication usually centered around the unrelenting growth of the periodical literature and the inability of the subject specialist to keep up with his field. Several American abstract journals cited the need to provide bibliographic coverage of the domestic literature which they felt was neglected by the European abstract journals. The interruption of European abstract service, particularly the German, during the War seems to have provided added impetus for the launching of American services. Other comments alluded to the usefulness of the abstract as a surrogate for the original article, particularly so when the original was in a language unfamiliar to the reader.

The Abstracts

A word should be inserted here about the nature of the abstract themselves, though this study has not concerned itself primarily with that aspect of abstract journal development. Entry seems to have evolved from a mixture of author, author/title, and title form, with the latter form being especially common in the early part of the period, to entry by author and title becoming the common form in the latter part of the period. Citations have evolved from poor ones, incomplete and ambiguous, or even non-existent, to the beginnings of standardization with complete and well abbreviated citations, though the practice still varied widely in 1920. The abstract itself changed over the period under review from a long, discursive format to a briefer, more informative one, though again there was a wide range of practice in 1920.

Geographic Scope

A study of the geographic coverage of abstract journals was not undertaken since this would have involved tedious analysis of lists of journals abstracted, if, indeed, such lists were even available (and in most cases they were not). A few general observations in this regard can, however, be made.

The early abstract journals encountered in this study were generally parochial in coverage and concerned with developing the state of the art in their respective subject fields within their own countries. Increasingly, however, there developed a desire to learn of foreign experiences as the realization grew that knowledge had no national boundaries. By mid-nineteenth century nearly all abstract journals were international in their coverage to a greater or lesser degree.

American journals through the greater part of the nineteenth century reflected their European counterparts,

presenting extracts, translations, bibliographical notices from
them, and giving little notice to American developments.
Likewise the European journals took little note of American
developments.   This lack of notice and bibliographical control of the growing American literature, as mentioned before,
was instrumental in giving rise to American abstract journals.

Notes

1. It should be borne in mind that the figures for the
    1820's and 1830's are distorted upward by the eight
    series of the Bulletin universel counted as eight
    separate entities in this study.
2. Some of the responsibility for this increased growth is
    undoubtedly due to the impetus given to abstracting
    activities on the international level from the Interna-
    tional Conference on International Scientific Organi-
    zation held in 1918 and from which the International
    Research Council (later the International Council of
    Scientific Unions (ICSU)) emerged.   The activities of
    ICSU in encouraging the spread of abstracting are
    well known.
3. Price, Little Science, Big Science, pp. 8-11.
4. This point of the hypothesis, originally broached in
    Price's Science Since Babylon, was subsequently par-
    tially cleared up in his Little Science, Big Science
    in which he explicitly states that his figures for
    scientific journal growth are for cumulative titles
    (p. 9).   He then (1963) estimated that about 30,000
    titles were being published.
5. Iwinski, Boleslas, "La Statistique internationale des
    périodiques (journeaux et revues)," Bulletin de
    l'Institut International de Bibliographie 15 (1910):
    p. 6, Table 1.
6. Though isolated examples persisted well into the last
    half of the nineteenth century, such as Just's Botan-
    ischer Jahresbericht.
7. On this point see especially Ornstein, pp. 198-209.
8. Appendix III contains a complete classified and chron-
    ological list of the abstract journals covered in this
    study.
9. Karol Maichel, "Soviet Scientific Abstracting Journals,"
    Special Libraries 50 (October 1959): 398.
10. Piscataqua Evangelical Magazine 1 (January/February
    1805): iii.

CHAPTER VI

SUMMARY AND CONCLUSIONS

Findings

The findings of this study with respect to the origins of the abstract journal show that, while learned journals included sections of abstracts from the earliest times and while independent journals comprised entirely of abstracts can be traced as far back as 1714, the abstract journal as we know it today, a specialized bibliographic tool designed to provide retrospective and current access to the contents of journals, did not begin to appear in a sustained manner until the 1820's and 1830's. These earlier efforts were largely polymathic, highly selective, rarely confined to the journal literature, and often short lived. Further, their contents are difficult to classify, often partaking equally of the nature of abstracts, extracts, and reviews. As such they should more properly be regarded in the nature of bibliographical precursors of the abstract journal than as early examples of it.

Regarding the reasons for the emergence of the abstract journal, this study found little primary evidence of the intentions of sponsors of abstract journals. Such evidence as was found, consisting usually of editorial statements of purpose, suggested that they were undertaken to provide a convenient, current digest and index to the journal literature to enable scholars to keep abreast of new developments. The reasons given for launching a new abstract journal generally centered upon the unrelenting growth of the journal literature and the inability of the subject specialist to keep up with his field.

The secondary literature was found generally to repeat this theme, referring to the emergence of the abstract journal as deriving from the need to provide for scholars effective bibliographic control of the ever-growing body of journal literature on both a current and a retrospective basis.

185

Some writers additionally saw the emergence of the abstract journal as a response to the need for a surrogate for the original materials thereby precluding the need, in many cases, for seeing the original. Still others viewed this emergence as a response to the need for access to foreign language materials, given the proliferation of scholarship and publication. On a broader plane, several writers and editors spoke of the development of the abstract journal as a device to assist in improving the quality of a field by delineating the current state of knowledge and, thereby, suggesting further areas for research.

Many American abstract journals of the nineteenth century cited the need to provide effective bibliographic coverage of the domestic literature which they felt was neglected by the European abstract journals; while a number of American abstract journals begun during and after World War I cited the interruption of European abstracting services (particularly the German), as impetus for launching American ones.

The findings of this study with respect to the nature of the overall bibliographic apparatus which evolved in the period under study to provide access to the journal literature support the controlling assumption that the abstract journal was but one element of a larger system, a system comprised in addition of the index journal and the review journal.

The abstract journal seems to have been the earliest of these devices to have emerged as an independent, specialized tool, doing so in the first decades of the nineteenth century. Its importance derived chiefly from its response to the need for both current awareness and retrospective coverage of the rapidly growing learned journal literature.

Soon after the middle of the nineteenth century the index journal emerged apparently in response to the need for access to the rapidly expanding general periodical literature and as a more efficiently produced alternative, principally in a number of highly specialized subject fields, to the abstract journal, already showing signs of being burdened by the growth and proliferation of the journal literature. By the beginning of the twentieth century, the last of the three elements to appear in the period covered by this study, the review journal, emerged as a specialized bibliographic tool in its own right, primarily in response to the need for a device to provide evaluation and synthesis of the vast population of journal articles which by then had become too large for the typical user.

This chronology demonstrates how the index journal and the review journal, which, like the abstract journal, can be traced to seventeenth and eighteenth century precursors, emerged in the nineteenth century in a new form and role, as current, serial bibliography to provide still further layers of control beyond the abstract journal in response to the new demands created by the rise of the general periodical literature and because of the inability of the abstract journal to meet the increasing requirements placed on it as the volume of learned publications grew unchecked.

Growth of the abstract journal throughout the period was, with the exception of some early anomalous behavior due to small sample size, quite vigorous, there being an overall average decennial percentage growth rate of 36.4 percent for cumulative titles, 38.9 percent for active titles (the number which were extant throughout a given decade). Further, the percentage of active titles increased steadily with time (though this trend was reversed temporarily during World War I).

A test of the validity of Price's hypothesis regarding the correlation between journal growth in the sciences and technology and the emergence and growth of abstract journals, with the recognition that his hypothesis covers a time period (1665 to the present) different from that covered by this study and that his data are based on cumulative journal growth while active journal growth is used here, yielded the following results.

The growth rate of abstract journals was found to be, as Price hypothesized, exponential, and growing at a rate of 2.6 percent per year (compared with Price's observation of 5 percent), with a doubling time observed of twenty-eight years (as compared with Price's observation of fifteen years). When plotted semi-logarithmically active scientific and technical journal growth (2.3 percent per year) essentially parallels that of abstract journal growth. (While the growth of both scientific and technical journals and abstract journals was found to be correlated, there was insufficient evidence to suggest a causal relationship between them.)

Price observed "emergence" around the year 1830 which was also observed in this study, i.e., at about this time occurred the beginnings of sustained growth of the modern abstract journal. However, the size of the "archive," i.e., the size of the population of journal titles at emergence was observed to be more nearly in the neighborhood of seven hundred active scientific and technical journal titles than the three hundred cumulative titles postulated by Price. The reasons for the discrepancy between the findings is not immediately clear.

Analysis of the 310 abstract journals surveyed led to the following findings concerning sponsorship, subject development, geographic origins, and various other developmental characteristics.

Five principal types of sponsorship were identified: personal enterprise, both lone and collaborative; the learned and professional society; the industrial research institute; governmental; and commercial enterprise. A small number of titles were sponsored by educational institutions and research institutes.

Historically, the pattern of development was from initial sponsorship by lone scholars, with the abstracts often constituting bibliographic sections of primary journals and typically written by subject specialists; then with the passing of time and the growth of the literature (and given the obvious vulnerability of such a system based on individual effort), increasingly the lone scholar was replaced by a collaboration of individuals in a subject field reflecting the growth of teamwork and cooperation in these areas. The motivating factor seems to have been one of pure bibliographic concern and concern with the development of one's field, the suggestion of personal gain, never appearing in the monetary sense, though the enhancement of professional status was undoubtedly a factor. As subject fields became more mature, more academically accepted, and more organized in the nineteenth century, professional and learned societies began to take over these previously individually-sponsored abstract publications, or to initiate their own. Still later in the century other forms of sponsorship emerged, such as governmental and industrial, but, numerically, these formed only a small part of the total. Commercial sponsorship was never statistically significant and personal sponsorship, principally of the collaborative variety, remained, in terms of numbers at least, the primary form throughout the period. The trend, though, was clearly toward sponsorship by professional and learned societies. Industrial sponsorship, also numerically small, was manifested interestingly only in the United States.

At the turn of the twentieth century a pattern appeared,

particularly in the sciences, of national responsibility for the
publication of abstract journals on a subject basis, usually by
the responsible national society in a given field.   As the volume of literature to be dealt with grew, and with an increasing recognition of the international nature of knowledge, the
wastefulness and inefficiency of such a system led to a considerable expenditure of effort to organize bibliographic undertakings, including abstract journals, internationally, reflected
in the federation of national societies and the establishment
of international bibliographic schemes designed to provide
universal bibliographic control.   This trend was manifested
in the appearance around the beginnings of this century of
abstract journals jointly sponsored on an international basis
by cooperating professional and learned societies, and, occasionally, abstract journals sponsored by international agencies.   World War I dealt this activity a severe setback.

As mentioned previously, change of sponsorship in the
period under study was primarily from personal to society
sponsorship, though only a surprisingly low 7 percent changed
sponsorship.   Personal and society sponsorship were both
strong in the pure sciences, while personal sponsorship was
the primary form in the field of medicine, where society
sponsorship, with one or two notable exceptions, was never
important.   Governmental and industrial sponsorship, as
might be expected, were important in the applied sciences
and technology.   Sponsorship in the social sciences and
humanities was so sparse, because of the few titles encountered, as to preclude any valid observations on the distribution of sponsorship in these areas.

Similarly, no observations concerning correlation between type of sponsorship and country of origin could be
made, with the exception of industrial sponsorship being confined to the United States and commercial sponsorship being
limited to the United States and England.

As might be expected, the pattern of subject development of abstract journals strongly reflects the pattern of the
development of scholarship in the period under study.
Broadly speaking, this pattern of the subject development,
or diffusion, of abstract journals is one of initial appearance
in the field of general learning (the polymathic journals), dying out with the passing of the polymaths and the polymathic
journals of the last decades of the eighteenth century, followed by almost simultaneous appearance in the pure sciences
and medicine, proliferating and becoming increasingly

specialized throughout the nineteenth century. From the middle of the nineteenth century onward abstract journals began to appear increasingly in the applied sciences and technology as these fields began to come into their own. Only toward the end of the century did they begin to appear in the social sciences, with a very few, near the end of the period under review, appearing in the humanities.

In terms of numbers, the overall predominance was surprisingly in the field of medicine, accounting for 126 of the 310 titles examined. Coverage in medicine, however, was greatly fragmented, being widely dispersed among many specialties, with little attempt at overall control or coordination of effort, and with many publications constituting only highly selective sections of primary journals. This lack of good abstract journal coverage in the field of medicine has been attributed to the nature of medical research in the period (where cooperation among researchers was not yet a custom).

The pure sciences were represented by some eighty-two titles. By the end of the period under study every major subfield of the pure sciences was represented by abstract coverage. Many areas were well covered by publications sponsored by the responsible professional or learned societies in those fields. It is here in the pure sciences that much of the national and international bibliographic efforts described above were expended. This generally thorough abstract coverage of the pure sciences is attributed to the competitive nature of the fields, their high degree of academic maturity, the quantitative nature of their data, and their well developed organizational structures.

The applied sciences and technology accounted for fifty-two titles, all fields, with the not surprising exceptions of the domestic arts, managerial sciences, and construction, being represented. Early activity in this area seems largely to have been pre-empted by the emergence of the patent abstract bulletin, though most abstract journals continued to cover the patent literature of their fields. Abstract journals in the applied sciences and technology were characterized by a high degree of society sponsorship and a low mortality.

In the period under review, abstract publications in the social sciences had appeared only sporadically, and in a few, highly specialized areas, such as psychology, economics, and history, and these often provided only selective coverage

of the literature, generally comprising abstract sections of
primary journals. The eight abstract journals encountered
in the study in the field of the humanities were generally
highly selective sections of abstracts in primary journals
(with the notable exception of the <u>Monthly Abstract Bulletin</u>
of the Eastman Kodak Company's Research Laboratory), a
major abstract publication. [1] Major areas of knowledge not
represented by abstract journal coverage in the period under
review are: law, librarianship, and literature.

Regarding geographic origins, the evidence adduced in
this study shows the initial appearance of the abstract journal
in Germany, France, and England, with the earliest sustained
efforts coming from Germany. The United States, France,
and England accounted for the bulk of the remainder of titles.
German emphasis was about equally divided among the pure
sciences, medicine, and the applied sciences and technology;
France placed somewhat more emphasis on the social sciences; England concentrated largely in the pure sciences and
medicine; while the emphasis in the United States was largely
on medicine, followed by the pure sciences and the applied
sciences and technology. No Russian abstract journals were
identified as being published in this period.

Language diffusion followed a similar pattern from
German to French to English, with English language abstract
publications superseding the German as English and American
abstract journals replaced the long-dominant German ones
during and after World War I.

Overall, longevity of the abstract journals was high,
with 70 percent of those identified and examined still extant
at the end of 1920. A surprising 87 percent lasted ten years
or more. The highest mortality rate was in the generalities;
lowest mortality being in medicine.

Three basic types of abstract journals were identified;
1) the cover-to-cover abstract journal, comprised entirely of
abstracts (though it was not uncommon for some of the German abstract journals to carry an occasional original article);
2) the continuously paged abstract section of a primary journal; and 3) the separately paged abstract section of a primary
journal. One journal was encountered which was issued in
insertion format and one issued also in journal format printed
on one side of the page only, the latter being also available
separately on cards. Publication type was about evenly divided
in the pure sciences and the applied sciences and technology

between cover-to-cover and continuously paged sections.   In
other subject areas the continuously paged section of abstracts
was the rule, while the separately paged section of abstracts
accounted for only a handful of titles.   Change of type of publication generally was from continuously paged section to
cover-to-cover, independent publication, though this change
occurred in only fifteen of the 310 titles.

Various types of bibliographic changes were encountered.   These were: title changes (generally of the supersession type), discontinuance, and changes in the status of
sections of abstracts (discontinuing the carrying of abstracts,
transferring abstract sections from one publication to another,
changing from separately paged to continuously paged sections,
etc.).

The most common form of arrangement, accounting
for over 60 percent, was broad systematic subject arrangement, underscoring the current awareness function of the abstract journal, with 142 of these numbering their abstracts.
Random arrangement persisted well into the twentieth century,
accounting for sixty-two titles.   A significant number arranged their abstracts by the titles of the journals from which
the abstracts were taken.   The overall trend was from random arrangement to increasingly systematic arrangement and
with the increasing inclusion of subject and author indexes,
included generally from the earliest but becoming the rule
by 1900.

The frequency of abstract journal issuance varied
widely from weekly to biennially, with monthly being the most
common.   The trend overall was toward increasing frequency
of publication.

The abstracts themselves became increasingly standard-
ized in entry, format, citation, and content, but practices
still varied widely at the end of 1920.

The geographical scope of abstract journals seems
generally to have been international although some journals
in the early nineteenth century restricted their coverage na-
tionally, or segregated foreign and domestic materials, perhaps because of the restricted distribution of foreign materials, the language limitations of users, or, as some suggested,
to foster the national development of their fields.   This practice seems largely to have disappeared after the middle of
the nineteenth century, except for some French publications

which retained a policy of segregation throughout the period
studied.

Conclusions

The findings outlined above concerning the nature of
the emergence and development of the abstract journal, the
reasons for its appearance, its growth, and its developmental
characteristics strongly indicate that the guiding hypothesis of
this study with regard to the origins and development of the
abstract journal has been validated. To recapitulate, this
study has proceeded under the controlling assumption that the
abstract journal emerged and achieved its sustained beginnings
in the early nineteenth century as one element of a larger
bibliographic apparatus which had evolved in the period under
study in response to the need for control of the contents of
the learned journal literature, an apparatus comprised, beside
the abstract journal, of the index journal and the major review journal. As such this apparatus represents an organic
synthesis and logical extension of the bibliographic tools used
by scholars of an earlier period--the pandects, encyclopedias,
handbooks, and other compendia; the bibliographic sections of
primary journals, and the independently issued abstract, index,
and review journals of the eighteenth century--now in a new
form and role, as specialized bibliographic tools: current,
serially issued subject bibliography.

This conclusion is an important one since, by confirm-
ing the guiding hypothesis of the study, it tends to resolve
the competing and conflicting explanations in the literature
regarding this development.

Several writers, for example Clarke,[2] have seen the
development of the abstract journal as the logical outgrowth
of the practice of periodical indexing which is viewed by
them as having gone through two principal stages: the retrospective stage of the eighteenth and nineteenth centuries characterized in its beginnings by indexes to individual periodicals,
later by cumulative indexes to individual periodicals, and finally by collective indexes to more than one periodical; and
the second stage from the late nineteenth century onward:
current, ongoing, indexes to more than one periodical, as
typified by the Wilson and other subject-oriented indexes.
The abstract journal is thought of by these writers as having
developed as a result of the addition of the abstract to this
tool in the nineteenth century. Others, like Collison,[3] view

the abstract journal as having appeared with the first learned journal, the <u>Journal des sçavans</u>, in 1665 since it contained summaries of books and periodical articles published elsewhere and was widely emulated in this practice.

Still others, like Price and Bradford,[4] see the abstract journal as the nineteenth century "innovation" of the documentalist seeking to meet his bibliographic needs. We have here a problem of semantics. If these writers mean by "innovation" the introduction of something completely new (which appears to this writer to be the logical inference) this study does not bear this out. If, however, they mean by "innovation" the alteration of an established practice by the introduction of new or different elements or techniques this is closer to what has been observed here.

The findings of the study with respect to the developmental characteristics of the abstract journal lead this writer to conclude that a number of overall trends have been at work shaping this development. Broadly, these trends can be summarized as:

1) the rise of bibliography new in role, form, and type, and comprised of a mixture of devices each designed to meet a special need;

2) the rapid growth and increasing specialization of bibliography paralleling the growth and specialization of scholarship and its primary record;

3) the development of different means of support for bibliographical activities as the value of such efforts became increasingly recognized;

4) the maturing and acceptance of practical bibliography as a recognized discipline with its own standards, system, and method;

5) the rise of popular bibliographic tools.

However, these trends, manifested in the development of bibliography and its component parts, are but reflections of larger forces, principally: the shifting emphases of scholarship, the increasing organization of scholarship, the influence of international cultural relationships and the fortuitous convergence of independent social, political, and economic events.

One of the most salient characteristics of the nineteenth century scholarship was the rise of science and technology with their emphasis on periodical publication, their

increasing specialization, and their continuing demand for research, resulting in greatly increased publication, and, in
turn, greatly increased demands for bibliographic control of
this publication.   In response to this demand a bibliographic
apparatus, comprised of the abstract journal, the index journal, and the review journal, developed, an apparatus serial
in form, subject specialized, and increasing in volume along
side that of primary publication.

The growth of scholarship in the nineteenth century
was marked by increasing organization and institutionalization,
with the founding of many learned and professional societies,
colleges and universities, libraries and archives.   Not a few
of these institutions saw it as their proper responsibility, in
an effort to advance their respective subject fields and to control their burgeoning literature, to undertake bibliographic
publications.   With the recognition late in the nineteenth century of the international nature of knowledge and the first attempts at the international organization of scholarly activities,
international bibliographic enterprise appeared on the scene.

Certain international cultural factors beyond that just
mentioned of the organization of scholarly activities on an international basis, principally the increase of intercourse between nations and the spread of democracy, contributed to the
shaping of bibliography.   This was especially true in the rise
of the general periodical and the resulting need for a device
to provide access to it.   All of these factors reinforced the
belief in the universal good of bibliographic control which
flowered late in the nineteenth century and fostered its propagation.

A series of independent events (social, economic, and
political) converged in the period under study to have an effect on the development of bibliography.   Primarily these are
such factors as the rise of the journal as a device for the
quick reporting of information (a development facilitated by
technological innovations in printing, postal reform, and the
growth and establization of the book trade); the growth in
mass education calling for a new, popular bibliographic effort;
and the new social, economic, and political conditions brought
about by World War I which interrupted the bibliographic tradition which had developed in the previous century, a tradition based largely on individual initiative, comprehensive control, and a German model.

Stated in another way, it can be concluded that the

development of the abstract journal, as well as that of the
index and review journals, has been characterized by the con-
stants of growth, differentiation, increasing specialization,
and an increasing recognition of its value, especially on the
national and international levels. At the same time, this development has been characterized by such variables as the
shifting emphases of scholarship, the changing form of the
record of scholarship, and varied means of support.

The bibliographic apparatus, then, that we have seen
emerge for the control of the contents of the journal literature, has done so by applying methods and techniques of bibliography in a new way in response to these constant and variable factors. It is not unreasonable to conclude that these
same factors will continue to influence the development of
periodical bibliography, which may be thought of as characterized by a continuing evolution of a mixture of devices designed to meet the changing needs of scholars (and others)
for the control of the records of mankind.

Thus it is important for those concerned with the future direction and potential of periodical bibliography to rec-
ognize in their policies that the devices for bibliographic control are not isolated or static. Rather, they constitute a
dynamic system which will continue to evolve in response to
these factors just mentioned. Accordingly, bibliographical
control should be conceived of as being achieved through a
system comprised of a range of devices meeting differing
needs at differing levels, fully rationalized and anticipating
the shifting emphases of scholarship, and enjoying support
at the national and international levels.

Finally, one can reasonably infer from the data presented here that the development of the abstract journal has
been accompanied by a number of persistent problems.

Probably the most striking problem which can be
gleaned from the text is that of agency. The diversity of effort which characterized sponsorship in the nineteenth century,
and which resulted in fragmentation of control, was not seen
as a serious problem until the events associated with World
War I caused a re-examination of bibliographic undertakings
and the goals of bibliography. Then, as energies or universal control, were re-directed toward these new goals of judi-
cious selection, evaluation, and synthesis, the central problem of the inter-relationships of producers and users (individuals and libraries) of bibliographic devices came to be

recognized. The problem of agency, i.e., who is responsible for what aspect of abstract journal production remains
a problem to this day. The present study has shown a clear
trend from personal to professional society and governmental
sponsorship of abstract journals. It can be assumed that
these latter forms of sponsorship will continue to be important, possibly with an increase in cooperation within subject
groupings.

Another problem which can be inferred from the text
derives from the nonevaluative role of the abstract journal,
only reacting to the growth of the literature rather than providing any qualitative control of it. This problem, as pointed
out earlier, has led to the decreasing importance of the current awareness role of the abstract journal and its replace-
ment, in the period under study, by the major review journal.

One problem which resulted from the increased bibliographic activity of the past one hundred years in general, not
solely due to the abstract journal, has been the concomitant
demand for devices to provide physical access along with intellectual access to materials.

The general problems of coverage, overlapping in some
cases, non-existent in others, and coordination of activities
are also apparent in this study.

These conclusions regarding the persistent problems of
abstract journal production underline strongly the need for cooperation among all elements of the information community in
producing a range of coordinated devices at various levels,
as mentioned above; and a mutual recognition of the unity of
our goals if we are to achieve a rationalized bibliography.

Notes

1. Here classified as a member of the humanities group
   since photography is considered a humanity in the
   Universal Decimal Classification.
2. Clarke, p. 40.
3. Collison, Abstracts and Abstracting Services, pp. 59-60.
4. Price, Little Science, Big Science, p. 96. Bradford,
   p. 27.

ABSTRACT JOURNALS, 1790-1920†

*Abstract of the Literature of Industrial Hygiene and Toxi-
cology. Cambridge, Mass.; etc., 1919-

*Abstracts from Recent Medical and Public Health Papers.
Washington, 1920-

*Abstracts of Bacteriology. Baltimore, 1917-

Abstracts of Physical Papers from Foreign Sources. London, 1895-1897.

*Abstracts of Tuberculosis. Baltimore, 1917-

Allgemeines Repertorium der gesamten deutschen medizinisch-
chirurgischen Journalistik. Leipzig, 1827-1847.

*American Economic Review. Ithaca, N.Y., 1911-

*American Gas Association, Bulletin of Abstracts. Easton,
Pa., 1907-

*American Journal of Archaeology. Concord, N.H.; etc.,
1885-

American Journal of Diseases of Children. Chicago, 1911-
1912.

---

†Titles as of 1920 (or latest if ceased) and years in
which they contained abstracts.
*An asterisk beside a title in this list (and in Appendixes
II and III) indicates that the publication continued beyond 1920,
the termination date for this study. No claim is made concerning the abstract content of these publications beyond that
date.

*American Journal of Obstetrics and Gynecology. St. Louis, 1920-

*American Journal of Pharmacy. Philadelphia, 1856-

*American Journal of Physical Anthropology. Washington, 1918-

*Amèrican Journal of Science. New Haven, Conn., 1820-

*American Journal of Sociology. Chicago, 1896-

*American Journal of Syphilis. St. Louis, 1917-

*American Medical Association, Journal. Chicago, 1883-

American Medical Intelligencer. Philadelphia, 1837-1842.

*American Veterinary Medical Association, Journal. New York, 1889-

*Analecta Bollandiana. Brussels, 1895-

*Analyst. London, 1884-

Analytical Review. London, 1788-1799.

*Ancient Egypt. London, 1914-

Annalen der Physik, Beiblätter. Halle; Leipzig, 1877-1919.

*Annales de chimie analytique et de chimie appliquée. Paris, 1896-

Annales de chimie et de physique. Paris, 1851-1873.

*Annales de dermatologie et de syphilographie. Paris, 1868-

*Annales de Gembloux. Brussels, 1893-

*Annales de médecine vétérinaire. Brussels, 1903-

*Annales des maladies de l'oreille, du larynx, du nez et du pharynx. Paris, 1875-

*Annales des postes, télégraphes et téléphones. Paris, 1910-

*Annales d'hygiène publique. Paris, 1872-

*Annales d'oculistique. Paris, 1867-

*Annales médico-psychologiques. Paris, 1843-

Annales Mycologici. Berlin, 1903-1917.

*Année biologique. Paris, 1895-

Année pédogogique. Paris, 1911-1913.

*Année psychologique. Paris, 1897-

Année sociologique. Paris, 1896-1912.

Arcana of Science and Art. London, 1828-1838.

Archiv der Pharmazie. Berlin, 1843-1889.

*Archiv für Kinderheilkunde. Stuttgart, 1880-

*Archiv für Reformations-Geschichte. Leipzig; Berlin, 1903-

*Archives de médecine des enfants. Paris, 1898-

*Archives des maladies de l'appareil digestif et de la nutri-
tion. Paris, 1907-

*Archives italiennes de biologie. Pisa; Rome; etc. , 1894-

*Archives of Dermatology and Syphilology. Chicago, 1920-

*Archives of Neurology and Psychiatry. Chicago, 1919-

*Archives of Pediatrics. New York; etc. , 1884-

*Archives suisses d'anthropologie générale. Geneva, 1914-

*Association des Chimistes de Sucrerie, Distilleries et In-
dustries Agricoles de France et de l'Union Française,
Bulletin. Paris, 1893-

*Astronomischer Jahresbericht. Berlin, 1899-

*Auk. Boston; New York; etc. , 1914-

Berichte über die gesamte Physiologie und experimentelle
    Pharmakologie. Berlin, 1920-

*Berliner philologische Wochenschrift. Berlin; Leipzig,
    1881-

*Bibliographia Evolutionis. Paris, 1910-1914; 1919-

*Bibliographie géographique. Paris, 1891-

*Biedermanns Zentralblatt für Agrikulturchemie und ration-
    ellen Landwirtschaftsbetrieb. Leipzig, 1872-

Biochemisches Zentralblatt. Berlin; Leipzig, 1902-1909.

Bolletino delle scienze mediche. Bologna, 1829-1835.

*Botanical Abstracts. Baltimore, 1918-

*Botanische Jahrbücher für Systematik, Pflanzengeschichte und
    Pflanzengeographie. Leipzig, 1884-

*Botanischer Jahresbericht. Berlin; Leipzig, 1873-

*Botanisches Zentralblatt. Cassel; Jena, 1880-

*Brasil-medico. Rio de Janeiro, 1887-

*British Dental Journal. London, 1881-

*British Journal of Dermatology and Syphilis. London,
    1888-

British Medical Journal. London, 1857-1867.

Bulletin des Neuesten und Wissenwürdigsten aus der Natur-
    wissenschaft. Berlin, 1809-1813.

Bulletin des sciences agricoles et économiques. Paris, 1824-
    1831.

Bulletin des sciences géographiques. Paris, 1824-1831.

Bulletin des sciences historiques, antiquités, philologie.
    Paris, 1824-1831.

*Bulletin des sciences mathématiques. Paris, 1870-

Bulletin des sciences mathématiques, astronomiques, physiques et chimiques. Paris, 1824-1831.

Bulletin des sciences médicales. Paris, 1824-1831.

Bulletin des sciences militaires. Paris, 1824-1831.

Bulletin des sciences naturelles et de géologie. Paris, 1824-1831.

*Bulletin des sciences pharmacologiques. Paris, 1899-

Bulletin des sciences technologiques. Paris, 1824-1831.

Bulletin générale et universel des annonces et des nouvelles scientifiques. Paris, 1823.

*Ceramic Abstracts. Easton, Pa. , 1919-

*Ceramic Society, Transactions. Stoke-on-Trent, 1906-

*Chemical Abstracts. Columbus, 1907-

*Chemical Society, Journal. London, 1871-

Chemische Annalen für die Freunde der Naturlehre, Arzney-gelahrtheit, Haushaltungskunst und Manufacturen. Helm-staedt; Leipzig, 1784-1804.

Chemische Annalen für die Freunde der Naturlehre, Arzney-gelahrtheit, Haushaltungskunst und Manufacturen, Beiträge. Helmstaedt; Leipzig, 1785-1799.

*Chemische Umschau auf dem Gebiete der Fette, Oele, Wachse und Harze. Hamburg, 1894-

*Chemisches Zentralblatt. Leipzig; Berlin, 1830-

Chemisch-technische Mitteilungen der neuesten Zeit. Berlin, 1849-1887.

*Chemisch-technische Übersicht. Cöthen; etc. , 1885-

Chemisch-technisches Repertorium. Berlin, 1862-1901.

*Chimie et industrie. Paris, 1918-

*Creamery and Milk Plant Monthly.   Chicago, 1912-

Dental Cosmos.   Philadelphia, 1860-

*Dermatologische Wochenschrift.   Leipzig, 1882-

Dermatologisches Zentralblatt.   Leipzig, 1897-1920.

*Deutsche tierärztliche Wochenschrift.   Karlsruhe; Hanover,
1893-

*Eastman Kodak Co., Research Laboratory, Monthly Abstract
Bulletin.   Rochester, N.Y., 1915-

Ecole Française d'Extrême-Orient, Bulletin.   Hanoi, 1901-
1916.

Economic Geology.   Lancaster, Pa., 1908-1918.

*Economic Journal.   London, 1891-

*Electrical World.   New York, 1894-

Encyclographie médicale.   Paris, 1842-1846.

*Engineering Index.   New York, 1884-

Epitome; a Monthly Retrospect.   New York, 1880-1889.

*Epitome of Current Medical Literature.   London, 1890-

Epitome of Medicine.   New York, 1884-1893.

Esprit des journaux, français et étrangers.   Paris, 1772-
1815; 1817-1818.

*Excerpta Medica.   Leipzig, 1891-

*Experiment Station Record.   Washington, 1889-

*Folia Haematologica.   Berlin; Leipzig, 1904-

*Forstliche Rundschau.   Neudamm, 1900-

*Fortschritte der Medizin.   Berlin, 1883-

Fortschritte der Physik.   Berlin; Brunswick, 1845-1918.

Fortschritte der Technik.   Berlin, 1909-1910.

*General Electric Co., Lamp Development Laboratory, Abstract Bulletin.   Cleveland, 1913-

Geological Record.   London, 1874-1879.

*Geologisches Zentralblatt.   Leipzig; Berlin, 1901-

*Giesserei.   Munich, 1914-

*Goerres-Gesellschaft zur Pflege der Wissenschaft im katholischen Deutschland, Historisches Jahrbuch.   Bonn, 1882-

*Great Britain, Imperial Institute, Bulletin.   London, 1911-

*Gynécologie et obstétrique.   Paris, 1920-

*Hahnemannian Monthly.   Philadelphia, 1917-

Half-Yearly Abstract of the Medical Sciences.   London, 1845-1873.

*Hedwigia.   Dresden, 1863-

*Hygienische Rundschau.   Berlin, 1891-

Hygienisches Zentralblatt.   Leipzig, 1906-1909

*Igiene moderna.   Genoa, 1908-

Institut Pasteur, Annales.   Paris, 1887-1888.

*Institut Pasteur, Bulletin.   Paris, 1903-

*Institute of Metals, Journal.   London, 1909-

*Institution of Civil Engineers, Abstracts of Papers.   London, 1875-

*International Abstract of Surgery.   Chicago, 1913-

*International Institute of Refrigeration, Monthly Bulletin.   Paris, 1910-

*International Journal of Orthodontia, Oral Surgery and Radiography.   St. Louis, 1919-

*International Medical and Surgical Survey. New York, 1920-

*International Medical Digest. New York, 1920-

*International Review of the Science and Practice of Agriculture. Rome, 1910-

*International Sugar Journal. Manchester; London; etc., 1909-

*Internationale Mitteilungen für Bodenkunde. Berlin; etc., 1911-

*Internationale Revue der gesamten Hydrobiologie und Hydrographie. Leipzig, 1908-

*Internationales Zentralblatt für Laryngologie, Rhinologie und verwandte Wissenschaften. Berlin, 1884-

*Internationales Zentralblatt für Ohrenheilkunde und Rhinolaryngologie. Wurzburg; Leipzig, 1903-

*Jahrbuch der Moorkunde. Hanover, 1912-

*Jahrbuch für Kinderheilkunde. Berlin, 1858-

*Jahrbuch über die Fortschritte der Mathematik. Berlin, 1868-

*Jahrbücher für Nationalökonomie und Statistik. Jena, 1863-1870.

Jahresbericht über die Fischereiliteratur. Neudamm, 1911-1912.

Journal de chimie physique et de physico-chimie biologique. Geneva, 1903-1905.

*Journal de chirurgie. Paris, 1908-

*Journal de médecine vétérinaire et de zootechnie. Lyons, 1876-

*Journal de pharmacie et de chimie. Paris, 1845-

*Journal de physiologie et de pathologie générale. Paris, 1899-

*Journal de physique et le radium.   Paris, 1872-

*Journal de radiologie et d'électrologie.   Paris, 1914-

Journal des sçavans.   Paris, 1665-1792; 1797.

*Journal d'urologie médicale et chirurgicale.   Paris, 1912-

Journal encyclopédique ou universel.   Liège; Brussels, 1756-
     1793.

Journal of Abnormal Psychology.   Boston; Albany, N.Y.,
     1906-1914.

Journal of American Folklore.   Boston; New York; Lancaster,
     Pa. , 1910-1911.

Journal of Applied Psychology.   Worcester, Mass.; Blooming-
     ton, Ind. , 1917.

*Journal of Ecology.   London, 1913-

*Journal of Forestry.   Washington, 1902-

*Journal of Laryngology, Rhinology, and Otology.   London,
     1887-

*Journal of Nervous and Mental Disease.   Chicago, 1874-

*Journal of Obstetrics and Gynecology of the British Empire.
     London, 1902-

*Journal of Philosophy, Psychology and Scientific Method.
     New York, 1904-

Kinderarzt.   Neuwied; etc. , 1890-1920.

*Kolloid-Zeitschrift.   Dresden; Leipzig, 1906-

*Kongresszentralblatt für die gesamte innere Medizin und
     ihre Grenzgebiete.   Berlin, 1912-

Laryngoscope.   St. Louis, 1896-1918.

*Malattie del cuore.   Rome, 1916-

*Marcellia.   Avellino, 1902-

*Mechanical Engineering. New York, 1912-

Medical Chronicle. Manchester, Eng. , 1884-1916.

Medical News. Philadelphia; New York, 1843-1905.

*Medical Science Abstracts and Reviews. London, 1919-

*Mental Hygiene. Concord, N. H. , 1917-

*Mind. London; etc. , 1876-

*Mineralogical Abstracts. London, 1920-

Mineralogical Magazine. London, 1876-1903.

*Mining Magazine. London, 1909-

*Mitteilungen zur Geschichte der Medizin und der Naturwis-
senschaften. Hamburg; etc. , 1902-

Mois scientifique et industriel. Paris, 1899-1919.

*Monatsschrift für Ohrenheilkunde und Laryngo-Rhinologie.
Berlin, 1877-

Monitore zoologico Italiano. Sienna, 1890-1913.

Monthly Abstract of Medical Science. Philadelphia, 1874-
1879.

Monthly Review. London, 1749-1844.

*Moslem World. New York, 1913-

*Münchener medizinische Wochenschrift. Munich, 1859-

Naturwissenschaftliche Rundschau. Brunswick, 1886-1912.

*Nederlandsch Tijdschrift voor Geneeskunde. Amsterdam,
1906-

Neues chemisches Archiv. Leipzig, 1783-1791.

*Neues Jahrbuch für Mineralogie, Geologie, und Paläontologie.
Heidelberg; Stuttgart, 1830-

*Neurologisches Zentralblatt. Leipzig, 1882-

*New York Medical Journal. New York, 1865-

*New York Times Index. New York, 1913-

Notizen aus dem Gebiete der Natur- und Heilkunde.   Erfurt;
    Weimar, 1821-1849.

Numismatic Chronicle. London, 1861-1896.

*Office Internationale d'Hygiène Publique, Bulletin mensuel.
    Paris, 1909-

*Petermanns Mitteilungen aus Justus Perthes' Geographischer
    Anstalt. Gotha, 1885-

Physikalisch-chemisches Zentralblatt. Leipzig, 1904-1909.

*Physikalische Berichte. Brunswick, 1920-

*Physiological Abstracts. London, 1916-

*Psychological Bulletin. Lancaster, Pa.; etc., 1904-

Psychological Review. Lancaster, Pa.; etc., 1894-1903.

*Radiologia medica. Milan; Turin, 1914-

Répertoire de chimie appliquée. Paris, 1858-1864.

Répertoire de chimie pure. Paris, 1858-1863.

Repertorium der analytischen Chemie. Hamburg, 1881-1887.

Repertorium der technischen Journal-Literatur. Berlin;
    Leipzig, 1899-1908.

Retrospect of Medicine. New York; London, 1840-1901.

Retrospect of Philosophical, Mechanical, Chemical and
    Agricultural Discoveries. London, 1805-1813.

Review of American Chemical Research. Cambridge, Mass.;
    Easton, Pa., 1895-1906.

*Review of Applied Entomology. London, 1913-

Review of Bacteriology. London, 1911-1919.

Review of Neurology and Psychiatry. Edinburgh, 1903-1919.

*Revue bryologique. Caen; Paris, 1882-

*Revue de géologie et des sciences connexes. Liège, 1920-

*Revue de laryngologie, d'otologie et de rhinologie. Paris, 1880-

Revue de l'histoire des religions. Paris, 1880-1901.

*Revue de métallurgie. Paris, 1904-

*Revue des questions scientifiques. Louvain; etc., 1877-

Revue des sciences médicales en France et à l'étranger. Paris, 1873-1898.

*Revue des sciences philosophiques et théologiques. Paris; etc., 1907-

*Revue d'hygiène et de police sanitaire. Paris, 1879-

*Revue d'orthopédie. Paris, 1908-

Revue du droit et de la science politique en France et à l'étranger. Paris, 1894-1906.

*Revue française de gynécologie et d'obstétrique. Paris, 1906-

Revue générale des sciences pures et appliquées. Paris, 1890-1891.

*Revue générale des travaux astronomiques. Paris, 1920-

*Revue historique. Paris, 1876-

*Revue neurologique. Paris, 1893-

*Revue semestrielle des publications mathématiques. Amsterdam, 1893-

*Revue universelle des mines. Liège, 1919-

*Revue vétérinaire. Toulouse, 1876-

*Rivista di clinica pediatrica. Florence, 1903-

*Rivista internazionale di scienze sociali e discipline ausiliarie. Rome, 1895-

*Rivista storica Italiana. Turin, 1896-

*Rocznik slawistyczny. Krakow, 1908-

*Royal Microscopical Society, Journal. London, 1878-

*Schmidts Jahrbücher der in- und ausländischen Medicin. Bonn; Leipzig, 1834-

Science. New York; etc. , 1883.

*Science Abstracts. London, 1898-

*Sociedad Española de Física y Química, Anales. Madrid, 1912-

*Société Botanique de France, Bulletin. Paris, 1854-

*Société Chimique de France, Bulletin. Paris, 1863-

Société Mycologique de France, Bulletin trimestriel. Paris, 1902-1914.

Société National d'Horticulture, Journal. Paris, 1855-1918.

*Société Scientifique d'Hygiène Alimentaire et de l'Alimentation Rationelle de l'Homme, Bulletin. Paris, 1904-

*Society of Chemical Industry, Journal. London, 1882-

*Society of Glass Technology, Journal. London, 1917-

*Society of Leather Trades' Chemists, Journal. Leeds; London, 1917-

Summarium des Neuesten aus der gesamten Medicin. Leipzig, 1828-1843.

Tagsberichte über die Fortschritte der Natur- und Heilkunde. Weimar, 1850-1852.

Taschenbuch für die gesamte Mineralogie.   Frankfurt a. M.;
    Heidelberg, 1807-1829.

*Technical Review. London, 1918-

Technische Auskunft. Berlin, 1909-1913.

*Textile Institute, Journal. Manchester, Eng., 1918-

*Therapeutic Notes. Detroit, 1894-

*Tijdschrift voor Diergeneeskunde. Utrecht; Amsterdam,
    1892-

Tijdschrift voor Geschiedenis. Utrecht, 1898-1903.

*Times Official Index. London, 1906-

*Tropical Diseases Bulletin. London, 1912-

*Tropical Veterinary Bulletin. London, 1912-

Universal Magazine of Knowledge and Pleasure. London,
    1747-1815.

*Wiener tierärztliche Monatsschrift. Vienna, 1914-

Year-Book of Facts in Science and Art. London, 1838-1879/81.

*Yearbook of Pharmacy. London, 1864-

*Zeitschrift für angewandte Chemie. Berlin; Leipzig, 1888-

*Zeitschrift für angewandte Entomologie. Berlin, 1914-

*Zeitschrift für Botanik. Jena, 1909-

*Zeitschrift für die gesamte Neurologie und Psychiatrie.
    Munich; Breslau; Berlin, 1910-

*Zeitschrift für Kristallographie. Leipzig, 1877-

*Zeitschrift für orthopädische Chirurgie. Stuttgart; Berlin,
    1891-

*Zeitschrift für Pflanzenkrankheiten und Gallenkunde. Stutt-
    gart, 1890-

*Zeitschrift für Pflanzenzüchtung. Berlin, 1912-

*Zeitschrift für physikalische und diätetische Therapie. Leipzig; Berlin, 1898-

Zeitschrift für Psychologie und Physiologie der Sinnesorgane. Hamburg; Leipzig, 1890-1906.

*Zeitschrift für technische Biologie. Leipzig, 1912-

*Zeitschrift für Tuberkulose. Leipzig, 1900-

*Zeitschrift für Urologie. Berlin; Leipzig, 1907-

*Zeitschrift für wissenschaftliche Mikroskopie und für mikroskopische Technik. Stuttgart, 1884-

*Zentralblatt der experimentellen Medizin. Berlin; Vienna, 1912-1914.

Zentralblatt für allgemeine Gesundheitspflege. Bonn, 1882-1915.

*Zentralblatt für allgemeine Pathologie und pathologische Anatomie. Jena; Wurzburg, 1890-

Zentralblatt für Anthropologie. Brunswick; etc., 1896-1912.

*Zentralblatt für Bakteriologie und Parasitenkunde. Jena, 1887-

*Zentralblatt für Biochemie und Biophysik. Leipzig, 1910-

*Zentralblatt für Chirurgie. Leipzig, 1874-

Zentralblatt für chirurgische und mechanische Orthopädie. Berlin, 1907-1919.

Zentralblatt für die gesamte Gynäkologie. Berlin, 1913-1914.

*Zentralblatt für die gesamte Kinderheilkunde. Berlin, 1911-

*Zentralblatt für die gesamte Landwirtschaft. Leipzig, 1920-

*Zentralblatt für die gesamte Ophthalmologie und ihre Grenzgebiete. Berlin, 1914-

Zentralblatt für die gesamte Physiologie und Pathologie des
Stoffwechsels. Berlin; etc. , 1900-1911.

Zentralblatt für die gesamte Therapie. Vienna; Berlin, 1883-
1917.

*Zentralblatt für die gesamte Tuberkuloseforschung. Berlin;
Wurzburg, 1906-

Zentralblatt für die Grenzgebiete der Medizin und Chirurgie.
Jena, 1897-1917.

Zentralblatt für die Krankheiten der Harn- und Sexual-Organe.
Hamburg; Leipzig, 1889-1906.

Zentralblatt für die medizinischen Wissenschaften. Berlin,
1863-1915.

Zentralblatt für Gewerbehygiene und Unfallverhutüng. Berlin,
1913-1915.

*Zentralblatt für Gynäkologie. Leipzig, 1877-

*Zentralblatt für Herz- und Gefässkrankheiten. Dresden;
Leipzig, 1909-

*Zentralblatt für innere Medizin. Leipzig, 1880-

Zentralblatt für Kinderheilkunde. Leipzig, 1896-1917.

Zentralblatt für Nervenheilkunde und Psychiatrie. Leipzig;
etc. , 1878-1910.

Zentralblatt für normale Anatomie und Mikrotechnik. Berlin;
Vienna, 1904-1914.

*Zentralblatt für Physiologie. Leipzig, 1887-

Zentralblatt für praktische Augenheilkunde. Leipzig, 1877-
1919.

Zentralblatt für Roentgenstrahlen und verwandte Gebiete.
Wiesbaden, 1910-1919.

Zentralblatt für Zoologie. Leipzig, 1912-1918.

*Zentralorgan für die gesamte Chirurgie.   Berlin; Leipzig,
    1913-

Zoologisches Zentralblatt.   Leipzig, 1894-1911.

APPENDIX II

CHRONOLOGY OF ABSTRACT JOURNALS, 1790-1920

1665   Journal des sçavans.   Paris, 1665-1792; 1797.

1747   Universal Magazine of Knowledge and Pleasure.   London, 1747-1815.

1749   Monthly Review.   1749-1844.

1756   Journal encyclopédique ou universel.   Liège; Brussels, 1756-1793.

1772   Esprit des journaux, français et étrangers.   Paris, 1772-1815; 1817-1818.

1783   Neues chemisches Archiv.   Leipzig, 1783-1791.

1784   Chemische Annalen für die Freunde der Naturlehre, Arzneygelahrtheit, Haushaltungskunst und Manufacturen.   Helmstaedt; Leipzig, 1784-1804.

1785   Chemische Annalen für die Freunde der Naturlehre, Arzneygelahrtheit, Haushaltungskunst und Manufacturen, Beiträge.   Helmstaedt; Leipzig, 1785-1799.

1788   Analytical Review.   London, 1788-1799.

1805   Retrospect of Philosophical, Mechanical, Chemical and Agricultural Discoveries.   London, 1805-1813.

1807   Taschenbuch für die gesamte Mineralogie.   Frankfurt a. M.; Heidelberg, 1807-1829.

1809   Bulletin des Neuesten und Wissenwürdigsten aus der Naturwissenschaft.   Berlin, 1809-1813.

1820   *American Journal of Science. New Haven, Conn.,
        1820-

1821   Notizen aus dem Gebiete der Natur- und Heilkunde.
        Erfurt; Weimar, 1821-1849.

1823   Bulletin générale et universel des annonces et des
        nouvelles scientifiques. Paris, 1823.

1824   Bulletin des sciences agricoles et économiques. Paris,
        1824-1831.
        Bulletin des sciences géographiques. Paris, 1824-1831.
        Bulletin des sciences historiques, antiquités, philologie.
        Paris, 1824-1831.
        Bulletin des sciences mathématiques, astronomiques,
        physiques et chimiques. Paris, 1824-1831.
        Bulletin des sciences médicales. Paris, 1824-1831.
        Bulletin des sciences militaires. Paris, 1824-1831.
        Bulletin des sciences naturelles et de géologie. Paris,
        1824-1831.
        Bulletin des sciences technologiques. Paris, 1824-
        1831.

1827   Allgemeines Repertorium der gesamten deutschen
        medizinisch-chirurgischen Journalistik. Leipzig,
        1827-1847.

1828   Arcana of Science and Art. London, 1828-1838.
        Summarium des Neuesten aus der gesamten Medicin.
        Leipzig, 1828-1843.

1829   Bolletino delle scienze mediche. Bologna, 1829-1835.

1830   *Chemisches Zentralblatt. Leipzig; Berlin, 1830-
        *Neues Jahrbuch für Mineralogie, Geologie, und
        Paläontologie. Heidelberg; Stuttgart, 1830-

1834   *Schmidts Jahrbücher der in- und ausländischen Medi-
        cin. Bonn; Leipzig, 1834-

1837   American Medical Intelligencer. Philadelphia, 1837-
        1842.

1838   Year-Book of Facts in Science and Art. London,
        1838-1879/81.

*See footnote to Appendix I, p. 198.

1840   Retrospect of Medicine.   New York; London, 1840-
        1901.

1842   Encyclographie médicale.   Paris, 1842-1846.

1843   *Annales médico-psychologiques.   Paris, 1843-
        Archiv der Pharmazie.   Berlin, 1843-1889.
        Medical News.   Philadelphia; New York, 1843-1905.

1845   Fortschritte der Physik.   Berlin; Brunswick, 1845-1918.
        Half-Yearly Abstract of the Medical Sciences.   Lon-
           don, 1845-1873.
        *Journal de pharmacie et de chimie.   Paris, 1845-

1849   Chemisch-technische Mitteilungen der neuesten Zeit.
        Berlin, 1849-1887.

1850   Tagsberichte über die Fortschritte der Natur- und
        Heilkunde.   Weimar, 1850-1852.

1851   Annales de chimie et de physique.   Paris, 1851-1873.

1854   *Société Botanique de France, Bulletin.   Paris, 1854-

1855   Société Nationale d'Horticulture, Journal.   Paris,
        1855-1918.

1856   *American Journal of Pharmacy.   Philadelphia, 1856-

1857   British Medical Journal.   London, 1857-1867.

1858   *Jahrbuch für Kinderheilkunde.   Berlin, 1858-
        Répertoire de chimie appliquée.   Paris, 1858-1864.
        Répertoire de chimie pure.   Paris, 1858-1863.

1859   *Münchener medizinische Wochenschrift.   Munich,
        1859-

1860   *Dental Cosmos.   Philadelphia, 1860-

1861   Numismatic Chronicle.   London, 1861-1896.

1862   Chemisch-technisches Repertorium.   Berlin, 1862-
        1901.

1863   *Hedwigia.   Dresden, 1863-

[1863] Jahrbücher für Nationalökonomie und Statistik.   Jena,
       1863-1870.
       *Société Chimique de France, Bulletin.   Paris, 1863-
       Zentralblatt für die medizinischen Wissenschaften.
       Berlin, 1863-1915.

1864   *Yearbook of Pharmacy.   London, 1864-

1865   *New York Medical Journal.   New York, 1865-

1867   *Annales d'oculistique.   Paris, 1867-

1868   *Annales de dermatologie et de syphilographie.   Paris,
       1868-
       *Jahrbuch über die Fortschritte der Mathematik.
       Berlin, 1868-

1870   *Bulletin des sciences mathématiques.   Paris, 1870-

1871   *Chemical Society, Journal.   London, 1871-

1872   *Annales d'hygiène publique.   Paris, 1872-
       *Biedermanns Zentralblatt für Agrikulturchemie und
           rationellen Landwirtschaftsbetrieb.   Leipzig, 1872-
       *Journal de physique et le radium.   Paris, 1872-

1873   *Botanischer Jahresbericht.   Berlin; Leipzig, 1873-
       Revue des sciences médicales en France et à l'étran-
           ger.   Paris, 1873-1898.

1874   Geological Record.   London, 1874-1879.
       *Journal of Nervous and Mental Disease.   Chicago,
       1874-
       Monthly Abstract of Medical Science.   Philadelphia,
       1874-1879.
       *Zentralblatt für Chirurgie.   Leipzig, 1874-

1875   *Annales des maladies de l'oreille, du larynx, du nez
           et du pharynx.   Paris, 1875-
       *Institution of Civil Engineers, Abstracts of Papers.
       London, 1875-

1876   *Journal de médecine vétérinaire et de zootechnie.
       Lyons, 1876-
       *Mind.   London; etc. , 1876-
       Mineralogical Magazine.   London, 1876-1903.
       *Revue historique.   Paris, 1876-

*Revue vétérinaire. Toulouse, 1876-

1877   Annalen der Physik, Beiblätter. Halle; Leipzig,
           1877-1919.
        *Monatsschrift für Ohrenheilkunde und Laryngo-Rhino-
           logie. Berlin, 1877-
        *Revue des questions scientifiques. Louvain; etc.,
           1877-
        *Zeitschrift für Kristallographie. Leipzig, 1877-
        Zentralblatt für praktische Augenheilkunde. Leipzig,
           1877-1919.

1878   *Royal Microscopical Society, Journal. London, 1878-
        Zentralblatt für Nervenheilkunde und Psychiatrie.
           Leipzig; etc., 1878-1910.

1879   *Revue d'hygiène et de police sanitaire. Paris, 1879-

1880   *Archiv für Kinderheilkunde. Stuttgart, 1880-
        *Botanisches Zentralblatt. Cassel; Jena, 1880-
        Epitome; a Monthly Retrospect. New York, 1880-
           1889.
        Revue de l'histoire des religions. Paris, 1880-1901.
        *Revue de laryngologie, d'otologie et de rhinologie.
           Paris, 1880-
        *Zentralblatt für innere Medizin. Leipzig, 1880-

1881   *Berliner philologische Wochenschrift. Berlin; Leip-
           zig, 1881-
        *British Dental Journal. London, 1881-
        Repertorium der analytischen Chemie. Hamburg,
           1881-1887.

1882   *Dermatologische Wochenschrift. Leipzig, 1882-
        *Goerres-Gesellschaft zur Pflege der Wissenschaft im
           katholischen Deutschland, Historisches Jahrbuch.
           Bonn, 1882-
        *Neurologisches Zentralblatt. Leipzig, 1882-
        *Revue bryologique. Caen; Paris, 1882-
        *Society of Chemical Industry, Journal. London,
           1882-
        Zentralblatt für allgemeine Gesundheitspflege. Bonn,
           1882-1915.

1883   *American Medical Association, Journal. Chicago,
           1883-
        *Fortschritte der Medizin. Berlin, 1883-

[1883] Science. New York; etc. , 1883.
       Zentralblatt für die gesamte Therapie. Vienna; Ber-
           lin, 1883-1917.

1884   *Analyst. London, 1884-
       *Archives of Pediatrics. New York; etc. , 1884-
       *Botanische Jahrbücher für Systematik, Pflanzenges-
           chichte und Pflanzengeographie. Leipzig, 1884-
       *Engineering Index. New York, 1884-
       Epitome of Medicine. New York, 1884-1893.
       *Internationales Zentralblatt für Laryngologie, Rhinol-
           ogie und verwandte Wissenschaften. Berlin,
           1884-
       Medical Chronicle. Manchester, Eng. , 1884-1916.
       *Zeitschrift für wissenschaftliche Mikroskopie und für
           mikroskopische Technik. Stuttgart, 1884-

1885   *American Journal of Archaeology. Concord, N.H. ;
           etc. , 1885-
       *Chemisch-technische Übersicht. Cöthen; etc. , 1885-
       *Petermanns Mitteilungen aus Justus Perthes' Geo-
           graphischer Anstalt. Gotha, 1885-

1886   Naturwissenschaftliche Rundschau. Brunswick, 1886-
           1912.

1887   *Brasil-medico. Rio de Janeiro, 1887-
       Institut Pasteur, Annales. Paris, 1887-1888.
       *Journal of Laryngology, Rhinology, and Otology.
           London, 1887-
       *Zentralblatt für Bakteriologie und Parasitenkunde.
           Jena, 1887-
       *Zentralblatt für Physiologie. Leipzig, 1887-

1888   *British Journal of Dermatology and Syphilis. London,
           1888-
       *Zeitschrift für angewandte Chemie. Berlin; Leipzig,
           1888-

1889   *American Veterinary Medical Association, Journal.
           New York, 1889-
       *Experiment Station Record. Washington, 1889-
       Zentralblatt für die Krankheiten der Harn- und Sexual-
           Organe. Hamburg; Leipzig, 1889-1906.

1890   *Epitome of Current Medical Literature. London,
           1890-

Kinderarzt. Neuwied; etc., 1890-1920.
Monitore zoologico Italiano. Sienna, 1890-1913.
Revue générale des sciences pures et appliquées.
   Paris, 1890-1891.
*Zeitschrift für Pflanzenkrankheiten und Gallenkunde.
   Stuttgart, 1890-
Zeitschrift für Psychologie und Physiologie der Sinnes-
   organe. Hamburg; Leipzig, 1890-1906.
*Zentralblatt für allgemeine Pathologie und patholo-
   gische Anatomie. Jena; Wurzburg, 1890-

1891   *Bibliographie géographique. Paris, 1891-
        *Economic Journal. London, 1891-
        *Excerpta Medica. Leipzig, 1891-
        *Hygienische Rundschau. Berlin, 1891-
        *Zeitschrift für orthopädische Chirurgie. Stuttgart;
           Berlin, 1891.

1892   *Tijdschrift voor Diergeneeskunde. Utrecht; Amster-
           dam, 1892-

1893   *Annales de Gembloux. Brussels, 1893-
        *Association des Chimistes de Sucrerie, Distilleries
           et Industries Agricoles de France et de l'Union
           Française, Bulletin. Paris, 1893-
        *Deutsche tierärztliche Wochenschrift. Karlsruhe;
           Hanover, 1893-
        *Revue neurologique. Paris, 1893-
        *Revue semestrielle des publications mathématiques.
           Amsterdam, 1893-

1894   *Archives italiennes de biologie. Pisa; Rome; etc.,
           1894-
        *Chemische Umschau auf dem Gebiete der Fette,
           Oele, Wachse und Harze. Hamburg, 1894-
        *Electrical World. New York, 1894-
        Psychological Review. Lancaster, Pa.; etc., 1894-
           1903.
        Revue du droit et de la science politique en France
           et à l'étranger. Paris, 1894-1906.
        *Therapeutic Notes. Detroit, 1894-
        Zoologisches Zentralblatt. Leipzig, 1894-1911.

1895   Abstracts of Physical Papers from Foreign Sources.
           London, 1895-1897.
        *Analecta Bollandiana. Brussels, 1895-
        *Année biologique. Paris, 1895-

[1895] Review of American Chemical Research. Cambridge,
         Mass.; Easton, Pa. , 1895-1906.
       *Rivista internazionale di scienze sociali e discipline
         ausiliarie. Rome, 1895-

1896   *American Journal of Sociology. Chicago, 1896-
       *Annales de chimie analytique et de chimie appliquée.
         Paris, 1896-
       Année sociologique. Paris, 1896-1912.
       Laryngoscope. St. Louis, 1896-1918.
       *Rivista storica Italiana. Turin, 1896-
       Zentralblatt für Anthropologie. Brunswick; etc. ,
         1896-1912.
       Zentralblatt für Kinderheilkunde. Leipzig, 1896-1917.

1897   *Année psychologique. Paris, 1897-
       Dermatologisches Zentralblatt. Leipzig, 1897-1920.
       Zentralblatt für die Grenzgebiete der Medizin und
         Chirurgie. Jena, 1897-1917.

1898   *Archives de médecine des enfants. Paris, 1898-
       *Science Abstracts. London, 1898-
       Tijdschrift voor Geschiedenis. Utrecht, 1898-1903.
       *Zeitschrift für physikalische und diätetische Therapie.
         Leipzig; Berlin, 1898-

1899   *Astronomischer Jahresbericht. Berlin, 1899-
       *Bulletin des sciences pharmacologiques. Paris,
         1899-
       *Journal de physiologie et de pathologie générale.
         Paris, 1899-
       Mois scientifique et industriel. Paris, 1899-1919.
       Repertorium der technischen Journal-Literatur. Ber-
         lin; Leipzig, 1899-1908.

1900   *Forstliche Rundschau. Neudamm, 1900-
       *Zeitschrift für Tuberkulose. Leipzig, 1900-
       Zentralblatt für die gesamte Physiologie und Pathologie
         des Stoffwechsels. Berlin; etc. , 1900-1911.

1901   Ecole Française d'Extrême-Orient, Bulletin. Hanoi,
         1901-1916.
       *Geologisches Zentralblatt. Leipzig; Berlin, 1901-

1902   Biochemisches Zentralblatt. Berlin; Leipzig, 1902-
         1909.
       *Journal of Forestry. Washington, 1902-

*Journal of Obstetrics and Gynecology of the British
Empire. London, 1902-
*Marcellia. Avellino, 1902-
*Mitteilungen zur Geschichte der Medizin und der
Naturwissenschaften. Hamburg; etc., 1902-
Société Mycologique de France, Bulletin trimestriel.
Paris, 1902-1914.

1903   *Annales de médecine vétérinaire. Brussels, 1903-
Annales Mycologici. Berlin, 1903-1917.
*Archiv für Reformations-Geschichte. Leipzig, 1903-
*Institut Pasteur, Bulletin. Paris, 1903-
*Internationales Zentralblatt für Ohrenheilkunde und
Rhinolaryngologie. Wurzburg; Leipzig, 1903-
Journal de chimie physique et de physico-chimie bio-
logique. Geneva, 1903-1905.
Review of Neurology and Psychiatry. Edinburgh, 1903-
1919.
*Rivista di clinica pediatrica. Florence, 1903-

1904   *Folia Haematologica. Berlin; Leipzig, 1904-
*Journal of Philosophy, Psychology and Scientific
Method. New York, 1904-
Physikalisch-chemisches Zentralblatt. Leipzig, 1904-
1909.
*Psychological Bulletin. Lancaster, Pa.; etc., 1904-
*Revue de métallurgie. Paris, 1904-
*Société Scientifique d'Hygiène Alimentaire et de
l'Alimentation Rationelle de l'Homme, Bulletin.
Paris, 1904-
Zentralblatt für normale Anatomie und Mikrotechnik.
Berlin; Vienna, 1904-1914.

1906   *Ceramic Society, Transactions. Stoke-on-Trent,
1906-
Hygienisches Zentralblatt. Leipzig, 1906-1909.
Journal of Abnormal Psychology. Boston; Albany,
N.Y., 1906-1914.
*Kolloid-Zeitschrift. Dresden; Leipzig, 1906-
*Nederlandsch Tijdschrift voor Geneeskunde. Amster-
dam, 1906-
*Revue française de gynécologie et d'obstétrique.
Paris, 1906-
*Times Official Index. London, 1906-
*Zentralblatt für die gesamte Tuberkuloseforschung.
Berlin; Wurzburg, 1906-

1907   *American Gas Association, Bulletin of Abstracts.
            Easton, Pa. , 1907-
        *Archives des maladies de l'appareil digestif et de la
            nutrition. Paris, 1907-
        *Chemical Abstracts. Columbus, 1907-
        *Revue des sciences philosophiques et théologiques.
            Paris; etc. , 1907-
        *Zeitschrift für Urologie. Berlin; Leipzig, 1907-
        Zentralblatt für chirurgische und mechanische Ortho-
            pädie. Berlin, 1907-1919.

1908   Economic Geology. Lancaster, Pa. , 1908-1918.
        *Igiene moderna. Genoa, 1908-
        *Internationale Revue der gesamten Hydrobiologie und
            Hydrographie. Leipzig, 1908-
        *Journal de chirurgie. Paris, 1908-
        *Revue d'orthopédie. Paris, 1908-
        *Rocznik slawistyczny. Krakow, 1908-

1909   Fortschritte der Technik. Berlin, 1909-1910.
        *Institute of Metals, Journal. London, 1909-
        *International Sugar Journal. Manchester; London;
            etc. , 1909-
        *Mining Magazine. London, 1909-
        *Office Internationale d'Hygiène Publique, Bulletin
            mensuel. Paris, 1909-
        Technische Auskunft. Berlin, 1909-1913.
        *Zeitschrift für Botanik. Jena, 1909-
        *Zentralblatt für Herz- und Gefässkrankheiten. Dres-
            den; Leipzig, 1909-

1910   *Annales des postes, télégraphes et téléphones.
            Paris, 1910-
        *Bibliographia Evolutionis. Paris, 1910-1914; 1919-
        *International Institute of Refrigeration, Monthly Bulle-
            tin. Paris, 1910-
        *International Review of the Science and Practice of
            Agriculture. Rome, 1910-
        Journal of American Folklore. Boston; New York;
            Lancaster, Pa. , 1910-1911.
        *Zeitschrift für die gesamte Neurologie und Psychia-
            trie. Munich; Breslau; Berlin, 1910-
        *Zentralblatt für Biochemie und Biophysik. Leipzig,
            1910-
        Zentralblatt für Roentgenstrahlen und verwandte
            Gebiete. Wiesbaden, 1910-1919.

1911   *American Economic Review.   Ithaca, N.Y. , 1911-
        American Journal of Diseases of Children.   Chicago,
            1911-1912.
        Année pédogogique.   Paris, 1911-1913.
        *Great Britain, Imperial Institute, Bulletin.   London,
            1911-
        *Internationale Mitteilungen für Bodenkunde.   Berlin;
            etc. , 1911-
        Jahresbericht über die Fischereiliteratur.   Neudamm,
            1911-1912.
        Review of Bacteriology.   London, 1911-1919.
        *Zentralblatt für die gesamte Kinderheilkunde.   Ber-
            lin, 1911-

1912   *Creamery and Milk Plant Monthly.   Chicago, 1912-
        *Jahrbuch der Moorkunde.   Hanover, 1912-
        *Journal d'urologie médicale et chirurgicale.   Paris,
            1912-
        *Kongresszentralblatt für die gesamte innere Medizin
            und ihre Grenzgebiete.   Berlin, 1912-
        *Mechanical Engineering.   New York, 1912-
        *Sociedad Española de Física y Química, Anales.
            Madrid, 1912-
        *Tropical Diseases Bulletin.   London, 1912-
        *Tropical Veterinary Bulletin.   London, 1912-
        *Zeitschrift für Pflanzenzüchtung.   Berlin, 1912-
        *Zeitschrift für technische Biologie.   Leipzig, 1912-
        *Zentralblatt der experimentellen Medizin.   Berlin;
            Vienna, 1912-1914.
        Zentralblatt für Zoologie.   Leipzig, 1912-1918.

1913   *General Electric Co. , Lamp Development Laboratory,
            Abstract Bulletin.   Cleveland, 1913-
        *International Abstract of Surgery.   Chicago, 1913-
        *Journal of Ecology.   London, 1913-
        *Moslem World.   New York, 1913-
        *New York Times Index.   New York, 1913-
        *Review of Applied Entomology.   London, 1913-
        Zentralblatt für die gesamte Gynäkologie.   Berlin,
            1913-1914.
        Zentralblatt für Gewerbehygiene und Unfallverhütung.
            Berlin, 1913-1915.
        *Zentralorgan für die gesamte Chirurgie.   Berlin;
            Leipzig, 1913-

1914   *Ancient Egypt.   London, 1914-

[1914] *Archives suisses d'anthropologie générale. Geneva,
            1914-
        *Auk. Boston; New York; etc. , 1914-
        *Giesserei. Munich, 1914-
        *Journal de radiologie et d'électrologie. Paris, 1914-
        *Radiologia medica. Milan; Turin, 1914-
        *Wiener tierärztliche Monatsschrift. Vienna, 1914-
        *Zeitschrift für angewandte Entomologie. Berlin,
            1914-
        *Zentralblatt für die gesamte Ophthalmologie und ihre
            Grenzgebiete. Berlin, 1914-

1915   *Eastman Kodak Co. , Research Laboratory, Monthly
            Abstract Bulletin. Rochester, N.Y. , 1915-

1916   *Malattie del cuore. Rome, 1916-
        *Physiological Abstracts. London, 1916-

1917   *Abstracts of Bacteriology. Baltimore, 1917-
        *Abstracts of Tuberculosis. Baltimore, 1917-
        *American Journal of Syphilis. St. Louis, 1917-
        *Hahnemannian Monthly. Philadelphia, 1917-
        Journal of Applied Psychology. Worcester, Mass. ;
            Bloomington, Ind. , 1917.
        *Mental Hygiene. Concord, N.H. , 1917-
        *Society of Glass Technology, Journal. London,
            1917-
        *Society of Leather Trades' Chemists, Journal.
            Leeds; London, 1917-

1918   *American Journal of Physical Anthropology. Wash-
            ington, 1918-
        *Botanical Abstracts. Baltimore, 1918-
        *Chimie et industrie. Paris, 1918-
        *Technical Review. London, 1918-
        *Textile Institute, Journal. Manchester, Eng. , 1918-

1919   *Abstract of the Literature of Industrial Hygiene and
            Toxicology. Cambridge, Mass.; etc. , 1919-
        *Archives of Neurology and Psychiatry. Chicago,
            1919-
        *Ceramic Abstracts. Easton, Pa. , 1919-
        *International Journal of Orthodontia, Oral Surgery
            and Radiography. St. Louis, 1919-
        *Medical Science Abstracts and Reviews. London,
            1919-
        *Revue universelle des mines. Liège, 1919-

1920   *Abstracts from Recent Medical and Public Health
            Papers. Washington, 1920-
        *American Journal of Obstetrics and Gynecology.
            St. Louis, 1920-
        *Archives of Dermatology and Syphilology.   Chicago,
            1920-
        *Berichte über die gesamte Physiologie und experi-
            mentelle Pharmakologie. Berlin, 1920-
        *Gynécologie et obstétrique. Paris, 1920-
        *International Medical and Surgical Survey.   New
            York, 1920-
        *International Medical Digest.   New York, 1920-
        *Mineralogical Abstracts.   London, 1920-
        *Physikalische Berichte.   Brunswick, 1920-
        *Revue de géologie et des sciences connexes.   Liêge,
            1920-
        *Revue générale des travaux astronomiques.   Paris,
            1920-
        *Zentralblatt für die gesamte Landwirtschaft.   Leip-
            zig, 1920-

SUBJECT CLASSIFIED LIST OF ABSTRACT JOURNALS, 1790-1920†

Generalities

1. Journal des sçavans. Paris, 1665-1792; 1797.

2. Universal Magazine of Knowledge and Pleasure. London, 1747-1815.

3. Monthly Review. London, 1749-1844.

4. Journal encyclopédique ou universel. Liège; Brussels, 1756-1793.

5. Esprit des journaux, français et étrangers. Paris, 1772-1815; 1817-1818.

6. Analytical Review. London, 1788-1799.

7. *Times Official Index. London, 1906-

8. *New York Times Index. New York, 1913-

Pure Sciences

General

9. Retrospect of Philosophical, Mechanical, Chemical and Agricultural Discoveries. London, 1805-1813.

---

†The numbers in this list correspond to those in Fig. 7, Subject Diffusion of Abstract Journals, 1790-1920, pp. 138-144.

*See footnote to Appendix I, p. 198.

10. *American Journal of Science. New Haven, Conn.,
     1820-

11. Bulletin des sciences mathématiques, astronomiques,
     physiques et chimiques. Paris, 1823/24-1831.

12. Bulletin des sciences naturelles et de géologie. Paris,
     1823/24-1831.

13. Annales de chimie et de physique. Paris, 1851-1873.

14. *Revue des questions scientifiques. Louvain; etc.,
     1877-

15. Science. New York; etc., 1883.

16. Naturwissenschaftliche Rundschau. Brunswick, 1886-
     1912.

17. Revue générale des sciences pures et appliquées.
     Paris, 1890-1891.

18. *Mitteilungen zur Geschichte der Medizin und der
     Naturwissenschaften. Hamburg; etc., 1902-

Mathematics

19. *Jahrbuch über die Fortschritte der Mathematik. Ber-
     lin, 1868-

20. *Bulletin des sciences mathématiques. Paris, 1870-

21. *Revue semestrielle des publications mathématiques.
     Amsterdam, 1893-

Astronomy

22. *Astronomischer Jahresbericht. Berlin, 1899-

23. *Revue générale des travaux astronomiques. Paris,
     1920-

Physics

24. Fortschritte der Physik. Berlin; Brunswick, 1845-1918.

25. *Journal de physique et le radium. Paris, 1872-

26. Annalen der Physik, Beiblätter. Halle; Leipzig, 1877-
    1919.

27. *Abstracts of Physical Papers from Foreign Sources.
    London, 1895-1897.

28. *Science Abstracts. London, 1898-

29. *Sociedad Española de Física y Química, Anales.
    Madrid, 1912-

30. *Physikalische Berichte. Brunswick, 1920-

31. *Electrical World. New York, 1894-

32. *General Electric Co., Lamp Development Laboratory,
    Abstract Bulletin. Cleveland, 1913-

Chemistry

33. Neues chemisches Archiv. Leipzig, 1783-1791.

34. Chemische Annalen für die Freunde der Naturlehre,
    Arzneygelahrtheit, Haushaltungskunst und Manu-
    facturen. Helmstaedt; Leipzig, 1784-1804.

35. Chemische Annalen für die Freunde der Naturlehre,
    Arzneygelahrtheit, Haushaltungskunst und Manu-
    facturen, Beiträge. Helmstaedt; Leipzig, 1785-
    1799.

36. *Chemisches Zentralblatt. Leipzig; Berlin, 1830-

37. Répertoire de chimie pure. Paris, 1858-1863.

38. *Société Chimique de France, Bulletin. Paris, 1863-

39. *Chemical Society, Journal. London, 1871-

40. Repertorium der analytischen Chemie. Hamburg, 1881-
    1887.

41. *Analyst. London, 1884-

42. Review of American Chemical Research. Cambridge,
    Mass.; Easton, Pa., 1895-1906.

43. Journal de chimie physique et de physico-chimie biologique. Geneva, 1903-1905.

44. *Kolloid-Zeitschrift. Dresden; Leipzig, 1906-

45. *Chemical Abstracts. Columbus, 1907-

46. Physikalisch-chemisches Zentralblatt. Leipzig, 1904-
1909.

47. *Annales de chimie analytique et de chimie appliquée.
Paris, 1896-

Mineralogy

48. Taschenbuch für die gesamte Mineralogie. Frankfurt
a. M.; Heidelberg, 1807-1829.

49. *Neues Jahrbuch für Mineralogie, Geologie, und Paläontologie. Heidelberg; Stuttgart, 1830-

50. *Zeitschrift für Kristallographie. Leipzig, 1877-

51. Mineralogical Magazine. London, 1876-1903.

52. *Mineralogical Abstracts. London, 1920-

Geology

53. Geological Record. London, 1874-1879.

54. *Geologisches Zentralblatt. Leipzig; Berlin, 1901-

55. Economic Geology. Lancaster, Pa., 1908-1918.

56. *Revue de géologie et des sciences connexes. Liège,
1920-

Life Sciences

57. Institut Pasteur, Annales. Paris, 1887-1888.

58. *Zentralblatt für Bakteriologie und Parasitenkunde.
Jena, 1887-

59. *Royal Microscopical Society, Journal. London, 1878-

60.   *Zeitschrift für wissenschaftliche Mikroskopie und für
      mikroskopische Technik. Stuttgart, 1884-

61.   Zentralblatt für Anthropologie. Brunswick; etc. , 1896-
      1912.

62.   *Archives suisses d'anthropologie générale. Geneva,
      1914-

63.   *American Journal of Physical Anthropology. Washing-
      ton, 1918-

64.   *Archives italiennes de biologie. Pisa; Rome; etc. ,
      1894-

65.   *Année biologique. Paris, 1895-

66.   Biochemisches Zentralblatt. Berlin; Leipzig, 1902-1909.

67.   *Internationale Revue der gesamten Hydrobiologie und
      Hydrographie. Leipzig, 1908-

68.   *Bibliographia Evolutionis. Paris, 1910-1914; 1919-

69.   *Institut Pasteur, Bulletin. Paris, 1903-

70.   Review of Bacteriology. London, 1911-1919.

71.   *Abstracts of Bacteriology. Baltimore, 1917-

72.   *Berichte über die gesamte Physiologie und experimen-
      telle Pharmakologie. Berlin, 1920-

73.   *Zentralblatt für Biochemie und Biophysik. Leipzig,
      1910-

74.   *Journal of Ecology. London, 1913-

                              Botany

75.   *Société Botanique de France, Bulletin. Paris, 1854-

76.   Hedwigia. Dresden, 1863-

77.   *Botanischer Jahresbericht. Berlin; Leipzig, 1873-

78.   *Botanisches Zentralblatt. Cassel; Jena, 1880-

79. *Botanische Jahrbücher für Systematik, Pflanzenge-
     schichte und Pflanzengeographie. Leipzig, 1884-

80. *Revue bryologique. Caen; Paris, 1882-

81. *Zeitschrift für Botanik. Jena, 1909-

82. *Botanical Abstracts. Baltimore, 1918-

83. Annales Mycologici. Berlin, 1903-1917.

Zoology

84. Monitore zoologico Italiano. Sienna, 1890-1913.

85. Zoologisches Zentralblatt. Leipzig, 1894-1911.

86. Zentralblatt für Zoologie. Leipzig, 1912-1918.

87. Zentralblatt für normale Anatomie und Mikrotechnik.
     Berlin; Vienna, 1904-1914.

88. *Physiological Abstracts. London, 1916-

89. *Review of Applied Entomology. London, 1913-

90. *Auk. Boston; New York; etc. , 1914-

Medicine

General

91. Notizen aus dem Gebiete der Natur- und Heilkunde.
     Erfurt; Weimar, 1821-1849.

92. Bulletin des sciences médicales. Paris, 1823/24-1831.

93. Summarium des Neuesten aus der gesamten Medicin.
     Leipzig, 1828-1843.

94. Bolletino delle scienze mediche. Bologna, 1829-1835.

95. *Schmidts Jahrbücher der in- und ausländischen Medicin.
     Bonn; Leipzig, 1834-

96. American Medical Intelligencer. Philadelphia, 1837-
     1842.

97. Retrospect of Medicine. New York; London, 1840-1901.

98. Encyclographie médicale. Paris, 1842-1846.

99. Medical News. Philadelphia; New York, 1843-1905.

100. Half-Yearly Abstract of the Medical Sciences. London,
     1845-1873.

101. Tagsberichte über die Fortschritte der Natur- und
     Heilkunde. Weimar, 1850-1852.

102. British Medical Journal. London, 1857-1867.

103. *Münchener medizinische Wochenschrift. Munich,
     1859-

104. Zentralblatt für die medizinischen Wissenschaften.
     Berlin, 1863-1915.

105. *New York Medical Journal. New York, 1865-

106. Revue des sciences médicales en France et à l'étranger.
     Paris, 1873-1898.

107. Monthly Abstract of Medical Science. Philadelphia,
     1874-1879.

108. Epitome; a Monthly Retrospect. New York, 1880-1889.

109. *Zentralblatt für innere Medizin. Leipzig, 1880-

110. *American Medical Association, Journal. Chicago,
     1883-

111. *Fortschritte der Medizin. Berlin, 1883-

112. Epitome of Medicine. New York, 1884-1893.

113. Medical Chronicle. Manchester, Eng., 1884-1916.

114. *Brasil-medico. Rio de Janeiro, 1887-

115. *Epitome of Current Medical Literature. London,
     1890-

116. Zentralblatt für die Grenzgebiete der Medizin und

Chirurgie. Jena, 1897-1917.

117. *Nederlandsch Tijdschrift voor Geneeskunde. Amsterdam, 1906-

118. *Kongresszentralblatt für die gesamte innere Medizin und ihre Grenzgebiete. Berlin, 1912-

119. Zentralblatt der experimentellen Medizin. Berlin; Vienna, 1912-1914.

120. *Hahnemannian Monthly. Philadelphia, 1917-

121. *Medical Science Abstracts and Reviews. London, 1919-

122. *International Medical and Surgical Survey. New York, 1920-

123. *International Medical Digest. New York, 1920-

Physiology

124. *Zentralblatt für Physiologie. Leipzig, 1887-

125. Zeitschrift für Psychologie und Physiologie der Sinnesorgane. Hamburg; Leipzig, 1890-1906.

126. *Journal de physiologie et de pathologie générale. Paris, 1899-

127. *Société Scientifique d'Hygiène Alimentaire et de l'Alimentation Rationelle de l'Homme, Bulletin. Paris, 1904-

128. *Zentralblatt für Herz- und Gefässkrankheiten. Dresden; Leipzig, 1909-

129. *Zeitschrift für technische Biologie. Leipzig, 1912-

Hygiene

130. *Igiene moderna. Genoa, 1908-

131. *Office Internationale d'Hygiène Publique, Bulletin mensuel. Paris, 1909-

Public Health

132. *Annales d'hygiène publique. Paris, 1872-

133. *Revue d'hygiène et de police sanitaire. Paris, 1879-

134. Zentralblatt für allgemeine Gesundheitspflege. Bonn, 1882-1915.

135. *Hygienische Rundschau. Berlin, 1891-

136. Hygienisches Zentralblatt. Leipzig, 1906-1909.

137. *Abstracts from Recent Medical and Public Health Papers. Washington, 1920-

Pharmacology and Therapeutics

138. Archiv der Pharmazie. Berlin, 1843-1889.

139. *Journal de pharmacie et de chimie. Paris, 1845-

140. *American Journal of Pharmacy. Philadelphia, 1856-

141. *Yearbook of Pharmacy. London, 1864-

142. Zentralblatt für die gesamte Therapie. Vienna; Berlin, 1883-1917.

143. *Therapeutic Notes. Detroit, 1894-

144. *Zeitschrift für physikalische und diätetische Therapie. Leipzig; Berlin, 1898-

145. *Bulletin des sciences pharmacologiques. Paris, 1899-

146. Zentralblatt für Roentgenstrahlen und verwandte Gebiete. Wiesbaden, 1910-1919.

147. *Journal de radiologie et d'électrologie. Paris, 1914-

148. *Radiologia medica. Milan; Turin, 1914-

Diseases

149. *Annales médico-psychologiques. Paris, 1843-

150.   *Jahrbuch für Kinderheilkunde. Berlin, 1858-

151.   *Dental Cosmos. Philadelphia, 1860-

152.   *Annales de dermatologie et de syphilographie. Paris,
       1868-

153.   *Journal of Nervous and Mental Disease. Chicago,
       1874-

154.   *Annales des maladies de l'oreille, du larynx, du nez
       et du pharynx. Paris, 1875-

155.   *Monatsschrift für Ohrenheilkunde und Laryngo-Rhinol-
       ogie. Berlin, 1877-

156.   Zentralblatt für Nervenheilkunde und Psychiatrie.
       Leipzig; etc. , 1878-1910.

157.   *Archiv für Kinderheilkunde. Stuttgart, 1880-

158.   *Revue de laryngologie, d'otologie et de rhinologie.
       Paris, 1880-

159.   *British Dental Journal. London, 1881-

160.   *Dermatologische Wochenschrift. Leipzig, 1882-

161.   *Neurologisches Zentralblatt. Leipzig, 1882-

162.   *Archives of Pediatrics. New York; etc. , 1884-

163.   *Internationales Zentralblatt für Laryngologie, Rhinol-
       ogie und verwandte Wissenschaften. Berlin,
       1884-

164.   *Journal of Laryngology, Rhinology, and Otology.
       London, 1887-

165.   *British Journal of Dermatology and Syphilis. London,
       1888-

166.   Zentralblatt für die Krankheiten der Harn- und Sexual-
       Organe. Hamburg; Leipzig, 1889-1906.

167.   *Zentralblatt für allgemeine Pathologie und pathologische
       Anatomie. Jena; Wurzburg, 1890-

168. *Excerpta Medica. Leipzig, 1891-

169. *Revue neurologique. Paris, 1893-

170. Laryngoscope. St. Louis, 1896-1918.

171. Zentralblatt für Kinderheilkunde. Leipzig, 1896-1917.

172. Dermatologisches Zentralblatt. Leipzig, 1897-1920.

173. *Archives de médecine des enfants. Paris, 1898-

174. *Zeitschrift für Tuberkulose. Leipzig, 1900-

175. Zentralblatt für die gesamte Physiologie und Pathologie
        des Stoffwechsels. Berlin; etc., 1900-1911.

176. *Internationales Zentralblatt für Ohrenheilkunde und
        Rhinolaryngologie. Wurzburg; Leipzig, 1903-

177. Review of Neurology and Psychiatry. Edinburgh,
        1903-1919.

178. *Rivista di clinica pediatrica. Florence, 1903-

179. *Folia Haematologica. Berlin; Leipzig, 1904-

180. *Zentralblatt für die gesamte Tuberkuloseforschung.
        Berlin; Wurzburg, 1906-

181. *Archives des maladies de l'appareil digestif et de la
        nutrition. Paris, 1907-

182. *Zeitschrift für Urologie. Berlin; Leipzig, 1907-

183. *Zeitschrift für die gesamte Neurologie und Psychiatrie.
        Munich; Breslau; Berlin, 1910-

184. American Journal of Diseases of Children. Chicago,
        1911-1912.

185. *Zentralblatt für die gesamte Kinderheilkunde. Berlin,
        1911-

186. *Journal d'urologie médicale et chirurgicale. Paris,
        1912-

187.   *Tropical Diseases Bulletin.   London, 1912-

188.   *Malattie del cuore.   Rome, 1916-

189.   *Abstracts of Tuberculosis.   Baltimore, 1917-

190.   *American Journal of Syphilis.   St. Louis, 1917-

191.   *Archives of Neurology and Psychiatry.   Chicago,
       1919-

192.   *Archives of Dermatology and Syphilology.   Chicago,
       1920-

Surgery and Ophthalmology

193.   Allgemeines Repertorium der gesamten deutschen
       medizinisch-chirurgischen Journalistik.   Leipzig,
       1827-1847.

194.   *Annales d'oculistique.   Paris, 1867-

195.   *Zentralblatt für Chirurgie.   Leipzig, 1874-

196.   Zentralblatt für praktische Augenheilkunde.   Leipzig,
       1877-1919.

197.   *Zeitschrift für orthopädische Chirurgie.   Stuttgart;
       Berlin, 1891-

198.   Zentralblatt für chirurgische und mechanische Ortho-
       pädie.   Berlin, 1907-1919.

199.   *Journal de chirurgie.   Paris, 1908-

200.   *Revue d'orthopédie.   Paris, 1908-

201.   *International Abstract of Surgery.   Chicago, 1913-

202.   *Zentralorgan für die gesamte Chirurgie.   Berlin;
       Leipzig, 1913-

203.   *Zentralblatt für die gesamte Ophthalmologie und ihre
       Grenzgebiete.   Berlin, 1914-

204.   *International Journal of Orthodontia, Oral Surgery and
       Radiography.   St. Louis, 1919-

Gynecology and Obstetrics

205. *Zentralblatt für Gynäkologie. Leipzig, 1877-

206. Kinderarzt. Neuwied; etc. , 1890-1920.

207. *Journal of Obstetrics and Gynecology of the British
      Empire. London, 1902-

208. *Revue française de gynécologie et d'obstétrique.
      Paris, 1906-

209. Zentralblatt für die gesamte Gynäkologie. Berlin,
      1913-1914.

210. *American Journal of Obstetrics and Gynecology.
      St. Louis, 1920-

211. *Gynécologie et obstétrique. Paris, 1920-

Veterinary Medicine

212. *Journal de médecine vétérinaire et de zootechnie.
      Lyons, 1876-

213. *Revue vétérinaire. Toulouse, 1876-

214. *American Veterinary Medical Association, Journal.
      New York, 1889-

215. *Tijdschrift voor Diergeneeskunde. Utrecht; Amster-
      dam, 1892-

216. *Deutsche tierärztliche Wochenschrift. Karlsruhe;
      Hanover, 1893-

217. *Annales de médecine vétérinaire. Brussels, 1903-

218. *Tropical Veterinary Bulletin. London, 1912-

219. *Wiener tierärztliche Monatsschrift. Vienna, 1914-

Applied Sciences and Technology

Inventions and Discoveries

220. Bulletin des sciences technologiques. Paris, 1823/24-
      1831.

221. Arcana of Science and Art. London, 1828-1838.

222. Year-Book of Facts in Science and Art. London,
      1838-1879/81.

223. Mois scientifique et industriel. Paris, 1899-1919.

Engineering

224. Bulletin des Neuesten und Wissenwürdigsten aus der
      Naturwissenschaft. Berlin, 1809-1813.

225. *Institution of Civil Engineers, Abstracts of Papers.
      London, 1875-

226. *Engineering Index. New York, 1884-

227. Repertorium der technischen Journal-Literatur. Ber-
      lin; Leipzig, 1899-1908.

228. Fortschritte der Technik. Berlin, 1909-1910.

229. Technische Auskunft. Berlin, 1909-1913.

230. *Technical Review. London, 1918-

231. *International Institute of Refrigeration, Monthly Bulle-
      tin. Paris, 1910-

232. *Mechanical Engineering. New York, 1912-

233. *Giesserei. Munich, 1914-

234. *Mining Magazine. London, 1909-

235. *Revue universelle des mines. Liège, 1919-

Agriculture

236. Bulletin des sciences agricoles et économiques.
      Paris, 1823/24-1831.

237. Société Nationale d'Horticulture, Journal. Paris,
      1855-1918.

238. *Biedermanns Zentralblatt für Agrikulturchemie und
      rationellen Landwirtschaftsbetrieb. Leipzig,
      1872-

239.   *Experiment Station Record. Washington, 1889-

240.   *Annales de Gembloux. Brussels, 1893-

241.   *International Review of the Science and Practice of
        Agriculture. Rome, 1910-

242.   *Internationale Mitteilungen für Bodenkunde. Berlin;
        etc., 1911-

243.   *Jahrbuch der Moorkunde. Hanover, 1912-

244.   *Zeitschrift für Pflanzenzüchtung. Berlin, 1912-

245.   *Zentralblatt für die gesamte Landwirtschaft. Leipzig,
        1920-

246.   *Zeitschrift für Pflanzenkrankheiten und Gallenkunde.
        Stuttgart, 1890-

247.   *Marcellia. Avellino, 1902-

248.   Société Mycologique de France, Bulletin trimestriel.
        Paris, 1902-1914.

249.   *Zeitschrift für angewandte Entomologie. Berlin,
        1914-

250.   *Forstliche Rundschau. Neudamm, 1900-

251.   *Journal of Forestry. Washington, 1902-

252.   *Creamery and Milk Plant Monthly. Chicago, 1912-

253.   Jahresbericht über die Fischereiliteratur. Neudamm,
        1911-1912.

Chemical Technology

254.   Chemisch-technische Mitteilungen der neuesten Zeit.
        Berlin, 1849-1887.

255.   Répertoire de chimie appliquée. Paris, 1858-1864.

256.   Chemisch-technisches Repertorium. Berlin, 1862-
        1901.

257.   *Society of Chemical Industry, Journal.   London, 1882-

258.   *Chemisch-technische Übersicht.   Cöthen; etc. , 1885-

259.   *Zeitschrift für angewandte Chemie.   Berlin; Leipzig,
         1888-

260.   *Chimie et industrie.   Paris, 1918-

261.   *Association des Chimistes de Sucrerie, Distilleries
         et Industries Agricoles de France et de l'Union
         Française, Bulletin.   Paris, 1893-

262.   *International Sugar Journal.   Manchester; London;
         etc. , 1909-

263.   *Chemische Umschau auf dem Gebiete der Fette,
         Oele, Wachse und Harze.   Hamburg, 1894-

264.   *American Gas Association, Bulletin of Abstracts.
         Easton, Pa. , 1907-

265.   *Ceramic Society, Transactions.   Stoke-on-Trent,
         1906-

266.   *Society of Glass Technology, Journal.   London, 1917-

267.   *Ceramic Abstracts.   Easton, Pa. , 1919-

268.   *Revue de Métallurgie.   Paris, 1904-

269.   *Institute of Metals, Journal.   London, 1909-

Manufacturing

270.   *Society of Leather Trades' Chemists, Journal.   Leeds;
         London, 1917-

271.   *Textile Institute, Journal.   Manchester, Eng. , 1918-

Social Sciences

Psychology

272.   Psychological Review.   Lancaster, Pa. ; etc. , 1894-1903.

273. *Année psychologique. Paris, 1897-

274. *Psychological Bulletin. Lancaster, Pa.; etc., 1904-

275. Journal of Abnormal Psychology. Boston; Albany,
      N.Y., 1906-1914.

276. Journal of Applied Psychology. Worcester, Mass.;
      Bloomington, Ind., 1917.

277. *Mental Hygiene. Concord, N.H., 1917-

Sociology

278. *Rivista internazionale di scienze sociali e discipline
      ausiliarie. Rome, 1895-

279. *American Journal of Sociology. Chicago, 1896-

280. Année sociologique. Paris, 1896-1912.

Political Science

281. Revue du droit et de la science politique en France
      et à l'étranger. Paris, 1894-1906.

Economics

282. Jahrbücher für Nationalökonomie und Statistik. Jena,
      1863-1870.

283. *Economic Journal. London, 1891-

284. *American Economic Review. Ithaca, N.Y., 1911-

285. Zentralblatt für Gewerbehygiene und Unfallverhütung.
      Berlin, 1913-1915.

286. *Abstract of the Literature of Industrial Hygiene and
      Toxicology. Cambridge, Mass.; etc., 1919-

Military Science

287. Bulletin des sciences militaires. Paris, 1823/24-1831.

Education

288. Année pédogogique. Paris, 1911-1913.

Commerce, Trade, Communication

289. *Great Britain, Imperial Inst., Bulletin. London, 1911-

290. *Annales des postes, télégraphes et téléphones. Paris,
      1910-

Folklore

291. Journal of American Folklore. Boston; New York;
      Lancaster, Pa., 1910-1911.

Geography

292. Bulletin des sciences géographiques. Paris, 1823/24-
      1831.

293. *Petermanns Mitteilungen aus Justus Perthes' Geograph-
      ischer Anstalt. Gotha, 1885-

294. *Bibliographie géographique. Paris, 1891-

History

295. Bulletin des sciences historiques, antiquités, philologie.
      Paris, 1823/24-1831.

296. *Revue historique. Paris, 1876-

297. *Goerres-Gesellschaft zur Pflege der Wissenschaft im
      katholischen Deutschland, Historisches Jahrbuch.
      Bonn, 1882-

298. *American Journal of Archaeology. Concord, N.H.;
      etc., 1885-

299. Tijdschrift voor Geschiedenis. Utrecht, 1898-1903.

300. *Ancient Egypt. London, 1914-

301. *Rivista storica Italiana. Turin, 1896-

Humanities

Philosophy

302. *Mind. London; etc., 1876-

303.   *Journal of Philosophy, Psychology and Scientific
       Method. New York, 1904-

304.   *Revue des sciences philosophiques et théologiques.
       Paris; etc. , 1907-

Religion

305.   Revue de l'histoire des religions. Paris, 1880-1901.

306.   *Moslem World. New York, 1913-

307.   *Analecta Bollandiana. Brussels, 1895-

308.   *Archiv für Reformations-Geschichte. Leipzig; Berlin,
       1903-

Languages

309.   *Berliner philologische Wochenschrift. Berlin; Leipzig,
       1881-

310.   *Rocznik slawistyczny. Krakow, 1908-

311.   Ecole Française d'Extrême-Orient, Bulletin. Hanoi,
       1901-1916.

Numismatics

312.   Numismatic Chronicle. London, 1861-1896.

Photography

313.   *Eastman Kodak Co. , Research Laboratory, Monthly
       Abstract Bulletin. Rochester, N.Y. , 1915-

APPENDIX IV

INDEXING PUBLICATIONS APPEARING INDEPENDENTLY
OF JOURNAL PUBLICATION

Generalities

Poole's Index to Periodical Literature (Boston, 1848-1908).
  Comment: Covers the years 1802-1906: v. 1, 1802-
  1881; 1st suppl. 1882-86; 2d suppl. 1887-91; 3d
  suppl. 1892-96; 4th suppl. 1897-1901; 5th suppl.
  1902-06.

Index to Current Literature (London, 1859-61).
  Comment: Author-subject index; quarterly.

Monthly Index to Current Periodical Literature, Proceedings
  of Learned Societies, and Government Publications.
  (New York, 1880-1881).
  Comment: Originally published under the title: The
  Index April 1877-June, 1880; incorporated with
  American Bookseller.

Cooperative Index to Periodicals (New York, 1883-91).
  Comment: Continued by Annual Literary Index.

Periodical Press Index (London, 1889).
  Comment: No. 1, May 15, 1889. No more published.

Weekly Review of Newspapers and Periodical Literature
  (Boston, 1891-93).

Annual Literary Index (New York, 1892-1904).
  Comment: Continues the Cooperative Index to Periodicals; continued by Annual Library Index.

Bibliographie de belgique, sommaire des périodiques (The
  Hague, 1897-1914; 1921-25).

Bibliographie der deutschen Zeitschriftenliteratur (Leipzig, 1896-   ).

Cumulative Index to a Selected List of Periodicals (Cleveland, 1896-1903).
    Comment: Merged into Readers' Guide to Periodical Literature.

Répertoire bibliographique des principales revues françaises (Paris, 1897-99).

Readers' Guide to Periodical Literature (New York, 1901-   ).
    Comment: Absorbed Cumulative Index ... in 1903, and Annual Library Index in 1911.

Annual Library Index (New York, 1905-10).
    Comment: Continues Annual Literary Index; absorbed by Readers' Guide.

Library Index to Periodicals and Current Events (N.Y., 1905-07).

What's in the Magazines (Chicago, 1906-08).

International Index to Periodicals (New York, 1907/15-   ).
    Comment: 1907-19, supplement to Readers' Guide.

Annual Magazine Subject Index (Boston, 1907-49).
    Comment: 1908-12, in Bulletin of Bibliography.

Nijhoff's index op de Nederlandsche periodieken van algemeenen inhoud (The Hague, 1909-   ).

Bibliographie der fremdsprachigen Zeitschriftenliteratur (Leipzig, 1911-   ).

Repertorium op de Nederlandsche tijdsschriften (The Hague, 1914-21).

Dansk Tidsskrift Index (Copenhagen, 1915-   ).
    Comment: annual.

Subject-Index to Periodicals (London, 1915-61).

Norsk Tidsskrift Index (Oslo, 1918-   ).

Pure Sciences

General

Bibliographie scientifique française (Paris, 1902-   ).
  Comment: A bi-monthly, subject classified index to the
    periodical literature.

Royal Society of London, International Catalog of Scientific
  Literature (London, 1902-21).
  Comment: An annual bibliography of books and articles
    in a large number of periodicals; its purpose was to
    attempt to record all original contributions since
    January 1, 1901; publication suspended after the is-
    sue for 1914; continued its Catalogue of Scientific
    Papers, 1867-1925, which covered the scientific
    literature of the nineteenth century.

Physics

Halbmonatliches Literaturverzeichnis der Fortschritte der
  Physik (Berlin, 1902-19).
  Comment: A semi-monthly classified index to the liter-
    ature of physics; merged with Fortschritte der Phy-
    sik and Annalen der Physik Beiblätter to form Phy-
    sikalische Berichte.

Geology

Bibliografia Geologiczna Polski (Warsaw, 1914-   ).
  Comment: An annual classified subject bibliography.

Meteorological Office, London, Monthly Bibliography of Ac-
  cessions (London, 1919-   ).
  Comment: A UDC arrangement of references to current
    books and articles.

Zoology

Zoological Record (London, 1864-   ).
  Comment: An annual index to the zoological literature;
    v. 43-52, 1906-15 issued also as Section N of the
    International Catalogue of Scientific Literature.

Index to the Literature of American Economic Entomology
  (Melrose Highlands, Mass., 1905-   ).
  Comment: An annual publication.

Medicine

Index Medicus (Washington, 1879-1927).
 Comment: The standard current bibliography in medicine
  for the period covered; a classified list with annual
  author and subject indexes; included periodical articles and other analytics; merged into the Quarterly
  Cumulative Index Medicus.

Quarterly Cumulative Index to Current Medical Literature
 (Chicago, 1917-27).
 Comment: An author and subject index to medical per-
  iodical literature; merged with Index Medicus into
  Quarterly Cumulative Index Medicus.

Applied Sciences and Technology

General

Repertorium der technischen Journal-Literatur (Berlin, 1856-
 98).
 Comment: An alphabetical subject index to more than
  400 periodicals; covers the literature from 1823;
  from 1899 to 1908 included abstracts.

Bibliographie des sciences et de l'industrie (Paris, 1903-).

Industrial Arts Index (New York, 1913-).
 Comment: Monthly subject index to the periodical literature.

Agriculture

Agricultural Index (New York, 1916-).
 Comment: Alphabetical subject index to periodical literature.

Social Sciences

Sociology

Bibliographie der Sozialwissenschaft (Göttingen, 1905-).
 Comment: A classified list with annual author and subject indexes; comprehensive in scope.

Public Affairs Information Service, Bulletin (New York,
    1915-   ).
    Comment: A subject index to books, periodicals, pam-
        phlets, etc.

Law

Index to Legal Periodicals and Law Library Journal (New
    York, 1908-   ).
    Comment: Monthly author and subject index; 1936 is-
        sued in two independent parts.

Folklore

Volkskunde Bibliographie (Berlin, 1917-37/38).
    Comment: A very comprehensive bibliography of books
        and periodical articles; classified arrangement with
        author and subject indexes.

Geography

Bibliotheca Geographica (Berlin, 1891/92-1911/12).
    Comment: Important annual bibliography of books and
        periodical articles; classified arrangement; no anno-
        tations.

History

Bibliographie zur deutschen Geschichte (Leipzig, 1889-1927).
    Comment: An annual subject classified bibliography of
        books and periodical articles; issued as a supplement
        to the Historische Vierteljahrschrift.

Répertoire méthodique de l'histoire moderne et contemporaine
    de la France (Paris, 1898-1913).
    Comment: An annual classified bibliography.

Repertorium der verhandelingen en bijdragen betreffende de
    geschiedenis des vaderlands (Leiden, 1900-53).
    Comment: Comprehensive classified bibliography of books
        and periodical articles.

Writings on American History (Washington, 1902-   ).
    Comment: An annual classified bibliography of books
        and periodical articles.

Bibliographie der Schweizergeschichte (Zurich, 1913-).
   Comment: An annual classified bibliography.

Deutsches Archäologisches Institut, Archäologische Bibliographie (Berlin, 1913-).
   Comment: An annual bibliography of books and periodical articles.

Humanities

Psychology

Psychological Index (Lancaster, Pa. , 1894-1935).
   Comment: A classified subject bibliography of books
   and periodical articles.

Fine Arts

Handbuch der musikalischen Literatur (Leipzig, 1817-29).
   Comment: An alphabetical list, by composer or author,
   of music and musical writings; restricted to German
   works, subject and publishers' indexes, superseded
   by Deutsche Musikbibliographie.

Deutsche Musikbibliographie (Leipzig, 1829-).
   Comment: Supersedes Handbuch der musikalischen
   Literatur; cumulated in Hofmeister's Jahresverzeich-
   nis der deutschen Musikalien und Musikschriften.

Internationale Bibliographie der Kunstwissenschaft (Berlin,
   1902-17/18).
   Comment: An annual classified bibliography of books
   and periodical articles.

Répertoire d'art et d'archeologie (Paris, 1910-).
   Comment: An annual subject classified bibliography of
   books and periodical articles.

Literature

Bibliotheca Philologica Classica (Leipzig, 1874-1938).
   Comment: Annual.

Bibliographie Hispanique (New York, 1905-17).
   Comment: Annual bibliography of books and periodical
   articles.

Modern Humanities Research Association. Annual Bibliog-
  raphy of English Language and Literature (Cambridge,
  Eng. , 1920-).
  Comment: An annual bibliography of books and periodical
    articles.

Dramatic Index (Boston, 1909-).
  Comment: An annual subject index; issued also as part
    2 of the <u>Annual Magazine Subject Index.</u>

JOURNALS WHICH CONTAIN BIBLIOGRAPHIC SECTIONS NOTING CONTENTS OF OTHER JOURNALS

Generalities

Librarianship

Zentralblatt für Bibliothekswesens (Leipzig).
Section: "Neue Bücher und Aufsätze zum Bibliothek- und Buchwesen"
Dates: 1904-12; 1922-39
Comment: Subject classified bibliography of books and periodical articles; without annotations. Cumulated annually and issued separately as Bibliographie des Bibliotheks- und Buchwesens.

Library Work (Minneapolis).
Section: "Bibliography and Digest of Library Literature"
Dates: April 1906-October 1911
Comment: Bibliography of periodical articles relating to librarianship; cumulated in Library Work Cumulated with some additions to bring it down to the close of 1911, after which the work of indexing the periodical literature was continued by a section of Library Journal.

Het Boek (The Hague).
Section: "Inhoud van Tijdschriften"
Dates: 1912-
Comment: Bibliography of periodical articles; journal title arrangement; without annotations.

Library Journal (New York).
Section: "Bibliography and Digest of Library Literature" (varies)
Dates: 1911/12-1917/18
Comment: Bibliography of periodical articles; no annota-

tions; continues the work of Library Work; cumulated
annually in the American Library Annual, 1911/12-
1917/18. Replaced by Cannon's Bibliography of Library Economy, which was in turn superseded by
Library Literature.

Pure Sciences

General

Archiv für Naturgeschichte (Berlin).
  Section: "Auszüge"
  Dates: 1838-
  Comment: An annotated subject classified bibliography
    of periodical articles.

Nature (London).
  Section: "Scientific Serials"
  Dates: 1870-1902
  Comment: Bibliography of periodical articles; some an-
    notations; journal title arrangement.

Revue générale des sciences pures et appliquées (Paris).
  Section: "Sommaires des journaux scientifiques"
  Dates: 1901-
  Comment: Subject classified bibliography of periodical
    articles; without annotations; issued as a supplement
    to the Revue.

Astronomische Nachrichten (Kiel).
  Section: "Literarisches Beiblatt"
  Dates: 1912-1938
  Comment: An annual review type of bibliography.

Isis (Brussels).
  Section: "Bibliographie analytique" (Later "Critical Bib-
    liography of the History and Philosophy of Science
    and the History of Civilization")
  Dates: 1913-
  Comment: A quarterly classified bibliography of period-
    ical articles; with annotations.

Science Progress in the Twentieth Century (London).
  Section: "Recent Advances in Science"
  Dates: 1915-
  Comment: An annual review type of bibliography.

General Science Quarterly (Salem, Mass.).
   Section: "Science in Current Periodicals"
   Dates: 1917-
   Comment: Subject classified bibliography of periodical
      articles; without annotations.

Archivio di Storia della Scienze (Rome).
   Section: "Sommario dei Periodici"
   Dates: 1919-
   Comment: Bibliography of periodical articles; without
      annotations; journal title arrangement.

Chemistry

Fresnius Zeitschrift für analytische Chemie (Wiesbaden).
   Section: "Bericht über die Fortschritte der analytischen
      Chemie"
   Dates: 1862-
   Comment: An annual review type of bibliography

Journal de chimie physique et de physiochimie biologique
   (Geveva).
   Section: "Index des périodiques"
   Dates: 1906-
   Comment: Unannotated subject classified bibliography of
      periodical articles.

Life Sciences

Institut Pasteur, Annales (Paris).
   Section: "Revue et analyses"
   Dates: 1889-93
   Comment: An annual review type of bibliography.

Anthropologie (Paris).
   Section: "Bulletin bibliographique"
   Dates: 1894-1917
   Comment: Bibliography of periodical articles; without
      annotations; journal title arrangement.

Botany

Botanisk Tidsskrift (Copenhagen).
   Section: "Litteratur"
   Dates: 1866-
   Comment: Unannotated subject classified bibliography of
      periodical articles.

Botanische Jahrbücher für Systematik, Pflanzengeschichte und
    Pflanzengeographie (Leipzig).
    Section: "Übersicht der wichtigeren und umfassenden,
        im Jahre ... über Systematik, Pflanzengeschichte
        und Pflanzengeographie erschienen Arbeiten"
    Dates: 1881-
    Comment: 1881-83 issued as Part II; 1884- issued
        separately as a "Beiblatt;" subject classified bibliog-
        raphy of periodical articles; some annotations.

Revue bryologique (Caen).
    Section: "Bibliographie allemande [etc.]"
    Dates: 1882-
    Comment: Unannotated subject classified bibliography of
        periodical articles grouped by country of journal ori-
        gin.

Torrey Botanical Club, Bulletin (New York).
    Section: "Index to American Botanical Literature"
    Dates: 1886-
    Comment: A bi-monthly unannotated subject classified
        bibliography.

Annals of Botany (London).
    Section: "Record of Current Literature--Periodical
        Literature"
    Dates: 1887-91
    Comment: Bibliography of periodical articles; geographic
        arrangement; no annotations.

Zeitschrift für Botanik (Jena).
    Section: "Neue Literatur"
    Dates: 1909-
    Comment: Unannotated subject classified bibliography of
        periodical articles.

Botanischer Jahresbericht (Berlin).
    Section: "Verzeichnis der neuen Arten, Varietäten,
        Formen, Namen und wichtigsten Synonyme ..."
    Dates: 1920-
    Comment: An important classified bibliography on fungi;
        without annotations.

Zoology

Ibis (London).
    Section: "Recent Ornithological Publications"
    Dates: 1859-

Zoologischer Anzeiger (Leipzig).
>Section: "Bibliographia Zoologica" (through 1895 as "Literatur")
>Dates: 1878-
>Comment: Unannotated subject classified bibliography of periodical articles; 1896- , contains the zoological references as given by the Concilium Bibliographicum in book form, and issued separately as a supplement to Zoologischer Anzeiger.

Entomological News (Philadelphia).
>Section: "Entomological Literature"
>Dates: 1890-1902
>Comment: Annotated subject classified bibliography of periodical articles; 1890-96, journal title arrangement.

Monitore zoologico Italiano (Sienna).
>Section: "Bibliografia"
>Dates: 1890-1918
>Comment: Unannotated subject classified bibliography of periodical articles; appears intermittently during World War I and not again after 1918.

Medicine

Schmidt's Jahrbücher der in- und ausländischen gesamten Medizin (Bonn).
>Section: "Medizinische Bibliographie des In- und Auslands"
>Dates: 1834-
>Comment: Very extensive unannotated subject classified bibliography of books and periodical articles in the field of general medicine.

Half-Yearly Abstract of the Medical Sciences (London).
>Section: "Reports on the Progress of Medical Science"
>Dates: 1845-1873
>Comment: An annual review type of bibliography.

Pharmazeutische Zeitung (Berlin).
>Section: "Referate"
>Dates: 1855-
>Comment: Weekly unannotated bibliography of periodical articles.

Archiv für Augenheilkunde (Karlsruhe).
>Section: "Referate"

Dates: 1869-1937
Comment: An annual review type of bibliography.

Anatomischer Anzeiger (Jena).
    Section: "Internationale Bibliographie der Anatomie des
        Menschens und der Wirbeltiere" (varies)
    Dates: 1886-
    Comment: Important unannotated subject classified bib-
        liography of periodical articles.

Dental Cosmos (Philadelphia).
    Section: "Monthly Bibliography of Dental Literature"
    Dates: 1889-1902
    Comment: Unannotated subject classified bibliography of
        periodical articles.

Ergebnisse der allgemeine Pathologie und pathologischen
    Anatomie (Wiesbaden).
    Section: "Referate"
    Dates: 1894-
    Comment: An annual review type of bibliography.

Revista de ciencias veterinarias (Lisbon).
    Section: "Das Revistas"
    Dates: 1903-
    Comment: Quarterly unannotated bibliography of period-
        ical articles.

Eugenics Review (London).
    Section: "Periodical Literature"
    Dates: 1909-
    Comment: An annual review type of bibliography.

Laryngoscope (St. Louis).
    Section: "Index Medicus of Oto-Laryngology" (varies)
    Dates: 1909-18.
    Comment: Annotated subject classified bibliography of
        periodical articles; appeared annually.

Minerva Medica (Rome).
    Section: "Bibliografia"
    Dates: 1909-
    Comment: Extensive subject classified bibliography of
        periodical articles.

American Journal of Diseases of Children (Chicago)
    Section: "Index of Current Pediatric Literature" (varies)

Dates: 1912-19
Comment: Unannotated subject classified bibliography of
periodical articles.

American Journal of Public Health (Boston).
Section: "Current Public Health Literature"
Dates: 1914-
Comment: Unannotated bibliography of books and period-
ical articles; divided into American and foreign jour-
nals; subarranged by journal title.

Mental Hygiene (Concord, N. H.)
Section: "Current Bibliography"
Dates: 1917-
Comment: Author list of periodical articles with brief
annotations.

Social Hygiene (Baltimore).
Section: "Bibliography"
Dates: 1919-
Comment: Quarterly bibliography of books and periodical
articles; arranged by author; no annotations.

Applied Sciences and Technology

Engineering

Glückauf (Essen).
Section: "Zeitschriftenschau"
Dates: 1865-
Comment: Extensive unannotated subject classified bib-
liography of periodical articles.

Agriculture

Société Mycologique de France, Bulletin (Paris).
Section: "Index analytique"
Dates: 1885
Comment: Unannotated subject classified bibliography of
books and periodical articles.

Pochvovedenie (Leningrad).
Section: "Bibliografiya"
Dates: 1899-

Domestic Arts and Sciences

Journal of Home Economics (Baltimore).
    Section: "Bibliography of Home Economics"
    Dates: 1911
    Comment: Subject classified bibliography of periodical
        articles with some annotations.

Managerial services

Finanz-Archiv (Berlin)
    Section: "Bibliographie der finanzwissenschaftlichen
        Literatur für den Jahre ..."
    Dates: 1884-
    Comment: Unannotated subject classified bibliography of
        books and periodical articles.

Journal of Accountancy (New York).
    Section: "Periodical Literature" (varies)
    Dates: 1905-08
    Comment: Subject classified bibliography of periodical
        articles; no annotations; 1906-08; annual review type
        of bibliography.

Chemical Technology

Journal of Applied Chemistry (New York).
    Section: "Literature"
    Dates: 1866-75

Iron and Steel Institute, Journal (London).
    Section: 1874-85, "Report of the Progress of the Iron
        and Steel Industries of the United Kingdom in 18 ..."
        1886-   , "Notes on the progress of the Home and
        Foreign Iron and Steel Industries"
    Dates: 1874-
    Comment: An annual review type of bibliography.

Stahl und Eisen (Düsseldorf).
    Section: "Zeitschriftenschau"
    Dates: 1881-
    Comment: Bi-weekly unannotated subject classified
        bibliography of periodical articles.

Tages-zeitung für Brauerei (Berlin).
    Section: "Beziehungen"
    Dates: 1903-15

Chemical and Metallurgical Engineering (New York).
    Section: "Synopsis of Recent Chemical and Metallurgical
        Literature"
    Dates: 1905-
    Comment: An annual review type of bibliography.

Brennstoff-Chemie (Essen).
    Section: "Zeitschriftenschau"
    Dates: 1920-
    Comment: Monthly unannotated subject classified bibliog-
        raphy of periodical articles.

Glass Industry (New York).
    Section: "Bibliography"
    Dates: 1920-
    Comment: Subject classified bibliography of books and
        periodical articles; some annotations.

Manufacturing

Textile Institute, Journal (Manchester, Eng.).
    Section: "Textile Bibliography"
    Dates: 1910-15
    Comment: A subject classified bibliography of periodical
        articles and patents; includes some annotations.

Social Sciences

Sociology

Zeitschrift für die gesamte Staatswissenschaft (Tübingen).
    Section: "Zeitschriftenschau"
    Dates: 1883-85
    Comment: Unannotated bibliography of periodical arti-
        cles; journal title arrangement.

American Journal of Sociology (Chicago).
    Section: "Bibliography of Sociology" (varies)
    Dates: 1896-
    Comment: An author list of current books and articles.

Statistics

Royal Statistical Society, Journal (London).
    Section: "Statistical and Economic Articles in Recent
        Periodicals"

Dates: 1906-
Comment: Unannotated bibliography of periodical articles;
geographic arrangement.

Political Science

American Political Science Review (Baltimore).
Section: "Periodical Articles in Political Science"
Dates: 1906-
Comment: Unannotated subject classified bibliography of
periodical articles, books and government publica-
tions.

Economics

Jahrbücher für Nationalökonomie und Statistik (Jena).
Section: "Die periodische Presse des Auslands;" "Die
periodische Presse in Deutschland"
Dates: 1878-
Comment: Unannotated bibliography of periodical articles; continues the section which formerly carried
abstracts of the periodical literature.

Revue socialiste (Paris)
Section: "Revue des revues"
Dates: 1894-1906
Comment: An annual revue type of bibliography; 1903-
04; unannotated bibliography of periodical articles,
journal title arrangement.

Indian Journal of Economics (Allahabad).
Section: "Principal Contents of American Journals"
(through 1919 as "Principal Contents of Foreign
Journals")
Dates: 1916-
Comment: Unannotated bibliography of periodical articles;
journal title arrangement.

Law

Zeitschrift für das gesamte Handelsrecht und Konkursrecht
(Erlangen).
Section: "Literaturbericht" (varies)
Dates: 1858-89
Comment: Unannotated subject classified bibliography of
books and articles; through 1873 alphabetically ar-
ranged by author.

Journal du droit international (Paris).
    Section: "Bibliographie systématique de droit interna-
        tional privé ..."
    Dates: 1888-
    Comment: Annual unannotated subject classified bibliog-
        raphy of periodical articles.

Revue générale du droit (Paris).
    Section: "Bulletin bibliographique"
    Dates: 1894-

American Journal of International Law (New York).
    Section: "Periodical Literature of International Law"
    Dates: 1907-
    Comment: Unannotated subject classified bibliography of
        periodical articles.

American Institute of Criminal Law and Criminology, Journal
    (Chicago).
    Section: "Bibliography of Periodical Literature" (varies)
    Dates: 1910-Sept. 1914
    Comment: Unannotated subject classified (from 1912)
        bibliography of periodical articles.

Social Pathology

Oeuvre national de l'enfance (Paris).   Revue trimestriel.
    Section: "Chronique bibliographique"
    Dates: 1919-
    Comment: Unannotated bibliography of periodical arti-
        cles; journal title arrangement.

Education

Journal of Educational Psychology (Baltimore).
    Section: "Current Periodicals"
    Dates: 1911-16
    Comment: Unannotated bibliography of periodical arti-
        cles; journal title arrangement.

Folklore

Journal of American Folklore (Boston)
    Section: "Bibliographical Notes - Journals"
    Dates: 1888-1902
    Comment: Highly selective bibliography of periodical
        articles with brief annotations.

Zeitschrift des Vereins für Volkskunde (Berlin).
    Section: "Literatur des Jahres ..."
    Dates: 1891-
    Comment: Annual unannotated subject classified bibliography of periodical articles.

Geography

Petermanns Mitteilungen (Gotha).
    Section: "Literatur"
    Dates: 1857-84
    Comment: Highly selective bibliography of periodical articles; brief annotations.

Società Geografica Italiana, Bolletino (Rome).
    Selection: "Sommario di Articoli Geografici"
    Dates: 1875-
    Comment: Unannotated bibliography of periodical; arranged by author alphabetically.

Annales de geographie (Paris).
    Section: "Bibliographie géographique internationale"
        (varies)
    Dates: 1891-
    Comment: Extensive subject classified bibliography of periodical articles and books; 1891-1913/14 issued in or as a supplement to the Annales; 1915/19- issued independently.

Geographical Journal (London).
    Section: "Geographical Literature of the Month" (varies)
    Dates: 1893-
    Comment: Bibliography of periodical articles; geographical arrangement; annotated through 1909; 1918- issued as a supplement to Geographical Journal.

Journal of Geography (Lancaster, Pa.).
    Section: "Geographical Publications"
    Dates: 1902-

Geographical Review (New York).
    Section: "Geographical Publications"
    Dates: 1916-19
    Comment: Bibliography of periodical articles and books; geographical arrangement; some annotations.

Société Royale de Géographie d'Egypte, Bulletin (Cairo).
    Section: "Bulletin bibliographique"
    Dates: 1919-

History

Società Romana di Storia Patria, Archivio (Rome).
    Section: "Bibliografia"
    Dates: 1877-
    Comment: Bibliography of periodical articles; journal
        title arrangement; some annotations.

Historisk Tidsskrift (Copenhagen).
    Section: "Fortegnelse over dansk historisk Litteratur"
        and "Fortegnelse over fremmed historisk Litteratur"
    Dates: 1878-
    Comment: Bibliography of periodical articles; 1878-96,
        journal title arrangement, no annotations; 1897-   ,
        classified subject arrangement, no annotations.

Vienna, Institut für österreichische Geschichtsforschung,
        Mitteilungen (Vienna).
    Section: "Kurzerer Notizen"
    Dates: 1880-

Aachener Geschichts-Verein, Zeitschrift (Aachen).
    Section: "Literatur aus Zeitschriften" (varies)
    Dates: 1882-91; 1893-96
    Comment: Unannotated subject classified bibliography of
        periodical articles.

Rivista Storica Italiana (Turin).
    Section: "Spoglio delle Pubblicazione Periodice"
    Dates: 1884-1895
    Comment: Extensive bibliography of selected journal
        articles arranged by language then by journal title;
        many have annotations.

English Historical Review (London).
    Section: "Periodical Notices" (through 1894 as "Contents
        of Periodical Publications")
    Dates: 1886-1905
    Comment: Bibliography of periodical articles; 1886-94
        arranged by country and journal title and with anno-
        tations; 1895-1905, unannotated alphabetical title
        listing.

Zeitschrift für die Geschichte des Oberrheins (Karlsruhe).
    Section: "Zeitschriftenschau und Literatur Notizen"
    Dates: 1886-
    Comment: Unannotated subject classified bibliography of
       books and periodical articles.

Le Moyen age (Paris).
    Section: "Périodiques"
    Dates: 1888-1896; 1903-
    Comment: Journal title arrangement; contents noted with
       some annotations. For 1898 a classified bibliography
       without annotations was provided.

Revue des études grecques (Paris).
    Section: "Bibliographie annuelle des études grecques ..."
    Dates: 1888-
    Comment: 1800-1910 an annual unannotated subject clas-
       sified bibliography of books and periodical articles;
       1911- an annual revue type of bibliography.

Historische Zeitschrift (Munich).
    Section: "Bibliographie"
    Dates: 1890-
    Comment: Highly selective classified bibliography of
       periodical articles.

Tijdsschrift voor Geschiedenis (Utrecht).
    Section: "Bibliographie"
    Dates: 1904-
    Comment: An annual review type of bibliography

Personalhistorisk Tidsskrift (Stockholm).
    Section: "Fortegnelse over den danske og norske
       stamtavle litteratur ..."
    Dates: 1910-
    Comment: An annual unannotated bibliography of period-
       ical articles; arranged alphabetically by author.

Revue des études napoléoniennes (Paris).
    Section: "Bibliographie napoléonienne de l'année ..."
       (varies)
    Date: 1912-
    Comment: Bibliography of periodical articles and books;
       issued as an annual supplement to F. M. Kircheisen's
       "Bibliographie du temps de Napoleon."

Journal of Egyptian Archaeology (London)
    Section: "Bibliography"
    Dates: 1914
    Comment: An annual unannotated subject classified bibliography of periodical articles and books.

Hispanic American Historical Review (Baltimore).
    Section: "Recent Publications"
    Dates: 1918-
    Comment: Unannotated author list of recent articles; highly selective.

Canadian Historical Review (Toronto).
    Section: "Recent Publications Relating to Canada"
    Dates: 1920
    Comment: Subject classified bibliography of books and periodical articles; some annotations.

Syria (Paris).
    Section: "Bibliographie - Périodiques"
    Dates: 1920
    Comment: Selective annotated bibliography of periodical articles.

Humanities

Philosophy

Mind (London).
    Section: "Reports"
    Dates: 1879-88

Divus Thomas (Berlin).
    Section: "Bibliographie"
    Dates: 1887-
    Comment: Bibliography of periodical articles; journal title arrangement; no annotations.

Archiv für die gesamte Psychologie (Leipzig).
    Section: "Literaturbericht"
    Dates: 1903-15
    Comment: An annual review type of bibliography.

Rivista di Filosofia (Turin).
    Section: "Bibliografia"
    Dates: 1909-

Religion

Zeitschrift für katholische Theologie (Innsbruck).
Section: "Analecten"
Dates: 1876-

Zeitschrift für Kirchengeschichte (Gotha).
Section: "Bibliographie der kirchengeschichtlichen
Literatur ..."
Dates: 1884-97; 1905-
Comment: Unannotated subject classified bibliography of
books and periodical articles.

Journal of Theological Studies (London).
Section: "Periodicals"
Dates: 1899-

International Review of Missions (Edinburgh).
Section: "International Missionary Bibliography" (varies)
Dates: 1913-
Comment: Unannotated subject classified bibliography of
books and periodical articles.

Zeitschrift für Kirchengeschichte (Gotha, 1920-   ).
Section: "Literarische Umschau"
Dates: 1920-
Comment: An annual review type of bibliography.

Linguistics

American Journal of Philology (Baltimore).
Section: "Reports"
Dates: 1880-
Comment: Unannotated bibliography of periodical arti-
cles; journal title arrangement.

Studies in Philology (Chapel Hill, N. C.).
Section: "Recent Literature of the Renaissance"
Dates: 1917-
Comment: Annual classified bibliography of books and
periodical articles.

English Language

Modern Language Journal (New York).
Section: "Literature of Modern Language Methodology"
Dates: 1916-

Comment: An annual bibliography of periodical articles; journal title arrangement; some annotations.

Germanic Languages

Indogermanische Forschungen (Berlin).
   Section: "Bibliographie" (varies)
   Dates: 1891-

Leuvensche Bijdragen (The Hague).
   Section: "Inhoud van Tijdschriften"
   Dates: 1910-
   Comment: Unannotated bibliography of periodical articles; journal title arrangement.

Romance Languages

Jahrbuch für romanische und englische Sprache und Literatur (Berlin).
   Section: "Bibliographie"
   Dates: 1857-76
   Comment: An annual classified bibliography of periodical articles and books.

Revue des langues romanes (Montpellier).
   Section: "Bibliographie - Périodiques"
   Dates: 1872-1913
   Comment: Bibliography of periodical articles; journal title arrangement; no annotations.

Romania (Paris).
   Section: "Périodiques"
   Dates: 1872-
   Comment: Bibliography of periodical articles and books; journal title arrangement; no annotations.

Zeitschrift für romanische Philologie (Halle).
   Section: "Supplement Heft - Bibliographie"
   Dates: 1875-
   Comment: Unannotated bibliography of books and periodical articles.

Spanish and Portuguese Languages

Bulletin Hispanique (Bordeaux).
   Section: "Sommaire des revues"
   Dates: 1899-1911

    Comment: Bibliography of periodical articles; journal
       titles arrangement; some annotations.

Revista de Filologia Española (Madrid).
    Section: "Bibliografia"
    Dates: 1914-
    Comment: Unannotated subject classified bibliography of
       periodical articles.

Classical Languages

Revue de philologie (Paris).
    Section: "Bibliographie - Bulletin des Journaux"
    Dates: 1845-47
    Comment: Annotated bibliography of periodical articles;
       journal title arrangement.

Bolletino di Filologia Classica (Turin).
    Section: "Bibliografia"
    Dates: 1894-
    Comment: Highly selective bibliography of periodical
       articles; brief annotations.

Rivista di Filologia e di Istruzione Classica (Rome).
    Section: "Rassegna di Pubblicazione Periodiche"
    Dates: 1897-
    Comment: Unannotated bibliography of periodical arti-
       cles; journal title arrangement.

Classical Quarterly (London).
    Section: "Summaries of Periodicals"
    Dates: 1907-
    Comment: Bibliography of periodical articles; journal
       title arrangement; no annotations.

Other Languages

Deutsche Morgenländische Gesellschaft, Zeitschrift (Leip-
    zig).
    Section: "Bibliographische Anzeigen"
    Dates: 1849-60
    Comment: Bibliography of books and periodical articles;
       journal title arrangement; no annotations.

Zeitschrift für Assyriologie (Leipzig).
    Section: "Bibliographie"
    Dates: 1886-

Comment: Unannotated bibliography of periodical articles
and books; author arrangement.

Byzantinische Zeitschrift (Leipzig).
Section: "Bibliographische Notizen und kleine Mitteilungen"
Dates: 1892-
Comment: Unannotated subject classified bibliography of
books and periodical articles.

Orientalistische Literatur-Zeitung (Berlin).
Section: "Bibliographie"
Dates: 1898-

Deutsche Shakespeare Gesellschaft, Jahrbuch (Weimar).
Section: "Zeitschriftenschau"
Dates: 1899-
Comment: An annual review type of bibliography.

Finnisch-ugrische Forschungen (Helsinki).
Section: "Bibliographie der finnisch-ugrischen Sprache
und Volkskund für die Jahre ..."
Dates: 1901-

Rivista degli Studi Orientali (Rome).
Dates: 1907-
Comment: An annual review type of bibliography.

Fine Arts

Gazette des Beaux-Arts (Paris).
Section: "Bibliographie des ouvrages publiés en France
sur les beaux arts et à l'étranger"
Dates: 1859-
Comment: Unannotated subject classified bibliography of
books and periodical articles.

Literature

Deutsche Literaturzeitung (Leipzig).
Section: "Zeitschriften"
Dates: 1880-1919
Comment: Issued in three sections: 1) Books (classified
by subject; 2) Notices; 3) Periodical contents (subject
classified).   After 1920 covers books only.

Giornale Storico della Letteratura Italiana (Rome).
Section: "Cronaca - Periodici"

Dates: 1883-
Comment: Arranged by language, then journal title; no
annotations.

Euphorion (Leipzig).
Section: "Bibliographie"
Dates: 1894-1914
Comment: Extensive bibliography journal title arrange-
ment; contents notes without annotations.

Revue d'histoire littéraire de la France (Paris).
Section: "Périodiques"
Dates: 1894-
Comment: Unannotated bibliography of periodical arti-
cles; journal title arrangement.

Studi Medievali (Turin).
Section: "Bulletino Bibliografia"
Dates: 1904-11
Comment: Unannotated subject classified bibliography of
books and periodical articles.

MAJOR REVIEW JOURNALS

Pure Sciences

General
Naturhistorische Gesellschaft, Jahresbericht (Hannover, 1889-).

Mathematics
Deutsche Mathematiker Vereinigung, Jahresbericht (Bielefeld, 1892-).

Astronomy
Jahrbuch der Astronomie und Geophysik (Leipzig, 1890-1913).
Hamburg, Sternwarte, Jahresbericht (Hamburg, 1906-).

Physics
Physikalischer Verein, Jahresbericht (Frankfurt a. M., 1844/45-).

Chemistry
Annual Reports on the Progress of Chemistry (London, 1904-).
Fortschritte der Chemie, Physik und physikalische Chemie (Leipzig, 1909-1932).
Jahresbericht über die Fortschritte der Chemie und verwandte Theile anderer Wissenschaften (Brunswick, 1847-1910).

Geology
Oberrheinischer Geologischer Verein, Jahresberichte und Mitteilungen (Stuttgart, 18 -).

Life Sciences
Jahresbericht über die Fortschritte in der Lehre von den Gärungs-Organismen (Brunswick, 1890-1911).
Jahresbericht über die Fortschritte in der Lehre von den Pathogenen Mikroorganismen (Leipzig, 1885-1911).

Botany
Hamburg, Staatsinstitut für Angewandte Botanik, Jahresberichte (Hamburg, 1917/24-   ).

Zoology
Zoologischer Jahresbericht (Leipzig, 1879-1913)
Jahresbericht über die Fortschritte der Anatomie und Physi-
   ologie (Leipzig, 1892-1914).

Medicine

Jahresbericht über die Fortschritte der gesamten Medizin ...
   (Erlangen, 1841-65).
Yearbook of Medicine, Surgery, and Their Allied Sciences
   (London, 1859-64).
Jahresbericht der Pharmazie (Göttingen, 1866-   ).
Jahresbericht über die Leistungen und Fortschritte in der
   gesamten Medizin (Berlin, 1866-1916).
Jahresbericht über die Fortschritte der Thier Chemie ...
   (Wiesbaden, 1871-1919).
Jahresbericht über die Leistungen auf dem Gebiete der Veter-
   inär-Medizin (Berlin, 1880-1943).
Medical Annual and Practitioners Index (London, 1883-   ).
Annual of the Universal Medical Sciences (Philadelphia,
   1888-96).
Jahresbericht über die gesamte Chirurgie ... (Munich,
   1895-   ).
American Year-Book of Medicine and Surgery (Philadelphia,
   1896-1905).
Jahresbericht über die Leistungen und Fortschritte auf dem
   Gebiete der Neurologie und Psychiatrie (Berlin, 1897-
   1919).
Bibliographischer Jahresbericht über soziale Hygiene (Berlin,
   1900-21).
Medizinischer Klinik, Beiheft (Berlin, 1905-   ).

Applied Sciences and Technology

Agriculture
Jahresbericht über die Erfahrungen und Fortschritte auf dem
   Gesamtgebiete der Landwirtschaft (Brunswick, 1886-1916).
Jahresbericht für Agrikultur Chemie (Berlin, 1858-1933).
Jahresbericht über das Gebiet der Pflanzenkrankheiten (Ber-
   lin, 1898-1913).
Jahresbericht über die Fortschritte, veröffentlichen und

wichtigeren Ereignisse im Gebiete der Forst-, Jagd-,
und Fischereiwesens (Frankfurt a. M. , 1858-1915).

Chemical and Related Technologies
Jahresbericht über die Leistungen der chemischen Technologie
    (Leipzig, 1855-   ).
Reports of the Progress of Applied Chemistry (London,
    1916-   ).

Social Sciences

Geography
Geographisches Jahrbuch (Gotha, 1866-   ).
Geographische Gesellschaft, Jahresbericht (Bern, 1878/79-   ).
Geographischer Jahresbericht über Österreich (Vienna,
    1894-   ).

History
Jahresberichte der Geschichtswissenschaft (Berlin, 1878-1913).
Historical Association, London, Annual Bulletin of Historical
    Literature (London, 1911-   ).

Humanities

Religion
Theologischer Jahresbericht (Tübingen, 1881-1913).

Language and Linguistics
Jahresbericht über die Erscheinungen auf dem Gebiete der
    germanischen Philologie (Berlin, 1879-1936/39).
Kritischer Jahresbericht über die Fortschritte der romanis-
    chen Philologie (Erlangen, 1890-1912).
Year's Work in Classical Studies (London, 1906-45/47).
Year's Work in English Studies (London, 1919-   ).

Literature
Jahresbericht für neuere deutsche Literaturgeschichte (Ber-
    lin, 1890-1915).

LIST OF REFERENCES

Allen, Walter C., ed. Serial Publications in Large Libraries. Urbana: University of Illinois, Graduate School of Library Science, 1970.

American Association for the Advancement of Science. Proceedings ... 1882. Washington: 1883.

_____. Proceedings ... 1883. Washington: 1884.

_____. Proceedings ... 1894. Washington: 1895.

American Library Association. "Proceedings of the First Annual Meeting." Library Journal 1 (November 30, 1876): 92-145.

_____. Proceedings of the Annual Meeting." Library Journal 20 (December 1895): 1C-93C.

Barnes, Sherman B. "The Beginnings of Learned Journalism." Scientific Monthly (March 1934): 257-260.

Barr, K. P. "Estimates of the Number of Currently Available Scientific and Technical Periodicals." Journal of Documentation 23 (June 1967): 110-116.

Besterman, Theodore. The Beginnings of Systematic Bibliography. 2d ed. London: Oxford University Press, 1936.

Bishop, William W. "Historic Development of Library Buildings." In Library Buildings for Library Service. Edited by Herman H. Fussler. Chicago: American Library Association, 1947. pp. 1-11.

Blake, John B. and Roos, Charles, eds. Medical Reference Works, 1679-1966; a Selected Bibliography. Chicago: Medical Library Association, 1967.

Blanchard, Joy R. and Ostvold, Harald. The Literature of

277

    Agricultural Research. Berkeley: University of Califor-
    nia Press, 1958.

Bolton, Henry C. A Catalogue of Scientific and Technical
    Periodicals, 1665-1895. 2d ed. Washington: Smithson-
    ian Institution, 1897.

_____. "An International Index to Chemical Literature."
    Journal of the American Chemical Society 15 (October
    1893): 574-579.

Bourne, Charles P. "The World's Technical Journal Litera-
    ture: an Estimate of Volume, Origin, Language, Field,
    Indexing, and Abstracting." American Documentation 13
    (April 1962): 159-168.

Bradford, Samuel C. Documentation. Introduction by Jesse
    H. Shera and Margaret E. Egan. 2d ed. London:
    Lockwood, 1953.

British Association for the Advancement of Science. Report
    of the Twenty-Fifth Meeting ... Glasgow, 1855. London:
    John Murray, 1856.

Brockhaus Enzyklopädie in zwanzig Bänden, 17. Aufl. S.v.
    "Dokumentation."

Brodman, Estelle. The Development of Medical Bibliography.
    Washington: Medical Library Association, 1954.

Browne, Charles A. and Weeks, Mary E. A History of the
    American Chemical Society. Washington: American
    Chemical Society, 1952.

California. University. University at Los Angeles. School
    of Library Service. The Annals of Abstracting, 1665-
    1970. Edited by Robert L. Collison. Los Angeles:
    School of Library Service and University Library, Uni-
    versity of California, 1971.

Callisen, Adolph C. Medicinisches Schriftsteller-Lexicon der
    jetzt lebenden Aerzte, Wundarzte, Geburtshelfer, Apoth-
    eker, und Naturforscher aller gebildeten Volker. 33
    vols. Copenhagen: n.p., 1830-1845.

Casey, Robert S. and Perry, James W., eds. Punched
    Cards; Their Application to Science and Industry. 2d ed.
    New York: Reinhold, 1958.

Chandler, George. Libraries in the Modern World. New
York: Pergamon Press, 1965.

Clapp, Verner W. "Indexing and Abstracting; Recent Past
and Lines of Future Development." College and Research
Libraries 11 (July 1950): 197-206.

_____. "Indexing and Abstracting Services for Serial Lit-
erature." Library Trends 2 (April 1954): 509-521.

Clarke, Archibald. "Abstracts and Extracts in General Professional Literature." Library Association Record 13
(January 1911): 37-54.

Cobb, Ruth, comp. Periodical Bibliographies and Abstracts
for the Scientific and Technological Journals of the World.
Washington: National Research Council, 1920.

Collison, Robert L. Abstracts and Abstracting Services.
Santa Barbara, Calif., ABC-Clio, 1971.

Coulson, Thomas. Joseph Henry, His Life and Work.
Princeton: Princeton University Press, 1950.

Crane, Evan J.; Patterson, Austin M.; and Marr, Eleanor B.
A Guide to the Literature of Chemistry. 2d ed. New
York: Wiley, 1957.

Dane, Nathan. A General Abridgment and Digest of American Law. 9 vols. Boston: Cummings, Hilliard & Co.,
1823-29.

Davinson, Donald E. The Periodicals Collection; Its Purpose
and Uses in Libraries. London: Deutsch, 1969.

Dembowska, Maria. Documentation and Scientific Information;
Outline of Problems and Trends. Translated by Halina
Dunin. Warsaw: Scientific Publications Foreign Cooperation Center of the Central Institute for Scientific, Technical, and Economic Information, 1968.

Dictionary of American Biography. S. v. "Griswold, William McC," by Frederick W. Ashley.

Dictionary of Scientific Biography. S. v. "Arago, Dominique," by Roger Hahn.

_____. S. v. "Dunglison, Robley," by Samuel X. Radbill.

Dictionnaire de biographie française. S. v. "Delacour," by
    Roman d'Amat.

Dorosh, John, comp. A Guide to Soviet Bibliographies; a
    Selected List of References. New York: Greenwood
    Press, 1968.

Ember, George. Review of Adatok és felismerések a szakir-
    odalmi dokumentáció történerének kezdeteihez, by Iván
    Polzovics. American Documentation 16 (January 1965):
    39-40.

Encyclopedia Americana, 1974 ed. S. v. "Bibliography," by
    Verner W. Clapp.

Fleming, Thomas P. "Medical Abstracting Journals and Ser-
    vices." Special Libraries 52 (July 1962): 322-325.

Flynn, John E. A History of Biological Abstracts. Phila-
    delphia: 1951.

Foskett, D. J. Information Service in Libraries. 2d ed.
    Hamden, Conn.: Archon Books, 1967.

_____. Science, Humanism and Libraries. New York:
    Hafner, 1964.

Garrison, Fielding. "The Medical and the Scientific Period-
    icals of the Seventeenth and Eighteenth Centuries." Bul-
    letin of the Institute of the History of Medicine 2 (July
    1934): 285-343.

Gottschalk, Charles M. and Desmond, W. F. "Worldwide
    Census of Scientific and Technical Serials." American
    Documentation 14 (July 1963): 188-194.

Graham, Walter J. English Literary Periodicals. New
    York: T. Nelson, 1930.

Gray, Dwight E. and Bray, Robert S. "Abstracting and In-
    dexing Services of Physics Interest." American Journal
    of Physics 18 (May 1950): 274-299.

Grenfell, David. Periodicals and Serials; Their Treatment
    in Special Libraries. 2d ed. London: Aslib, 1965.

Grogan, Denis, J. Science and Technology; an Introduction

to the Literature. 2d ed. London: Clive Bingley, 1973.

Hale, Barbara. The Subject Bibliography of the Social Sciences and Humanities. New York: Pergamon Press, 1970.

Hanson, Christopher W. Introduction to Science-Information Work. London: Aslib, 1971.

Harrod, Leonard M. The Librarians' Glossary. 3d ed. New York: Seminar Press, 1971.

Hicks, Frederick G. Materials and Methods of Legal Research. 3d ed. Rochester, N.Y.: Lawyers' Cooperative Pub. Co., 1942.

Hulme, Edward W. Class Catalogue of Current Serial Digests and Indexes of the Literature of Pure and Applied Science. London: Library Association, 1912.

_____ and Kinzbrunner, C. "On Current Serial Digests and Indexes of the Literature of Science and Some Problems Connected Therewith." Library Association Record 15 (January 1913): 22-28.

Index Bibliographicus. 1st-4th eds. Paris [etc.] Unesco [etc.] 1925-64.

International Conference on Science Abstracting, Paris, 1949. Final Report. Paris: Unesco, 1957.

International Federation for Documentation. Abstracting Services; an Index to Material Collected by FID in 1962/63. The Hague: 1963.

_____. Abstracting Services in Science, Technology, Medicine, Agriculture, Social Sciences, Humanities. The Hague: 1965.

_____. List of Current Specialized Abstracting and Indexing Services. The Hague: 1949.

Iwinski, Boleslas. "La Statistique internationale des périodiques (journeaux et revues)." Bulletin de l'Institut International de Bibliographie 15 (1910): 1-40.

Kirchner, Joachim. Das deutsche Zeitschriftenwesen, seine

Geschichte und seine Probleme. 2d ed. 2 vols. Wiesbaden: Harrasowitz, 1958-62.

Kronick, David A. A History of Scientific and Technical Periodicals: The Origins and Development of the Scientific and Technological Press, 1665-1790. Metuchen, N.J.: Scarecrow Press, 1962 [c1961].

_____. _____. 2d ed. Metuchen, N.J.: Scarecrow Press, 1976.

Lawler, John L. The H. W. Wilson Company; Half a Century of Bibliographic Publishing. Minneapolis: University of Minnesota Press, 1950.

Lederman, Laura F. "Abstracting and Indexing Periodicals of Chemical Interest Published in the United States." Journal of Chemical Education 29 (August 1952): 396-401.

Lehmann, Ernst H. Einführung in die Zeitschriftenkunde. Leipzig: Hiersemann, 1936.

Littleton, Isaac T. The Literature of Agricultural Economics; Its Bibliographic Organization and Use. Raleigh, N.C.: Agricultural Experiment Station, 1969.

Loosjes, Th. P. On Documentation of Scientific Literature. Translated by A. J. Dickson. London: Butterworths, 1967.

McCutcheon, Roger P. "The Journal des sçavans and the Philosophical Transactions of the Royal Society." Studies in Philology 21 (October 1924): 626-628.

McKie, Douglas. "The Scientific Periodical from 1665-1798." Philosophical Magazine (July 1948): 128-138.

Maichel, Karol. "Soviet Scientific Abstracting Journals." Special Libraries 50 (October 1959): 398-402.

Malclès, Louise N. Bibliography. Translated by Theodore C. Hines. New York: Scarecrow Press, 1961.

_____. Les Sources du travail bibliographique. 3 vols. Geneva: Droz, 1950-58.

Mayer, Claudius F. "Abstracting and Review Journals." In

A Guide to the History of Science, by George Sarton.
Waltham, Mass.: Chronica Botanica, 1952. Pp. 105-
110.

Menz, Gerhard. Die Zeitschrift; Ihre Entwicklung und Ihre
Lebensbedingungen; eine Wirtschaftsgeschichtliche Studie.
Stuttgart: C. Poeschel, 1928.

Milek, John T. "Abstracting and Indexing Services in Electronics and Related Fields." American Documentation 8
(January 1957): 5-21.

Moran, Clarence G. The Heralds of the Law. London:
Stevens, 1948.

Mott, Frank L. History of American Magazines. 5 vols.
Cambridge, Mass.: Harvard University Press, 1938-68.

Murra, Katherine O. "History of Some Attempts to Organize
Bibliography Internationally." In Bibliographic Organization. Edited by Jesse H. Shera and Margaret E. Egan.
Chicago: University of Chicago Press, 1951. Pp. 24-
53.

_____. "Notes on the Development of the Concept of Cur-
rent Complete National Bibliography [from 1844 to 1939]."
In Bibliographical Services; Their Present State and Possibilities of Improvement; Report of the Unesco/Library
of Congress Bibliographical Survey. Washington: U.S.
Govt. Print. Off., 1950.

New York Public Library. A Check List of Cumulative Indexes to Individual Periodicals in the New York Public
Library. Compiled by Daniel C. Haskell. New York:
1942.

Ogburn, William F. "Recent Social Trends--Their Implica-
tions for Libraries." In Library Trends. Edited by
Louis R. Wilson. Chicago: University of Chicago Press,
1937. Pp. 1-12.

Ornstein, Martha. The Role of Scientific Societies in the
Seventeenth Century. Chicago: University of Chicago
Press, 1928.

Osborn, Andrew D. Serial Publications; Their Place and
Treatment in Libraries. 2d ed. Chicago: American
Library Association, 1973.

Otlet, Paul. Traité de documentation: le livre sur le livre,
théorie et pratique. Brussels: Editiones Mundaneum,
1934.

Passman, Sidney. Scientific and Technological Communication. New York: Pergamon Press, 1969.

Pearl, Richard M. Guide to Geologic Literature. New York:
McGraw-Hill, 1951.

Polzovics, Iván. Adatok és felismerések a szakirodalmi
dokumentáció történerének kezdeteihez [A Contribution to
the Early History of Documentation]. Budapest: Országos Müszaki Könyvtar és Dokumentációs Kozpont, 1964.

Porter, John R. "The Scientific Journal - 300th Anniversary."
Bacteriological Reviews 28 (September 1964): 211-230.

Price, Derek, Little Science, Big Science. New York:
Columbia University Press, 1963.

_____. Science since Babylon. New Haven: Yale Univer-
sity Press, 1961.

_____. _____. Enl. ed. New Haven: Yale University
Press, 1975.

Ricks, Christopher. "Learned Journals." Times Literary
Supplement. 4 July 1968, p. 709.

Robinson, Antony. Systematic Bibliography; A Practical
Guide to the Work of Compilation. 3d ed. Hamden,
Conn.: Linnet Books, 1971.

Sarton, George. A Guide to the History of Science. Waltham, Mass.: Chronica Botanica, 1952.

Schneider, Georg. Theory and History of Bibliography.
Translated by Ralph R. Shaw. New York: Columbia
University Press, 1934.

Science Museum Library, London. Bibliography of Current
Periodical Abstracts and Indexes Published in the British
Commonwealth and Contained in the Science Museum Li-
brary. London: 1939.

Scudder, Samuel H. A Catalogue of Scientific Serials of

All Countries; Including the Transactions of Learned Societies in the Natural, Physical and Mathematical Sciences, 1633-1876. Cambridge, Mass.: Library of Harvard University, 1879.

Shera, Jesse H. Documentation and the Organization of Knowledge. London: Lockwood, 1966.

_____ and Egan, Margaret E., eds. Bibliographic Organization. Chicago: University of Chicago Press, 1951.

Smithsonian Institution. Sixth Annual Report. Washington: U.S. Govt. Print. Off., 1852.

Staveley, Ronald. Notes on Modern Bibliography. London: Library Association, 1954.

_____. Notes on Subject Bibliography. London: Deutsch, 1962.

_____; McIlwaine, I. C.; and McIlwaine, J. Introduction to Subject Study. London: Deutsch, 1967.

Taylor, Archer. General Subject-Indexes Since 1548. Philadelphia: University of Pennsylvania Press, 1966.

_____. A History of Bibliographies of Bibliographies. New Brunswick, N.J.: Scarecrow Press, 1955.

Ulrich's Periodicals Directory. 7th-14th eds. New York: Bowker, 1953-1972.

U.S. Congress. House. Committee on Science and Astronuatics. Dissemination of Scientific Information, 86th Cong., 2d sess., 1959.

U.S. Library of Congress. Science and Technology Division. A Guide to the World's Abstracting and Indexing Services in Science and Technology. Washington: 1963.

Van Laer, H. "Des mesures destinées â faciliter aux chimistes et techniciens l'accès rapide de toutes les publications qui les interessant." In Congres international de chimie appliquée, Compte-rendu. Brussels: Deprey, 1894.

Vesenyi, Paul. An Introduction to Periodical Bibliography. Ann Arbor: Pierian Press, 1974.

Vickery, Brian C.   Techniques of Information Retrieval.
    Hamden, Conn. :   Archon Books, 1970.

World Health Organization, Library.   Current Indexing and
    Abstracting Periodicals in the Medical and Biological
    Sciences; An Annotated List.   2d ed.   Geneva: 1959.

Zittel, Karl von.   A History of Geology and Palaeontology to
    the End of the Nineteenth Century.   Translated by Maria
    Ogilvie-Gordon.   London: W. Scott, 1901.

NAME INDEX

Allen, W. 14, 277
Allgemeiner Deutscher
    Apotheker-Verein 79
Amat, R. d' 106, 280
Amer. Assoc. for the Advancement of Science 15,
    42, 277
Amer. Ceramic Society 104
Amer. Chemical Society 15,
    100
Amer. Electro-Chemical
    Society 99, 130
Amer. Gas Assoc. 104
Amer. Institute of Criminal
    Law and Criminology 264
Amer. Institute of Electrical
    Engineers 99, 130
Amer. Institute of Medicine
    102
Amer. Institute of Physics
    148
Amer. Library Assoc. 38,
    277
Amer. Medical Assoc. 93-4,
    126, 151
Amer. Neurological Assoc.
    130, 132
Amer. Physical Society 99,
    130
Amer. Physiological Society
    101, 130
Amer. Society of Mechanical
    Engineers 96, 132
Amer. Veterinary Medical
    Assoc. 95
Apotheker-Verein in Norddeutschland 79
Arago, D. 82, 146

Ashley, F. 279
Assoc. Internationale de
    Botanistes 130
Assoc. Internationale du
    Froid 103
Assoc. of Engineering Societies 95
Associazione Elettrotecnica
    Italiana 99
Astronomische Gesellschaft
    99, 150

Baillarger, J. 79
Barnes, S. 15, 55, 64,
    277
Barr, K. 277
Barreswil, C. 89
Beckurts, H. 79
Bergakademie, Berlin 103
Berthelot, P. 83
Besterman, T. 12, 26, 47,
    63, 277
Beughem, C. 36
Beutler, J. 36
Billings, J. 42
Bishop, W. 48, 277
Blake, J. 13, 21, 76, 106,
    277
Blanchard, J. 21, 277
Bolton, H. 21, 42, 43, 50,
    278
Botanischer Verein, Munich
    92, 132
Bourne, C. 113, 278
Boussingault, J. 83
Bowker, R. 39
Bradford, S. 14, 24, 47,

287

TITLE INDEX

SUBJECT INDEX

Abridgment   1-2
Abstract journals
  Arrangement   3, 179-80, 192
  Before 1790   55ff.
    1790-1799   66-7
    1800-1819   67-70
    1820-1849   70-82
    1850-1869   82-90
    1870-1889   90-8
    1890-1920   98-105
  Bibliographic characteristics   19, 176ff., 192
  Definition   2, 3, 57
  Duration   61, 172ff., 191
  Frequency   181-2, 192
  Geographic diffusion   19, 28, 30, 61, 161ff., 191
  Geographic scope   183-4, 192-3
  Growth   19, 108ff., 187-8
  Indexes   180-1
  Language diffusion   167ff., 191
  Literature relating to   11ff.
  Origins and development   7, 16-18, 19, 32, 185-7, 193-6
  Problems of   196-7
  Purpose   7-8, 182-3, 185-6
  Sponsorship   19, 116ff., 188-9
    and country of origin   134
    and subject category   132-4
    change of   131-2
    commercial   128
    government   127-8
    industrial   127
    learned and professional society   125ff.
    miscellaneous   128-9
    multiple   129-31
  Subject diffusion   18-19, 134ff., 189-91
    applied sciences and technology   67, 69-70, 80-2, 88-9, 95-7, 102-4, 155ff., 240ff., 250
    generalities   66-7, 105, 145, 228, 247ff.
    humanities   67, 70, 82, 90, 98, 105, 160ff., 245ff., 252-3

311